HUGH STRETTON

HUGH STRETTON

Selected Writings

Edited by
Graeme Davison

Published by La Trobe University Press in conjunction with Black Inc.
Level 1, 221 Drummond Street
Carlton VIC 3053, Australia
enquiries@blackincbooks.com
www.blackincbooks.com
www.latrobeuniversitypress.com.au

La Trobe University plays an integral role in Australia's public intellectual life, and is recognised globally for its research excellence and commitment to ideas and debate. La Trobe University Press publishes books of high intellectual quality, aimed at general readers. Titles range across the humanities and sciences, and are written by distinguished and innovative scholars. La Trobe University Press books are produced in conjunction with Black Inc., an independent Australian publishing house. The members of the LTUP Editorial Board are Vice-Chancellor's Fellows Emeritus Professor Robert Manne and Dr Elizabeth Finkel, and Morry Schwartz and Chris Feik of Black Inc.

9781760640743 (paperback)
9781743820612 (ebook)

 A catalogue record for this book is available from the National Library of Australia

Cover design by Marilyn de Castro
Text design by Peter Long and typesetting by Tristan Main
Cover portrait of Hugh Stretton by Rob Hannaford, image courtesy of the Art Gallery of South Australia.

CONTENTS

INTRODUCTION

Graeme Davison

I N HIS TIME, HUGH STRETTON WAS ADMIRED AS AUSTRALia's foremost public intellectual and a social-democratic thinker of international stature. His prolific writings on cities, housing, economics, history and the social sciences attracted appreciative readers on both sides of politics. His most popular book, *Ideas for Australian Cities* (1970), became the manifesto for a generation awakening to the distinctive features of our cities and suburbs. He gave the ABC's Boyer Lectures on housing policy, speculated on how new technologies and environmental change would reshape Western societies, and challenged the effects of neoliberal economics on their public life.

As powerful as his writing, however, was his personal influence. As a speaker, teacher and mentor, Stretton inspired a generation of academics, politicians, planners and public servants, people who shared his vision of a fairer Australia. His domed forehead, leonine good looks and gravitas made an immediate impression on all those who heard or met him. Colleagues were in awe of his speed and clarity of thought, the simplicity of his speech and his extraordinary breadth of knowledge, practical as well as theoretical. Yet he was modest, self-deprecatory and generous almost to a fault.

Among twentieth-century Australian intellectuals, perhaps only one other figure – the philosopher John Anderson – was similarly revered. In a country sometimes considered resistant to intellectual pursuits, each commanded attention for his intellectual charisma. Anderson developed a distinctive philosophical approach, Australian realism, and drew a band of devoted disciples, the Andersonians, although their influence hardly spread beyond Sydney. While drawing strength from the progressive traditions of Melbourne and Adelaide, Stretton reached a wider national and international readership. For a time, his ideas influenced social policy in Adelaide and Canberra, and even after his brand of social democracy faded he remained an incisive critic of its opponents. Yet while his writing was widely read, he won admirers rather than disciples. There are no Strettonians.

Like Anderson, Stretton was an Australian original, a big-picture thinker conversant with the wider currents of British and American thought, but with distinctively Australian attributes: a resistance to abstraction, a respect for the lessons of practical experience, and a preference for plain speech. Immune from the herd instinct of parties and schools, he defied conventional labels. He was sometimes called enigmatic or idiosyncratic, although there was really nothing mysterious or contrarian about him. While resistant to Marxism – he believed that 'the idea of having a theory of everything is death' – he defied Cold War suspicions and both encouraged and appointed individual Marxists.

The label most frequently applied to Stretton is 'social democrat', sometimes with the qualification 'pragmatic'. It is accurate as far as it goes, in capturing his belief in democratic state action to redress social disadvantage, but it misses a strain of paternalism that irked some critics. 'Moderate socialist or radical conservative' was how he described himself in *Ideas for Australian Cities*. Then and later he usually placed himself on the Left, but gave the term his own definition: 'I use the terms "Left" and "Right" not for forms of government but for attitudes to equality.' In that regard he was old-fashioned, for he had little interest in emerging leftist preoccupations with questions of identity and diversity. Asked about his beliefs, he offered 'Christian atheist'. His heroes included the Christian socialist R.H. Tawney, the sociologist and activist Michael Young, the old-school South Australian public servants J.W. Wainwright and Alf Ramsay, and the long-serving Australian Reserve Bank governor and advocate for Aboriginal Australians Herbert 'Nugget' Coombs.

The apparent contradictions in Stretton's outlook are best understood when set against the pattern of his life. The opening section of this book, 'Stretton on Himself', collects a number of short pieces drawn from various published and unpublished works in which he reflects on phases or aspects of his life. Written at different times and for different purposes, they nevertheless provide insights, variously earnest, wry and self-critical, on how he saw himself. In the following pages, I offer a brief overview of his life and an assessment of his work from the vantage point of an admirer, a fellow historian who knew Stretton (although not closely) and followed a similar path some years later from Melbourne via Oxford to Canberra, where I caught his interests in the social sciences and the history of Australian cities.

Hugh Stretton was a person of his time – World War II and the long post-war boom – and of the places where he lived – Melbourne, Oxford and Adelaide. He was born in 1924 into Melbourne's upper middle professional class. His father, Leonard, was a respected barrister and judge who chaired a series of landmark inquiries. His mother, Nora, a daughter of the vicarage and herself a brilliant student, devoted her life to her family and a range of public causes. At Melbourne University the Strettons had been friends of the young Robert Menzies, but as adults, their son recalled, they were 'almost perfectly non-political in the party sense'. Hugh was a child of the suburbs (beachside Beaumaris and upper-middle-class Kew), of the private schools (Mentone Grammar and Scotch College) and of a loving, encouraging family. Several of his abiding interests as a social theorist – such as the effects of housing on human welfare, the value of unpaid domestic work and the benefits of the suburban house and garden – were grounded in his own experience of home and family.

While the Strettons were well-off, there was nothing insular or complacent about them. 'Life didn't consist of having, or looking at or enjoying things,' Nora told her children. 'Life consisted of doing things.' At Scotch, Hugh came under the influence of a remarkable school chaplain, the Christian Socialist Stephen Yarnold. With Yarnold's support, he established a boys' club on a new Housing Commission estate in Port Melbourne, a working-class suburb on the other side of town. Reaching across the class divide would become a motif in his social thought. 'I like trotting about the class structure,' he later confessed. To some, it smacked of noblesse oblige. But, as Stretton persuasively argued, the barriers between rich and poor damaged both. He was convinced that a more equal society would also be a happier one for everyone.

Stretton left Scotch as dux on the eve of World War II, and enrolled to study Arts and Law at the University of Melbourne, although he intended to join the armed forces as soon as he was old enough. From the first, his intellectual prowess stunned his teachers. 'The word "genius" was one to be chary of,' his Ancient History lecturer, Jessie Webb, observed, but 'it was the word her mind associated with the name of Hugh Stretton'. Her colleague Max Crawford agreed: Stretton was 'a young man of quite exceptional promise'. His examination results were so outstanding that, under a manpower regulation designed to prevent Australia losing its best and brightest, as England had in the Great War, he was forbidden to enlist. With his father's support, Stretton successfully challenged the regulation and enlisted as an able seaman in the Royal Australian Navy. 'This got me three years' card-carrying membership of our working class, for which I'm grateful ever since,' he boasted.

Towards the end of the war, while serving on a corvette in the Timor Sea, Stretton noticed an advertisement calling for applications for the Victorian Rhodes Scholarship. He had barely begun his degree, but with glowing references from Menzies, Crawford, Kathleen Fitzpatrick and his school headmaster, he was selected ahead of his fellow Scotch Collegian and historian Geoffrey Serle, who was successful the following year. When he arrived in England in the autumn of 1946, London was still recovering from the Blitz but the political atmosphere was exhilarating. The election of Clement Attlee's Labour government promised 'a peaceful democratic transition' to a moderate socialist society. 'Bliss was it in that morn to be alive,' Stretton recalled.

At Balliol College, Oxford, he read Modern History, following in the path of other Australians, including Keith Hancock, Crawford and Manning Clark. There his brilliant career continued. At the age of twenty-four, even before taking his final examinations, he was elected to a college fellowship. His parents were amazed. 'I shall never understand how he happened to us,' Nora confided to Max Crawford. Stretton had been appointed to teach history without having written a book or even set foot in an archive. Like many Oxford high-flyers, he did not bother with a doctorate, a qualification most at the time regarded as a mere journeyman's ticket. For a while it hardly mattered. In Oxford, and later in Adelaide, the effortless superiority he displayed in the lecture theatre, common room and professorial board was enough. But the question of whether he was a real historian remained a sensitive point. 'There's no evidence I've got any historical imagination,' he told a surprised interviewer. 'I've never written any history books.' To a sympathetic one, he gave a more considered reply. 'I'm a historian. My field is the twentieth-century growth and influence of the social sciences.'

He had arrived at this answer only gradually. His father was a kind of contemporary historian, having written a masterly official report on the causes of the devastating 1939 Victorian bushfires. At Melbourne University, Hugh had joined the discussions stimulated by Max Crawford's 1942 paper 'History as a Science'. Such theoretical questions, he soon discovered, were of no interest to Oxford historians: 'I got to Oxford aghast at how unselfconscious they were and how little they seemed to understand about arguments that went on about what caused what, and how you knew what caused what.' He found more sympathetic intellectual company with his closest Oxford friend, the Austrian-born economist Paul Streeten, whose ideas about 'programs and prognoses' influenced Stretton's experiments with 'scenarios' as a way of rethinking histories and imagining possible futures.

In 1948, while waiting to take up his Balliol fellowship, Stretton spent a year sampling courses at Princeton. 'That was a fashionable thing for a young historian to think he should do at that time,' he explained. He audited courses in sociology, politics, economics and international relations. If Oxford's theoretical innocence surprised him, Princeton's scientific pretensions appalled him: 'Nearly all of what I met I thought was just simple intellectual fraud.' The abstractions, false claims to objectivity, attempts to quantify everything – the whole positivistic program that seemed to pervade the place – repelled him. It also left him in a quandary. Neither Oxford nor Princeton seemed to have answers to the questions that really interested him. It would take another twenty years before he found his own answers and published them.

Why did it take him so long? 'Sloth and incapacity,' he joked to one interviewer. Very few memorable or influential books were written by anyone under the age of forty, he claimed, perhaps defensively, on another occasion. The real answer was more complex. At Balliol he was a popular and respected teacher. But there were things about Oxford he disliked ('If Melbourne intellectuals are self-destructive, Oxford intellectuals are mutually destructive'), and he had begun to feel that he couldn't be a 'working effective' citizen in England as well as he could back in Australia. In 1954, when an invitation to the chair of history at Adelaide came, he jumped at it. 'I came home very happily,' he recalled. Not yet thirty, he became the youngest professor in Australia.

Over the next fifteen years, Stretton built a lively and democratic history department, taught some distinguished future historians, survived a painful marriage break-up, sole-parented two children, remarried happily and fathered two more. As much as that crowded life allowed, he continued to think about the nature and future of the social sciences. But it was a lonely task, with few to share its difficulties. Only in 1966, while on sabbatical leave at the Australian National University, was he able to complete *The Political Sciences*, a 400-page examination of the doctrine of value-free, positivistic social science. With its publication in 1969, the burden of impossible expectation grew lighter. At the ANU, the Research School of Social Sciences suspended its usual seminar program for two weeks to read and discuss what everyone believed to be a magnum opus.

While its Australian reviewers were enthusiastic, in Britain and America *The Political Sciences* was received more coolly. 'Brilliant' but 'wrong', declared the sociologist Arthur Stinchcombe. The book was not really wrong, but its arguments were less original than some Australian admirers supposed. During its long gestation, the scholarly landscape Stretton had observed at Princeton had changed. Other writers, such as the radical sociologist C. Wright Mills, had already attacked the pretensions of Parsonian 'grand theory'. Furthermore, as Stretton's friend the sociologist Jean Martin reminded him, not all American social scientists were quite as 'scientific' and 'quantitative' in style as he seemed to think. My own first acquaintance with the critique of 'value-free' social science was not through reading Stretton's book but in classes given by his friend, my economics tutor at Balliol, Paul Streeten, in the mid-1960s. When the book at last appeared in 1969, the scholarly world was feeling the after-shocks of the student revolts in Paris and Chicago. Although radical by the standards of the 1960s, *The Political Sciences* was soon overtaken by even more radical, although less subtle, critiques.

But if the book's conclusions were not entirely original, there was no doubting the originality of the mind behind it. Stretton's penetrating powers of analysis, persuasive prose and interdisciplinary breadth were his alone. When I read it now, some of the book seems dated, but its vision of the social sciences as an irreducibly moral and political activity remains memorable. Its conclusions informed virtually everything Stretton wrote over the next forty years. After his long, halting preparation, he had entered the most productive period of his life.

To make space to write, he resigned his chair to become plain Mr Hugh Stretton, Reader in History. He lived modestly at 61 Tynte Street, a terrace house in North Adelaide, which he bought in the 1950s and did up himself, employing his own carpentry skills. Asked what his ideal city would be like, he answered:

> I want what I've got. A home of my own where I can sit under a vine in my own backyard; a park somewhere near where kids can kick a football; a short walk to Tom the Cheap and a local pub; an easy trip to work in the city; half an hour's drive maybe to a beach, or some open country.

The Strettons lived simply. Hugh hated ostentation of any kind. He drove a small second-hand station wagon but sent his children to good private schools. 'I have made it a rule of life that the more radical you want to be, the more respectable you must try and look,' he remarked. On ceremonial occasions he took his own advice, but his everyday attire was casual, even scruffy. He liked to quote the results of an early student survey, which identified a need for improvement in his clothes.

The simplicity he applied to his personal life Stretton also pursued in his thinking and writing. In Oxford and Adelaide he encouraged his students 'to communicate as clearly as they can and to be as good as they are able'. He urged them not to adopt his values but to think critically and ethically about their own. Being explicit about one's values was a matter of simple honesty. 'I believe that people including social scientists should write "good", "bad", "right" and "wrong" when that is what they mean.' What to Stretton was simple honesty, however, could sometimes be construed as Olympian self-assurance.

'At the heart of Stretton's project,' Greg Melleuish writes, 'is the desire to use education in order to create an older type of statesman who will be able to act wisely and create a more equal and just society.' Stretton lived that project as well as promoting it. The trouble, Melleuish contends, is that people no longer want to be guided paternalistically by such 'wise administrators'. He may be right, but what is the alternative? In representative democracies, Stretton insisted, we should care about the quality of our leaders. After all, their decisions affect us all. If the age of the 'wise administrator' is over, we need to consider the likelihood that the vacuum will not be filled by the people alone but by a different kind of leader, more cynical, populist and authoritarian.

Stretton wrote *The Political Sciences* while living happily with his young family in Hughes, a new suburb in Canberra's Woden Valley. In what remained of his sabbatical, he began to think about what to do next. He knew now what social sciences should *not* be like. But what *should* they be like? It was a time when urban questions were in the air. The Australian National University had recently established an Urban Research Unit. Social democrats, including the new Labor leader, Gough Whitlam, were looking to the cities and their suburbs as laboratories of social reform. If you wanted to discover what social science should be, where better to begin than in one's own backyard?

Stretton began talking with neighbours, walking the streets, picking the brains of Canberra planners, academics and politicians, and reading fat government reports. Back in his home suburb, North Adelaide, in 1967 he continued to read, observe, talk and think about cities. He described *Ideas for Australian Cities*, published in 1970, as an 'amateur book'; in fact it was an inspired mixture of observation, self-taught planning theory, streetwise analysis and literary flair. Published under the author's own imprint, 'An Orphan Book' – because, as the jacket claimed, six commercial publishers had rejected it – it soon became a bestseller.

A tract for the times written for citizens rather than planners, *Ideas* was the reverse of a professional textbook or manual. It challenged the unthinking condescension of Australian intellectuals towards their cities and suburbs. As Donald Horne noted, Stretton 'could see beyond the clichés into the lives of ordinary Australians'. And much of what he saw was surprisingly good. The suburban house and garden was the best place to rear families. Owning the house increased one's security and wellbeing. 'You don't have to be a mindless conformist to choose suburban life,' Stretton decided. 'Many of the best poets and painters and inventors and protesters choose it too.'

If there was a problem about the suburbs, it was that their benefits were not shared fairly. Reducing the differences between rich and poor suburbs, and mixing rich and poor within them, would make them better for all. In planning their futures, each Australian city wrestled with legacies of its history. In deft thumbnail portraits,

Stretton sketched the forces hampering the overgrown metropolises of Sydney and Melbourne, and pointed to the smaller, better-planned outliers, Adelaide and Canberra, as the most promising models of what the rest might become.

Through the 1970s and '80s, Stretton continued to defend the suburbs, often against the consensus of economists and planners. In his 1974 Boyer Lectures, *Housing and Government*, for example, he argued for policies to support home ownership as well as generous public housing. He insisted that both public authorities and private enterprise had roles to play in housing Australians. In the looming conflict between advocates of 'big' and 'small' government, Stretton occupied the shrinking middle ground. Socialists accused him of advocating 'a housing policy for the middle class', while neoliberals portrayed him as a defender of moribund state welfare. In the 1970s, home ownership was at record levels but its future looked perilous. Stretton feared that rising land costs and unregulated housing finance could jeopardise the Australian Dream. Was there a technical fix that might avert it, he wondered, such as indexed interest rates? Forty years on, with real-estate prices at an all-time high and housing affordability at an all-time low, Stretton's worst forebodings have been realised.

In the 1980s planners launched a new urban agenda. For more than a century, they had warned against the dangers of urban sprawl. Economic stringency and environmental alarm reinforced their concern. The antidote, they argued, was what they called 'the compact city'. Most Australian capitals were soon committed, at least on paper, to policies of urban consolidation. Stretton was not against denser housing for those who wanted it, but he thought it worsened the lives of those who didn't, while hardly touching the problems it was supposed to solve. Housing had to be densified beyond tolerable limits to save much land. If you wanted to reduce carbon pollution, it was better to improve public transport or promote electric cars rather than tinker with residential densities. Since the 1980s, when Stretton advanced these criticisms, Australian cities have been substantially rebuilt. There are more high-rise apartments but also more huge, energy-consuming houses. A social scientist interested in Australia's new suburbs could no longer begin in their backyards because there aren't any. Meanwhile, the cities continue to sprawl. Readers of this book will be able to weigh the merits of Stretton's anti-consolidation arguments for themselves. To me, at least, many of them remain persuasive.

As the political pendulum in the 1980s swung to the Right and neoliberals displaced social democrats in academic and public life, Stretton's influence waned. In the late 1970s he had helped members of Labor's shadow cabinet draft policies to combat inflation and unemployment, but once Hawke and Keating came to power the policies were discarded in favour of radical deregulation. Henceforward, Stretton fought a valiant but largely unavailing battle to turn back a revolution in thought that he believed to be intellectually and morally flawed. His essay 'The Cult of Selfishness' distils the essence of his discontent. Neoliberalism, he feared, was grounded in the same ungoverned egotism as the liberation movements of the 1970s. His objection to it, however, was not just moral but intellectual. Sooner or later, he argued, neoliberalism would fail because it was based on a narrow and oversimplified view of human nature.

Each revolution writes its own history. To its champions, neoliberalism triumphed because of its inherent superiority. Stretton contested that history but recognised the flaws of the managed economy it replaced. 'Inflation and unemployment discredited the Keynesian regime,' he wrote – but the democracies compounded the harm by the way they handled the problem. With the demise of the old economy, the old politics had gone as well. Social democrats could no longer count on a skilled blue-collar workforce to deliver the votes they needed to legislate their program.

How, then, was the social democratic project – the vision of a prosperous and egalitarian society – to be reconstructed? Should its followers press forward along the old path, attempting, against the political odds, to revive the old redistributionist program of state-funded welfare? Or should they take a step sideways by applying social-democratic values of fairness to other relationships, such as those between the sexes, users of common resources or the generations? In 'Tasks for Social Democratic Intellectuals', Stretton returned to where he began, with the values of the good society. 'Stay generous, and keep on recommending it,' he urged. 'Restore the serious study of social values and purposes to a central place in the higher education of as many students as possible.'

Economics: A New Introduction was Stretton's last valiant attempt to achieve that goal. He called it his 'Anti-Samuelson', for it was designed to challenge the intellectual hegemony of *Economics: An Introductory Analysis*, the 'canonical' bestselling textbook by the American economist Paul Samuelson. An Australian edition by Stretton's colleagues Keith Hancock and Robert Wallace had appeared in 1970. Stretton admired the Samuelson model – 'orderly, clear, lively, engaging, humanely intended and useable' – and adopted it himself, with over 850 pages of double-column text. But he disagreed with Samuelson's conception of economics. He vowed his own text would be 'more practical, historical, institutional … with less simplifying abstraction [and] less deductive theory'. It would narrate more and measure less. Classical economic theory, Stretton argued, was made for a more stable world than ours; economists now needed to take greater account of the variability of human nature, historical contingency and uncertainty. The book is a *summa* of everything Stretton had thought and written over the previous forty years.

All the old themes – how values shape explanation; the importance of childhood and households; the purposes and effects of redistributionist policies – are there. Stretton considered it his most original work. Any student bound for business or government would be better off for reading it. It was an admirable but perhaps quixotic enterprise. 'Stretton's book is right for the times because the times are wrong,' an admiring reviewer remarked. Alas, neither the times nor an economic profession dominated by neoclassicism was ready for it. Perhaps another age, more receptive to Stretton's concerns, will rediscover and honour it.

When Hugh Stretton died in 2015, some of his friends and admirers began to discuss the idea of republishing his most famous book, *Ideas for Australian Cities*. I am grateful to Bill Randolph for beginning the conversation, and to Patrick Troy and Brendan Gleeson, who lent their support. I had already begun to research Hugh's life and writings for a chapter in my 2016 book *City Dreamers*. Soon afterwards, Robert Manne proposed an edited selection of Stretton's writings in his Australian Thinkers series. While much of *Ideas for Australian Cities* remains fresh and relevant, by 1989, when the third edition appeared, even its author recognised that some of its ideas, such as his enthusiasm for 'linear cities', were flawed. A collection of Stretton's best writings, selected from across his career, with an eye to those of most enduring value, was a more appealing way of keeping his legacy alive. I am grateful to Rob for nurturing the project at a time of personal difficulty. David Chandler, Ruth Fincher, Brendan Gleeson, Stuart Macintyre and Wilfrid Prest contributed helpful information or comments. I am especially grateful to Hugh's widow, Pat, for her encouragement and permission to reproduce works from his literary estate.

Selecting 90,000 words from the million or more he published was a daunting editorial challenge, so a few words about how I approached the task may be in order. My aim was to select writings that illustrate Stretton's bravura intellectual style, his acuity of mind and expression, the remarkable range and depth of his concerns, and the striking originality of his thought. 'Selection' was one of Hugh's favourite words: what the historian or social scientist selects, he insisted, reflects their values as much as the significance of what they select. In selecting chapters and essays from the larger body of his work, I am inevitably severing them from their original context and making my own judgements about their value for us now. As an Australian urban historian, I confess a bias towards Stretton's writings about Australian cities and housing; I have given less space than other editors might to his important writing on international planning, public-choice theory or economics. Some of his most ambitious projects, such as his first book, *The Political Sciences*, and his last, *Economics: A New Introduction*, defy abridgement and selection. The short extracts included here may convey their flavour, but not the intricate fabric of analysis and evidence on which they rest. In the interests of breadth or to retain what seems of enduring interest in Stretton's thinking, I have sometimes excised passages inspired by contemporary debates that no longer seem as interesting as the general insights or principles from which they derived.

So then: why read Stretton?

First, simply for the pleasure of following a brilliant thinker as he stretches his mind. We read him, as we may read Swift or Adam Smith or Orwell or Donald Horne, for the power of his words as well as for the freshness of his thinking. Like his parents, Hugh loved the English language and took writing seriously. He wrote as he spoke: crisply, plainly and concisely. While never using a long word or sentence where a short one would do, he could nevertheless require close attention from his readers. So compressed and subtle is his reasoning that at times the reader can be left gasping, figuratively, for breath at the end of the page. He admired successful journalists who could make abstract ideas vivid and concrete: 'He's writing about people whose faces and jumpers you can see,' he remarked of Donald Horne. His own sketches of Australian cityscapes and his keenly observed portraits of Coombs and Keating in this volume show how well he mastered that art. Some of Stretton's most attractive writing is in unpublished public addresses, magazine articles and broadcasts, where he allows more of his personality and wit to shine. In editing this volume, I have interspersed some of these shorter pieces with longer, more closely argued essays.

Second, Stretton shows us what it is to be a public intellectual. He addressed questions of high public importance. He regarded reasoned public debate as the right way to settle them. As the selections in this book illustrate, he wrote and spoke prolifically in public meetings; public lectures; public broadcasts; newspapers, both local and national; journals of comment; and reviews. He respected the conventions of civilised discussion. 'Always respect, as far as they're there, the good intentions of the folk you are arguing against,' he wrote in one of his last essays. 'All sorts of economic rationalists with whom you and I might disagree have the best of good intentions.' In the era of shock-jocks and spin doctors, as reasoned public debate gives way to naked partisanship and unsupported opinion, he shows us how citizens may productively disagree.

Third, Stretton memorably articulated a generous, humane and original vision of Australia. He was sometimes described as a maverick, yet he also voiced the best hopes of a generation: the progressive, university-educated moral middle class. The historian Judith Brett credits the moral middle class with the birth of the Liberal Party. 'The middle class,' she writes, 'rallied round a conception of citizenship which combined civic duty with a personal ethic of selfless service to challenge Labor's claim to be a party of government.'

Stretton reminds us of another face of the moral middle class, the progressive intellectuals, whose conception of civic duty drew them to the other side of politics. They were the brains of the Whitlam and Hawke governments. Educating and supporting them was Stretton's lifelong project. *Ideas for Australian Cities* was their manifesto as well as his. When applicants were interviewed for positions in the Whitlam government's Department of Urban Development, the first question was: 'What do you think of Stretton?'

But if Stretton was a force in the 1970s and '80s, why read him now? Surely his day has passed. Haven't his neoliberal adversaries won the battle of ideas? Hugh sometimes asked these questions himself. He was convinced that the battle of ideas had consequences for the whole society. But he was wary of siding with the big battalions or the newest arrivals on the field, or of declaring victory at any stage of the contest. 'New ways of doing things aren't neither necessarily better, nor necessarily worse, than old ways,' he wrote in 'How Not to Argue'. 'We can pick up ideas and historical experience from any place or time, if they promise well for us.' I think he would have applied the same test to himself, urging us to take only as much from his thinking – or from that of his adversaries – as 'promises well for us'.

Readers will decide for themselves what to take. Rereading Stretton for this book has confirmed my admiration for his generous vision, intellectual integrity and powers of argument, while prompting reconsideration of some of his theories and policies. On some matters, it seems to me, he saw further than on others. His was a vision grounded in the old Anglo-Protestant Australia. One of his planning slogans was 'Women and children first', but his views on gender roles were formed before the advent of second-wave feminism in the 1970s. He also underestimated the profound transformations that would occur as Australia grew closer to Asia.

If our cities now look different from the suburban cities of the 1960s and '70s, it is not only because economic and environmental circumstances have changed them, but also because the people who inhabit them are now different. Looking from North Adelaide rather than from, say, Cabramatta or Box Hill may have limited his vision.

A social scientist with Stretton's values now begins in different circumstances and with different questions. Some of the changes he resisted have now become so entrenched as to make their reversal difficult, if not impossible. Once you have sold off the family estate of state-owned enterprises, for example, it may be impossible to buy it back again. And once you have exposed the Australian economy to global forces, it will almost certainly be impossible to re-erect the protective structure of exchange controls and tariffs Stretton fought to keep intact.

There are now signs, however, that the neoliberal revolution may have run its course. Even one of its architects, Paul Keating, says so. There aren't too many state enterprises left to privatise. And, as a royal commission is finding, the so-called liberation of the financial system hasn't liberated everyone. The benefits of globalisation are more apparent at the top end of Collins Street and Pitt Street than in our rusting manufacturing towns and suburbs. The abandonment of any idea of a fair wage as a call on industry has condemned many Australians to low-paid casual employment. The dream of home ownership is out of the reach of many younger people. The disparities in income and life chances that Stretton observed and sought to reduce in the 1970s have only widened since. In short, Australia Fair is now suffering a fairness deficit.

The conditions are ripe for a change of political course. But if 'fairness' is now the agreed direction, it remains unclear how it will be followed. If the United States and Britain are any guide, it may produce a politics of suspicion, anger and indiscriminate redress rather than one of democratic, intelligently designed, progressive reform. For the democratic Left, the temptations of populism and the short-term political fix are ever-present. As they look ahead, those who hope for a fairer Australia could do worse than return to the writings of Hugh Stretton. They will not find readymade recipes, but they may be reminded of principles and policies that bear reconsideration and perhaps renovation. What they *will* find is a model of how to think rigorously, ethically and imaginatively about the good society. Such models are not so abundant that we can afford to dispose of them too soon.

1

STRETTON ON HIMSELF

Stretton's writing often drew on personal experience, but he was either too modest or too wary to attempt an autobiography. 'My reason for never writing an autobiography,' he explained to one interviewer, 'is that I have been so unbelievably lucky that I couldn't think how I would seem anything but a self-satisfied prig.' He was too defensive: there was nothing priggish or self-satisfied about him, although his intellectual and moral confidence sometimes daunted contemporaries – even those who knew him closely. In the following extracts from various sources – books, unpublished talks, letters and a scholarship application – he reflects on the experiences that formed his intellectual outlook.

Childhood

WHAT HAS SEEMED FAIR AND UNFAIR IN THE bits of real life I've experienced?

Back to the 1920s and '30s in Beaumaris, on a rocky bit of coast eighteen miles or so down the bay from Melbourne. It was part local and part commuter village. Two shops and a pub. Except for the main road through it, all the roads were dirt, mostly through ti-tree. No sewers. Our household lavatory, away behind the washhouse, had a black tub which two men with a truck emptied and replaced once a week. To avoid over-filling it, males peed instead into a heap of charcoal behind another wall of the washhouse. (Gender equity was achieved in 1932, when we could afford a septic tank.) My mother (ex–vice president of the Student Representative Council at Melbourne University, and thereafter on the board of Melbourne Church of England Girls Grammar School, of which she had been captain) did the laundry, boiling the copper over a chip-fire and hand-scrubbing in two cement troughs. Indoors, she had a sewing machine and a knitting machine, and among other things made the curtains for a new boarding house at her old school.

Every morning, one of us walked up Tramway Parade, which had long lost horse trams and their rails, leaving buried sleeper bolts to break pedestrians' feet, to the acre where a lady kept a cow and supplied our milk. My mother did the cooking and some other housekeeping, but we also had Elsie, a live-in lady-help (I scarcely heard the word 'servant' in that household). She was an English emigrant who had got the job soon after reaching Melbourne, for bed and board and the lawful wage. My father, among other things a poet who had edited the *Melbourne University Magazine*, worked in the city. He took a bus, or his wife drove him, to trains at Sandringham or Cheltenham. So he was a long day away, earning modestly as the partner of another solicitor.

The point of this cosy sketch is to acknowledge the gross class differences between the Beaumaris households of that time, but also to notice also how much experience the classes still shared. Most of the children met around the village and the state school, a two-roomed building between an orchard and the ti-tree bush, a mile or so inland from the village. Walking to and from school, the hazards included occasional school bullies, and sad men showing their dicks to passing kids. At school the headmaster, in the secondary classroom, was there by grace of returned soldiers' rights to public employment. He had a visible steel patch in his skull from World War I, and a dangerous temper. In the primary room was a young local resident, a teacher to dream of. I later passed three years of Greek, including Herodotus' account of the Persian invasion of Greece, but his vivid account of the Spartan betrayal and defeat at Thermopylae was no more moving than Miss Kissane's classroom account of it, with big blackboard outlines of the terrain, for seven- to ten-year-olds. She soon afterwards traded teaching for managing one of the early airlines in Central Australia.

From 'Is a Fair Society a Happier One?', unpublished paper, c. 1993

Beliefs

MY MOTHER WAS THE DAUGHTER AND GRAND-daughter of Anglican clergymen but had no religious beliefs – but no anti-religious feelings either, as far as I knew. My father had no religious beliefs. Religion was neither taught nor attacked in our family life. My secondary school was a Presbyterian private school [Scotch College]. Its chaplain was a strong social democrat: we used to say, joking, that he mentioned Jesus about once a fortnight, and then only to assure that Jesus was a socialist too. What he actually did was to use his Christian resources to teach social rather than individual principles of love and fairness and mutual responsibility. I was one of a self-consciously intellectual group who liked and admired him.

Partly from his influence, partly from many other influences, and partly (we fondly imagined) from our own thoughtful choice, we went some way towards living those principles. We developed nurturing rather than bullying ways of welcoming new boys to the school; we happened to be good at various sports, but insisted that giving every boy a game, and coaching the beginners and junior teams, was more important than teaching people to admire and cheer the competitive 'first' teams or crews in which we ourselves performed. Some of us – partly from other non-school connections but with the school's support and blessing – founded and ran the first boys' club on a Victorian Housing Commission estate (at Fishermans Bend, in a house which the commission lent us for the purpose, where we ran the club a couple of nights a week). We were also arty and liked the tall, pale, graceful school chapel that had recently been built. Though a day boy (we lived about two miles from the school), I often went to the boarders' Sunday evening service, for some mixture of moral and aesthetic reasons. Still with no belief in the Christian god, or life after death, but with great respect for the chaplain's (and the headmaster's) moral and social philosophy.

So I am a non-believer who has never been in any general way anti-religious.

From 'Biography and Opinions of HS', undated reply to a correspondent

Ambitions

I N 1941 I HAD ATTEMPTED TO ENTER THE MERCHANT Service, and in 1942 entered the Army but was withdrawn by the university. After some months of negotiations, the Universities Commission granted a release, and I entered the Royal Australian Navy, being there disqualified from the executive of the service by a slight confusion of colour vision. In the robust and colourful company of the lower deck lay experience which perhaps may prove valuable, and which is certainly not to be forgotten.

Before enlistment, my activities were chiefly the common ones of school and university life: sports and games, literary and debating societies, dramatics, school politics, and the more quiet interests of reading and study and argument; in Belloc's words, 'laughter and the love of friends'. The chief occupations of my leisure have been reading; walking in a more or less exploratory way; riding; hearing music; rowing and swimming, football, tennis and sailing; and enjoying the solitude of forest country and the sea.

In my final year at Scotch College I rowed in the Head of the River VIII, and represented the school at rugby. 'Organised' sports in those years seemed to us to be valuable for the companionship of common effort and the common endurance of stress. This valuation has been well proved in war. The coaching and encouragement of junior sportsmen demanded as much of our enthusiasm as did the participation in 'Firsts' matches and boat races; it was our aim to make of, say, the boatshed a community of oarsmen rather than an organisation devoted mainly to the success of the First VIII. For its mental as well as its physical discipline, and for hard work in good company, sport has remained one of my greatest interests.

During the last few years at school and the university I was fortunate in being able to assist in the management of some boys' clubs in industrial suburbs, and at holiday camps designed as physical and mental recreation for boys who were set to work at fourteen, and for those, younger, who lived in the twin environments of poverty at home and the rigorous and sometimes undiscriminating discipline of the state schools. I had charge of one such camp for the less privileged boys at Cowes, and began and led a boys' club on the Government Housing Estate at Fishermans Bend.

There remain two interests deeper than the rest.

When I was very young I was encouraged to read widely and indiscriminately. From that grew the habit of reading, which has persisted in whatever circumstances I have found myself. To have been led to discover for myself the literature of our race is something for which I am grateful. To have been so well guided in later years by sensitive and sympathetic minds adds an indebtedness to the pleasure which I have found in these fields of wisdom and grace and beauty. To know – though the field of English writing is so vast that the best of it cannot be encompassed by one mind in one life-time – that I may forever walk in the company of great men, in many countries and in many ages is something that I hope may sustain me as an abiding certainty in a world which may prove to be uncertain and insecure.

I feel that while the literature of the past is concerned not only with past things but with the unchanging spirit and character of humanity, it is the more immediate and material function of history to make ready the tests and lessons of the past for application to the problems of the future. I have found an absorbing interest in the history of trial and adventure, of great endeavour and great failure, of the abiding quality of ideas among the evanescent quality of human pretentions. But I feel that the mere interest must be comparatively barren unless it leads to the trial of present questions in the light of the experience of the past; that history cannot be allowed to be a mere misleading saga of armies and empires and notable men. There must be a place in worldly affairs for the dispassionate accuracy of scholastic judgement. I learn what I can of the history of ancient and modern civilisations so that I may better understand the tasks that lie ahead of my generation in the troubled and perilous future.

From Stretton's application for a Rhodes Scholarship, 1945

Politics

WHEN I FIRST SAW THEM IN 1946, LONDON and the Londoners seemed lovable as well as unbeatable. The fabric still blitzed, 'looped and windowed', full of ragged gaps and acres of rubble. Black with coal-smoke, no paint for seven years, but great fraternity. Beveridge's notions of social justice and compassion seemed to be shared by almost everyone. The class war seemed amiable, without much hatred. Rich and poor had died together in the war, now they grumbled together at bus stops and post offices. In those days 'millionaire' meant £30,000 a year, the notional yield of a million in capital; a 1946 report estimated that, after tax, only sixty remained of however many thousands there were in the 1930s. Two or three successive deaths could cost an earldom three-quarters of its acres in death duties. Stately homes were becoming museums, research centres, trade union colleges. The top rate of income tax was 95 per cent, and lot of the rich who owed it were believed to be paying it. Keynes had invented full employment.

That shabby, friendly equalising world was full of further promise. The Attlee government was nationalising the commanding heights of the economy. Wartime controls were adapted to reconstruction, directing resources to better rather than worse uses: industrial re-equipment rather than office-building; houses rather than hotels; public rather than private hospitals; holidays at home to protect the balance of payments. Bevan got three-quarters of the doctors to vote for the National Health Service.

And as fast as the old ideas were implemented, the best forward thinkers were feeding the government new ones. Socialist Bruce-Glazier, the able London manager of the Blue Funnel Line, was ready to manage nationalised shipping. (His conservative owners knew it, and thought he'd do it better than most. They were meanwhile financing the first of the Outward Bound Schools.) Richard Tawney was urging some inventive, less bureaucratic diversification of the forms of public ownership. Joan Robinson and Thomas Balogh and others were specifying the income policies to protect full employment from inflation, and boundary and exchange policies to protect it from other hazards. As the head of Labour Party research, Michael Young was recommending family policies and educational policies which look even more prescient now than they did then. He was also introducing Britain to consumer protection.

Labour had been elected in a landslide against the advice of 85 per cent of the national press. A peaceful democratic transition looked quite possible, if not to socialism then at least to a mixed economy with steadily improving welfare, dwindling private ownership and increasing equality. Bliss was it in that dawn to be alive and letter-boxing for Attlee's re-election.

From 'From London, with Love and Hindsight', Overland, 1985

Knowledge

I FIRST MET THE MODERN SOCIAL SCIENCES QUITE EARLY in their post-war career, at Princeton in 1948. As a history graduate looking for broader education, I took courses in economics, sociology, political science and international relations. It was a provoking experience. The economics was old-fashioned, perhaps wrong, but honestly meant. Large chunks of the other courses seemed to be simply fraudulent. Smart new operators were pointing the social sciences in smart new directions, trying to make them more abstract or more quantitative, more objective, more like physics – and whatever else, more profitable in the ordinary way of business. But on careful technical inspection, too much of the new business seemed to be strictly a sucker business, because too much of the new science was sterile, and certain to remain so. The models were inappropriate for their tasks, the theories were of types that could never deliver any new holds on the unknown, the objectivity was bogus, the jargon served chiefly to obscure the other shortcomings. Only the fund-hunting and the sales approach were effective.

The intellectual pretension and trickery we were getting were fair samples of what rising numbers of students were beginning to get all over the affluent world; as the production of social scientists and their sale to business and government multiplied, and more and more of the ruling classes' recruits were put through six or eight years of undergraduate and postgraduate training, often within a single discipline or at least a single philosophy of science. Of course, education has to direct people to some degree, and these trainees were all supposed to have democratic freedom to think as they pleased. But they were required to be scientific as their disciplines defined it, and many of the developing rules of 'discipline', 'objectivity' and 'science' were quite hostile to a genuinely observant, thoughtful, fruitful study of social life.

Such nasty-looking developments in the modes of conservatism, and in the selection of rich countries' ruling classes, seemed to be fit subjects for study by historians. But to study them usefully, a historian would need to understand the social sciences from the inside. I spent the spare time of the next fifteen years learning to understand the main structures and directions of theory in contemporary economics, sociology and political science – also in history, because (contrary to what most of both parties were saying at the time) it struck me that most of the main methodological problems of the social sciences were very like the problems that historians faced in selecting and constructing historical explanations. In both cases, the problems were less technical than political – they were questions of scientific purpose, but in the social sciences those tend to be questions of social purpose too.

I eventually arrived at reasons for believing that most social theory and research *had* to differ according to the personal values of the theorists and researchers, and certainly *ought* to do so. It must do so not just from human bias or frailty, but for strictly technical reasons. The structure of natural-scientific theory is ultimately determined by its subject matter and the scientists' purposes. Social theory is the same, but its subject matter and purposes are inevitably more contentious and changeable. Therefore (unless society itself has no conflicts of interest) widely agreed, universally serviceable theories are not to be expected except where their use relies on shared values or is enforced by political or academic coercion. Academic coercion is often associated with 'discipline', a portmanteau word whose meanings include rules and styles of work, and intellectual and administrative boundaries. Disciplines often define their boundaries and membership by the theories they elect to use, and the theories always incorporate somebody's values, however open or concealed.

Of course the values may be more professional than social. For example, plenty of economists have thought their political opinions less important than their ambition to build an exact, unified science, as deductive and mathematical as possible. But it makes sense to build a science like that only to the extent that life is like that; that is, to the extent that reliably regular economic behaviour can be abstracted from other social activity of which it is a part. If theory-builders push the exercise beyond those real-life limits, they get into two kinds of trouble. Theory becomes irrelevant, unreliable, unprovable or all three. And in choosing their constants and variables, the theorists may develop a systematic bias in favour of social constants and economic variables. The effects of that bias are likely to be politically conservative.

An opposite response to social complexity has always come from a school of institutional economists whose twentieth-century leaders have included Wicksell, Myrdal, Paul Streeten and (in odd, uneasy ways) those political opposites Joseph Schumpeter and Paul Sweezy, both of them doctrinaire in principle but institutionalists in practice. Any economic system is a social and political creation. It will rarely be well understood without understanding many determinants of economic activity, which are themselves neither economic nor stable. It may often include strands of repetitive behaviour which can be forecast by the use of local models and theories – but that is all, and even that is subject to historical change. It follows that useful economic understanding is always likely to depend in varying degrees on local knowledge. It will usually have to include a good deal of eclectic political, social and historical explanation. Most important of all, many technical beliefs about an economic system are part of it and affect its working; but they keep changing – so economists need to be able to step outside the going systems of technical belief (including their own) and observe *their* workings. Thinking through that last imperative, first Gunnar Myrdal and then Paul Streeten have contributed most of this century's best perceptions of the irreducible role of values in all the social sciences, not just in economics.

I had the extreme good fortune to be a fellow student, then a colleague of Streeten's. Besides friendship, he and I have shared some common methodological interests and also the experience of living and working with Thomas Balogh, that most instinctive, original, flamboyant and warlike of Anglo-Hungarian economists and advisers to British Labour leaders. I began my academic life living in a flat in Balogh's house, followed some of his professional and political warfare, and shared some of his and Streeten's pupils at a time when Balliol tutors were trying to give the School of Philosophy, Politics and Economics some of its intended unity. While Streeten was writing his powerful first paper, 'Programs and Prognoses', he was also translating some of Myrdal's methodological work for publication in English. I was trying to follow suit, writing my first papers about social and historical explanation, and translating some of Balogh's manuscripts from actionable Hungarian English into libel-free English English. I was less successful than Streeten – my papers were not published, and Balogh had a regrettable tendency to translate his books back again. But by the time I moved from Oxford to Adelaide I was equipped to follow the more general philosophical developments in economics, as far as my studies of the social sciences required.

Those studies were a long time getting done. At various dates, there were short, difficult papers which nobody would publish, then in 1966 a long book, which appeared three years later as *The Political Sciences: General principles of selection in social science and history*. Most of it had been lonely work. In Australia through these years, some sophisticated methodologists emerged from the Melbourne history school, but other social sciences either stayed old-fashioned or adopted fairly mindless ambitions. If you questioned those ambitions in a technical way, you would usually be sneered at for persecuting Copernicus and wanting to restore religious censorship and a flat earth. Economists were calmer than sociologists, but no likelier to listen to 'outsiders'; and none of them seemed to have read Wicksell or Myrdal or heard of Streeten. Meanwhile, I had picked up one easy skill: if dealing with one of the unoriginal majority of the profession, knowing two of his or her opinions was enough to guess the rest, and often also the textbooks they came from and the concealed values their owner didn't know they depended on. If we conversed at all, we were likely to irritate each other, and I learned to avoid it.

After *The Political Sciences*, I interviewed a great many town planners and administrators and wrote a more practical book called *Ideas for Australian Cities*. Unoriginally, its jacket blurb was headed: 'Women and children last?' That may have helped to get me appointed – I believe as token woman *and* token intellectual, a characteristic economy – to the South Australian Housing Trust. It was then necessary to learn the housing business in a practical way, from the work of that frugal and efficient organisation and from Alex Ramsay, the general manager who keeps it so. Among the lessons: public housing performance has intricate relations with the behaviour of private housing and money markets, so it is necessary to understand those too. In Australian conditions, housing commissions (public housing authorities) that do nothing but build houses can easily do less good than they should, so the trust was a town and community developer, a land dealer, a factory builder and the landlord of 400 shops. Not by uses of 'government power', but by its business operations in the market, it had been expected since its foundation to exercise a statewide influence on private land and housing prices and rents, and also on real wages, industrial investment and the geographical distribution of work and community services. As a first principle of management, whatever else such an operation needs, it needs a number of people engaged in it to be personally committed to its social purposes.

From 'A Capital Mistake', in Sol Encel (ed.), Inside the Whale:
Ten Personal Accounts of Social Research, *1978*

Values

YOU ARE ENTITLED TO A 'DECLARATION OF VALUES' by the author, so here it is, in four parts:

Motherhood values

I am for peace rather than war, and cooperation wherever possible. (But freedom sometimes has to be fought for, and competition works better than cooperation for some purposes.) I am for democracy, free speech and assembly, due process of law, the standard civil liberties. I value opportunities for personal diversity, individuality and self-expression: so I value a shared culture which encourages individual difference and non-conformity. The more the big bureaucracies of business and government can be humanised, the better: small is beautiful wherever it works well. One place it needs to work well is the household. Households not only do a third or more of economic production. They also do a lot to shape the character, skills and moralities of the children they bring up. Their resources for the task are important, and have been unduly neglected by most economists. But although upbringing is important, childhood should not be treated merely as a preparation for adult life. It can be a good, bad or indifferent experience in itself, and economic policies can have important effects on it. Young or old, each year of life should have equal value.

Economic concerns

I am for more equality within and between nations, more satisfying work, more active recreations and less 'consumerist' brainwashing than we have now. For all who want to earn – and for some, but by no means all, who don't – earned incomes are better than doles.

If changing conditions call for radical kinds of work-creation and work-sharing, we should work hard to provide them.

We should be thoughtful about the directions of economic development: about what we produce as well as about how we distribute it. In rich countries at least three values conflict with any policy of undiscriminating market-directed 'growth regardless'. There are severe resource and environmental problems. There are gross international inequalities, which call for various kinds of restraint in the rich countries, and intelligent international aid. And there is mounting evidence that the rich countries have now passed the threshold above which more material income does not increase the sum of human happiness. Materially, those countries now have more to gain by better distribution than by further growth. Socially, most of their people have more to gain by secure employment in good company than by any addition to national output that is expected (rightly or wrongly) to be won by turning rising numbers of them into increasingly anxious competitors for increasingly insecure jobs.

Capitalism or socialism?

Are these capitalist or socialist values? I think that is a wrong question. Developed modern economies are mixed economies in at least four senses:

- They mix public and private and cooperative and household *ownership* of the means of production.
- They mix public and private and cooperative and household *work* in the processes of production.
- To distribute wealth and income and goods and services, they mix market methods, administrative distribution, and household and cooperative and voluntary distribution.
- The fourth mixture deserves a heading of its own.

Human nature and culture

All those institutions run on mixtures of motive: desires for money, power, security, respect, love and other people's welfare; individual gain, mutual service, self-sacrifice, national, racial, religious, corporate, family and other loyalties ... No economic system could possibly run on universal selfishness. Nor on universal duty, universal love or any other single motive. And debating the mix of types of ownership and motivation, trying to improve it and adapting it to changed conditions are central concerns of economic policy ... So I think economists should be attentive students of the changing mixtures of motivation, and the alternative patterns of incentive, on which economic institutions can actually run.

From Economics: A new introduction, *1999*

2

A POLITICAL SCIENCE OF SOCIETY (1969)

Hugh Stretton was forty-five when he published his first book,
The Political Sciences. *Its subject – 'the mixtures of knowl-*
edge, imagination and persuasion' in the social sciences – was
timely and ambitious. Post-war hopes of social betterment had
boosted the prestige of the social sciences. Some practitioners,
especially in the United States, aspired to make their study as
mathematically precise, objective and predictive as physics.
Stretton's worries about this project had been slowly gather-
ing since his student days but became acute during his visit
to Princeton in 1948. The Political Sciences, *he later recalled,*
'arose one half out of disgust with the American social scien-
tists, and one half rationalising my own worries about what
kinds of historical explanation I was looking for'. The book took
another twenty years of reading and rumination, but from it
Stretton distilled an original vision of the social sciences as an
intrinsically moral and political activity. The following extracts
from the introduction and conclusion of The Political Sciences
summarise a position from which he hardly deviated over the
following forty years of prolific publication.

THIS BOOK IS ABOUT THE MIXTURES OF KNOWLedge, imagination and persuasion to be found in the work of historians and social scientists. They are influential people these days. They advise and staff governments and other institutions, and in rich countries they help to educate almost everybody. Most of them teach more than they discover. Their work wants watching, for its increasing social effect. Obviously, their values affect their work. Facts are facts, but theories order them and explanations select them. The political and professional values of the scientists affect these selections, which also get political direction from technical choices of method. Some nevertheless try to purge the values from the work, and attempt other irrational imitations of the forms of physical science. These efforts are called by their critics 'scientistic'. 'Scientism' flourishes in sociology like a cargo cult in Melanesia, invoking magical plenty wherever conventional production is scantiest.

Strict social scientists like to search for the regular, measurable, general and objective facts of social life. Will those principles of selection net much useful understanding of a life which is complex, changing and sometimes perhaps freely chosen? Softer social scientists think not. What is the difference between the strict scientific methods and their softer rivals? Most of the rivals would allow practical aims and social valuations to guide the detail of the research. Some such intrusion of values is inevitable, but strict scientists keep trying to exclude them, by increasingly curious principles of selection. The worst offenders when misused, sometimes with devastating effect, are various rules of objectivity. These were meant to make observation accurate. They are misapplied to the different business of selecting concepts and identities and classes, and causes and effects.

Value judgements seem so unscientific that even 'soft' authors are often content to confess them, and critics to detect them, so that readers can discount them. It is worth going further to see just what the valuations do and how they do it, and what the scientific rules would do instead. It is a conclusion of this study that valuations contribute rationally and indispensably to a wide range of scientific selections and constructions, from the most 'applied' to the most 'pure'. They should be improved, not replaced. Those who teach their students otherwise corrupt them.

*

In politicians' discourse we expect valuable arrangements of true information. That is the structure of any other knowledge of society; and that is the status of whoever discovers and publishes it.

The mixtures of fact, value, selection and reasoning will vary with the problems. But a non-valuing, laws-only program is simply mad. Social scientists who refused controversial work would be as useless as politicians who refused it. Unanimous social science would be as sinister as unanimous politics. Researchers might avoid responsibility by the public service method of silence under political control, but they would have to stop publishing and teaching. Scientists may well defer to the citizens' values, but like politicians they must choose which ones, and their work suffers technically if limited by the citizens' present visions and valuations of facts and options. Altogether a scientific program, though as political as any other, is not as conservative as is sometimes thought. It cripples causal analysis, distorts selection unhelpfully to any party, and preaches an uncaring morality hostile to most.

Facts are still sovereign, observation objective. Scientists need not adopt the false reporting, the one-eyed short-run commitments or the disreputable persuasions of bad political oratory, nor the blinkered, uncandid purposes of some of the science reviewed in this book. They may sometimes come nearer to the good politician's balancing and conciliation of interests. But generally their employments allow them to be honest, altruistic, far-sighted and fair, and the technical fertility of much of their work requires that their valuations be complicated, subtle and unstereotyped. And, above all, *good*. They need only fear the spurious simplicities of orators' or salesmen's values if they themselves adopt programs to conceal valuations, or make them unanimous, or 'deduce' them all from agreed value-premises. Or, of course, if they value things like height, rigour, abstraction and generality above useful truth.

Whatever the scientists intend, their activity is anyway made political by its subjects. Some social science is inventive or self-verifying. For some, social trial is a more appropriate test than 'proof'. The language of 'hypothesis', 'verification' and 'discovery' can report only a biased selection of the inescapable relations between scientists and the listening, choosing, disagreeing, self-changing subjects of their science. Nor can 'value-free' stand to 'value-structured' as pure to applied. Indeed, the more abstract and general the social theory, the more its construction must usually depend on valuations, and the likelier it is to be taught to people under authority. The language of 'application' and 'engineering' has to include in its meaning informing, persuading, tempting and coercing the people engineered. It makes no difference if they, rather than scientists or administrators, do these things for themselves and to each other; they still use the social scientist's work, including whatever values are (whether or not he intended or concealed them) built into the structure of the work.

Of course the tasks of social science are very various. The division of labour will usually provide a quiet life, unembarrassed unanimity and predominantly technical tasks for those who prefer them. This may be just as well, to keep out of mischief a multitude already brainwashed with the values of scientific imitation, careerism and the unconcerned acceptance of whatever is. Resignation from life is a personal matter. But now some of them want to make death the program for everybody.

The scientistic program seems to distinguish itself from science by the following principles, of which the second frustrates the first, the fourth contradicts the third, and the fifth forgets the third and any other respectable purposes of inquiry.

- Limit scientific activity to causal explanation.
- Omit or conceal the selective imagination and valuation required by most causal analysis of human society.
- Attempt universal laws.
- However systems differ in fact, speak only of classes of them; but do not limit your class to systems to which identical explanations sufficiently apply; instead, keep your class large and select only the causes which occur in all the disparate systems in it; then assert that these few causes constitute an independent system, and a sufficient explanation of each system in the class.
- When your scheme has discovered no new information and has finished reclassifying the old information, then let it pattern eclectic explanations wherever (as in higher education) you can protect a market for them.

In practice, this program sometimes selects politically indifferent phenomena for investigation – small details, uninteresting abstracts, such vast but unendangered effects as mere political or social survival. It often requires that socially recognised and valued phenomena be fragmented or compounded, conceptually, into socially unrecognised and morally indifferent identities. This may serve good purposes in particular cases, but as a generalised principle it has no general justification by results. Nor have the other principles which often accompany it – generalised preferences for quantities over qualities, for regulars over locals, for inferred relations over understood mechanisms of relation, for laws over skills, for letting methods choose problems rather than problems chose methods.

In the end, having thus atrophied some scientific skills, the program usually achieves one of three effects. It limits work to problems of no social interest. Or it limits work to areas of (at least among the scientists) political consensus. Or it plugs its own new moralities.

The first effect is obvious. The second is commoner. Most practical rules of objectivity simply require unanimous valuations. Conventional, trivial, diffuse and ambiguous values are the least likely to be criticised, the easiest to conceal and the easiest to contrive by authority or fashion – dissent can be dismissed as 'value-structured', not science at all. The technical effects of this are terrible. It inhibits whole ranges of perceptive observation, useful selection, original imagination of alternatives and possibilities and programs, and original discovery of facts and their relations.

Or, worst, objectivity begets its own politics. For a last example of the price of purity, exaggerate a current purification in urban theory. How can cities be measured, compared, explained? Past comparisons have been subjective, measurements untheoretical, purposes *ad hoc* and programmatic. From such impurity, rescue seems urgent. Find a measurable, objective indicator of an abstract, general and commanding quality or 'urbanity', and *then* you will have the beginnings of a pure science to unify and direct the brawling inconsistencies of 'applied' city planning: What are cities, essentially? They are systems of intense, hyper-efficient interaction. Interaction is quintessentially the transmission, reception and exchange of information. The basic unit of information is the simple clause or image, the 'bit'. The basic unit of interaction is the transmission of one bit from one human to another. Call this basic transaction a 'hubit'. Private, face-to-face hubits are not countable. But the public channels of communication are all metered, one way or another. Count the hubits they carry. Weight them for distance carried. Divide by time and population, and you have indexed the intensity of interaction. Indeed, you are on the way to a universal, abstract and reliable measure of urbanity, and a general theory of it. You also have a political program: to maximise urbanity. That may not mean maximising the intensity of interaction. Object studies, of the precise intensity at which neurosis overtakes productivity, will discover the urbane optimum. (Pretend you selected interaction and communication, isolated bits, identified neurosis and defined productivity, and chose the word 'urbanity', without valuing anything. Alternatively, you derived the value of urbanity objectively from the citizens' observed propensity to overcrowd. But refuse to value the bits themselves – the nature of the interactions or the substance of the communications. The pure science would become impure, and the applied science would continue quarrelsome, if some bits were valued above others.) Now that you are quantised and objective, there is no further call for divisive and subjective impressions of quality and desirability. You can revise the curriculum to tell the next generation of college-educated researchers and planners and legislators that two lies are more urbane than one truth. Two messages of hatred are better than one of love. Two crimes are better than one arrest. A minute of talk is better than two of thought. Taped commercials enhance the urbanity of public transport. Up to the optimum, that is – above the optimum, any silence is better than any protest. Now cross-fertilise with other disciplines which have similarly purified, indexed and quantified 'demand' and 'liberty', to show that ten lousy options enlarge consumers' choices more than five good options could.

Now at last city planning can cease to be utopian-directive. Instead, it can become empirical-adaptive, democratically responsive to the demands of whoever already has (objectively) the dollars, the land and the skills. Science, purged of its subjective and divisive valuations, can give its whole and pure authority to legitimising winners, and to asking and observing and contriving, neutrally, which victories the winners would like next.

Scientism prospers. It is preached by leaders in many disciplines, and by some of their ablest followers and likeliest supplanters. Not all of it is wilful sin, though I think some is. Its dangers will be underestimated by anyone who forgets its element of noble ambition, of high scientific hope and good social intention.

The many who suspect its sterility, or its vicious fertility, find themselves on the defensive. Fashion disarms them, making fun of their outmoded politics, their grandmotherly morals and literacy, their primitive notions of truth-telling. Promoters neglect them for teaching so much – or worrying so honestly – that they publish so little. Uncertainties of their own inhibit them – science is a most emotive word and they cannot always distinguish, reliably, science from its imitations. Most concede something – commonly, value-freedom – to modernity. But their confidence and skill are now very important. So are their weapons. Their appropriate rearmament is not so much moral, but is rather the coldest understanding of the principles of scientistic selection, and the reasons for their lack of yield.

For two centuries after Locke and Newton were colleagues, there were more social than natural scientists at work. Then and since, those who valued (and persuaded) the people they studied have helped with social achievements – from the disgrace of some tyrants to the decencies of some democracies, from the loving care of children to the higher education of millions, from safe streets to the modern grace of Stockholm, from the old-age pension to the conquest of unemployment and the billions of international aid. Meanwhile, the 'immaturity' of social scientism spans a hundred of those years. In the last forty, more resources, more numbers and man-hours and equipment and intelligence, have tried to scientise society than it took to get physics from the astrolabe through Newton to Einstein.

Their costs have been high. They include some arrest of honest science and some taming, or confusing, of the young. Their useful yield is trifling. Surely their excuses have run out?

But social evils can survive without excuses, whether by apathy, honest mistake or selfish intent. Most social scientists sit comfortably high in the hierarchies of race, class, income and power. That need not stop any one of them supplying to other people the services which poorer classes and reforming movements have commonly received, for one reason or another, from individuals richer than themselves. But comfort is seductive, and so is scientism. Scientistic selection avoids the radical imagination or discovery of poor men's chances for social choice or change or conservation. Like other censors, it hedges science and education into the service of established winners. Scientistic values may prompt the 'value-free' observation that this educational reinforcement is 'functional for the system'. But others' values should equip them to see in the methodological disputes about scientism a real social conflict: a competition for the talent, conscience, judgement and recruitment of scientists and students, the advisers and next inheritors of power.

In that conflict, the scientist is a citizen. His duty goes beyond discovering and understanding. It becomes his business to win.

3

AUSTRALIA AS A TALE OF THREE CITIES (1970)

In The Political Sciences *Stretton said what he thought social scientists should, and should not, do.* Ideas for Australian Cities, *published just a year later, put his ideas into practice by examining his own rapidly urbanising Australian society. He challenged the myopic focus of most contemporary observers of Australia on its two biggest cities, Sydney and Melbourne. Viewed from Canberra and Adelaide, smaller cities with stronger planning traditions, the shortcomings of the urban monoliths fell into sharp relief. In these brilliant thumbnail sketches, Stretton stressed the characteristics of most interest to the social-democratic planner: Adelaide's distinctive political legacy, Melbourne's tradition of private enterprise and Sydney's magical but confining landscape. Melbourne's middle class he had known as a boy, Adelaide's university and bureaucracy at first hand, as professor and deputy chairman of the South Australian Housing Trust, and Sydney's landscape more distantly, as a regular visitor. Deft combinations of history, contemporary observation and personal opinion, these sketches show Stretton's ease in the role previously monopolised by a long line of astute journalists from Anthony Trollope to Donald Horne, as interpreters of the Australian social and political scene.*

Adelaide as an estate agency

ADELAIDE IS REALLY TWO CITIES. A PROVINCIAL capital fattens comfortably through the second century of its slow growth. But through it like a cable, from twenty miles north to twenty miles south of it, deft men lately threaded a Detroit. Heavy industry, housing for its labour and services for both are strung along a forty-mile skein of roads and rails and pipes and wires. Public power contrived that, but can't now control one of its effects. Across the middle of the line, nourished as never before, middle-class Adelaide quickens its middle-aged spread; it begins to clog the new Detroit's transport and force distortions of its lean shape. If the old town would only conform to the new line's discipline, the two might thrive together. But the old town won't; knowing its wilful appetites, its planners don't even try. Instead, its engineers propose to drive clean through it the clear channels which Detroit must have. The lady resists the rape, understandably, but she was a fool to miss the chance of such an energetic marriage.

The old town began on a broad wedge of coastal plain. Halfway from the coast to an abrupt wall of hills, the plain steps up to firmer ground and the Torrens river cuts a shallow valley through the step. Here, on either side of the river, Colonel William Light laid out his famous plan: two patches of city grid around six generous squares, within a figure eight of parklands. Launched there in 1836, the town lived a few quarrelsome years on its imported capital, languished, then survived chiefly on copper, government, grain and wool until it was big enough to dignify its local trades as industries. It developed its shallow port and was early with local railways and horse trams, piped water and sewers and gas. Electricity waited for the twentieth century and never reached the railways, whose old black puffers pulled balconied cowboy-style carriages around the suburban tracks, and along a number of suburban streets, until the 1950s.

The plain had patches of brick clay and crumbling limestone, but not much useful timber. These, with the empty skies and pale seas of long summers and autumns, prompted various recollections of the Mediterranean. Cracked brick-and-stone slums with the instant charm of almost immediate pink and sandy decay; sundrenched gravelly streets; olives dark on the parched hillsides; vines all over the verandahs; cheap, abundant wine. Prosperity often depended on continued immigration, minerals and rainfall. Sometimes all three languished. Then there was another Mediterranean likeness – a hot, dry austerity of hard work on arid small holdings, and debt and unemployment in the dusty town.

It was at the end of its first century, with its population of a third of a million still clustered closely around Colonel Light's centre, that the city began suddenly to grow in quite new ways and new directions. These, with its modern efficiency and its modern problems, owe very little to any official town planning. They are the product of the industrial program which the state government launched in 1934. The way that program reshaped the city, though seldom thought of then or since as a method of metropolitan planning, is in fact a practical and powerful one, adaptable to other places and purposes. But it can only be as good as the men in charge of it, and to understand its Adelaide successes and shortcomings, it is necessary to look back to the character of a past generation of the state's oligarchy, and to the way in which a handful of unusually educated men came to control a few of its public services in the 1930s. This may strike some readers as an idle historical ramble, but it is really the shortest cut to grasping *one* way in which an Australian city can keep its land cheap, its costs low, its life peaceful and its growth easy, to the advantage of a large majority of its citizens.

It was easy to mock the respectable society of the old Adelaide oligarchy. They did tend to marry each other's money, meet at the Club, cultivate tennis and bougainvillea, attend chamber concerts and 'preserve standards' in quaintly Victorian ways. But they had other qualities, which were eventually to converge in sparking their industrial revolution. They were honest, often puritanical. Many original fortunes were lawfully based on reselling land bought from the government, or on mining or grazing leases granted by it; the rich were used to cosy but lawful relations between business and government. They were able gamblers, the steadiest source of risk capital for Australian mineral search. They had a high regard for a gentlemanly sort of education – they founded their own university early, hired some remarkable scholars into it, and kept many links with English universities. They were an open oligarchy, willing to recruit talent; and they seem to have conserved, in at least a few of themselves, some of the radical propensities that had founded the colony in the first place. In *Paradise of Dissent* (1957), Douglas Pike saw even in the latest generation 'a single-minded resolution which is the continuing feature of the state's history and its most distinguishing mark. Other parts of Australia may muddle through in the best British tradition: South Australians zealously attach themselves to some conscious theoretical purpose.'

These qualities, under leadership which usually mixed patricians with town and country radicals, led them to interesting achievements. In systematic colonisation, new land laws, attempts at workers' blocks and village settlements, voting methods, votes for women and some other democratic devices they were among the world's innovators. Though patchy, their early social services were often novel and generous by the standards of the nineteenth century. In 1872 Trollope saw '60,000 people in a new city, with more than all the appliances of humanity belonging to four times the number in old cities'. To those productions the next generation added another: it brought up and sent off Lawrence Bragg and Howard Florey to win Nobel prizes in physics and medicine, and Elton Mayo to apply similar ingenuity to American industrial psychology and management. After that, as elsewhere between the wars, the society became duller and less inventive, and its leaders more stodgily conservative. But not entirely so. The Industrial Revolution, and the shape of the modern city, had their origins in an odd practice of recruiting a few schoolteachers into the routine financial and administrative branches of the state civil service.

In this century all Australian states have recruited their civil services chiefly from modest families: state school leavers join the service at sixteen or so, a few of the ablest then pick up technical qualifications by part-time study, so in the normal course of events nobody gets either private business experience or a general education, or achieves much influence until he's past fifty. Between the elderly, philistine hierarchy this produces and the better-educated wealth in business and the professions there is rarely much affinity. The others look down on the 'petty officialdom' of the state service even when some of the 'petty officials' control larger enterprises than their own.

Adelaide was no different, except for a device by which a few of the same state school boys climbed to the same heights rather younger, and by way of a different educational experience, a decade or two before even the Commonwealth service got much educated leadership. Scholarships to the University of Adelaide were few and mean. So were South Australian schoolteachers' salaries. But there was *one* chance for able children without money: they could go to the teachers' college, which put the best of them through the university, and made sure that they did nothing 'useful' there – only pure arts and sciences. Educated thus, a few then transferred to other branches of state service. There they were noticed by more powerful men than were noticing junior public servants at that time in bigger bureaucracies in other places. The South Australian oligarchy was intimate. All sorts sat unpaid on the boards of the public utilities, and gentlemen still went into parliament. Between the wars, a small group of senior civil servants and patricians made a point of knowing the gifted few among the university students, and of contriving university courses for any talents that turned up in the public service. Among these patrons was Leslie Hunkin, and his own power was an example of the oligarchs' occasional eccentricity at its best.

Five facts about Hunkin distinguished him from the rest of his generation of public service leaders. He came from out of state, started life with a little money, went to a private as well as a state school, founded and ran a successful business, and was a radical Labor politician. In his spare time he was also secretary of the Public Service Association, its advocate in the industrial courts and the government's chief critic on public service matters. In 1929 the conservative premier Sir Richard Butler took the extraordinary step of appointing this natural enemy to be Public Service Commissioner. He was persuaded to do this by J.W. Wainwright, a subordinate in the state audit office, whom Hunkin and Butler presently appointed auditor-general. Between them, Wainwright and Hunkin then hauled up a few others like them.

Hunkin had a sure eye for talent. He himself had been removed from university after one year by a long illness, but he spent it reading much of what the university might have taught him. Though he knew talent was personal, he thought it also needed education, preferably general rather than specialised. Unless they had some compensating natural genius, he had no time for merely 'practical men'. Above all he looked for able youngsters, and sent them to the university if they had not been there already. When the first batch enrolled in economics and public administration, he enrolled and took the courses with them.

Numerically, the effect of all this was slight. Plenty of the state service continued to be managed by the old rules of thumb. But the few exceptions were important. One ex-teacher is now the very able registrar of one of the universities. Another is head of the state treasury. Another – the first, before Hunkin's time – was the auditor Wainwright himself. Hunkin planted another, A.M. Ramsay, in the Housing Trust. Its manager soon decided on his own initiative to change places with the newcomer, who thus at thirty-four got hold of very large public resources indeed. At the university, Wainwright was educated in science and arts, Ramsay in arts and economics; both were exceptionally lucky in having as teachers young men on their ways to high eminence, and Ramsay regards the experience as a watershed of much of his power and purpose since.

Meanwhile, back in 1934, as the weary old market and warehouse town emerged from another cycle of drought, depression and heavy unemployment, Wainwright persuaded Hunkin and a necessary half-dozen of its oligarchs to industrialise it. The methods they chose were like their grandfathers' methods of colonisation: highly theoretical. They ignored the obvious sources of industrial capital and practical knowhow in Melbourne and Sydney; those were the enemy. They unlearned most of the conventional wisdom of the day about private enterprise, crown land and public housing, and replaced it by a half-page logic of their own: local, ruthless, simple, new. Then, sticking tuppenny stamps on cheapish envelopes, they addressed themselves to a few of the biggest corporations in the world.

Melbourne as a private enterprise

THE METROPOLIS SPRAWLS, COMFORTABLY FOR THE well-off and in a dull, segregated, neglected way for many of the rest. It does house a lot of its workers reasonably near to the centre, to their jobs, or to both. From the better suburbs, people come in to work in the country's richest concentration of corporate head offices – especially the headquarters of manufacturing industry, and the legal and financial services that go with them. Apart from some office towers there, and some housing commission towers nearby, growth is an undramatic process of slow change, low skylines and (except inside the public and private gardens) a dreadful insensitivity to the detailed structure of the land. The place is already endless, tedious and average-dangerous to drive around. Hundreds of identical miles of straight tram-lined suburban main roads cross and congest at incessant shop-lined intersections. Many impressions of the character of Melbourne life have related it to the weary boredom of its suburban transport. One theorist ascribed the decline of the intellectual and artistic left to its dispersal beyond conversation range. Certainly the beards don't crowd the centre, or not enough to sustain more than a couple of Carlton pubs – they go and build pisé houses on bush hillsides fifteen miles out and hopefully christen the nearest main street 'the village'. Others have seen in the dull transport and the dullish locations it gets you to the key to an extreme emphasis by the middle classes on private life, private homes and gardens, and inviolable property rights.

Except to work (this theory says) Melbourne people don't travel in order to congregate or generate much public gaiety. It takes all their time and petrol to visit each other occasionally, and that is what they chiefly do. Family life and friendship and private hospitality make for quiet personalities with serious concerns. Excellent private schooling and higher education send their best talents into the professions, or the biggest business, or increasingly both. There are conservative cars and suits, Town Hall concerts, whatever last year's equivalents are of Gilbert and Sullivan and *My Fair Lady*, a responsible and unsensational press, a safe though philistine farmers' and liberals' government, and on every hand (across the river) understatements or dignified disclosures of wealth. And, of course, secure social segregations.

The lady wife of one lord mayor (knighted or not, Melbourne mayors are wed to good ladies, never to women) once appeared on television to defend Toorak. 'People think Toorak is full of millionaires with Bentleys and Rolls-Royces,' she said. 'This is quite wrong, not true. I have lots of very good friends with Bentleys and Rolls-Royces who don't live in Toorak at all.' Wherever they live, they help critics to write off respectable Melbourne society as absurd. But respectability gets an unduly bad press these days. Considered as a style for the rich, there is something to be said for it – it's better than chromium vulgarity, or the penthouse-jet-youth-thirdwife syndrome. The private lives of Melbourne's middle classes are often as thoughtfully cultivated as their private gardens, and as full of grace and individuality. Its best schoolboys write good verse, talk well about words and people and politics, and rarely have daddies with alcoholic yachts. Even its Old Boys seem more intent on making things (and of course money) than on selling things. Melbourne is not the centre of the advertising business.

A restrained public culture takes some of its colour from such educated values. The city's old gardens (there at all only because English governors reserved them) are quiet and beautiful; nannies wouldn't look amiss in them. Across a boulevard from one of them, the new cultural centre stands as the most private of all public buildings. Its austere fortress walls shut out the city's public sights and sounds from the country's finest collection of paintings, bought mostly from private endowments. But people who are fond of this city find it hard to focus their affections on any of its public structures or centres. They like its atmosphere, and many small parts of it; but chiefly they seem to think of the private life it affords them, and of the friends they find. They don't expect much of its public life – or its public officials.

All classes share that last understanding. It is known in Kew and Camberwell – rather as Englishmen used to know about 'The East' – that on either side of their slow routes to the city and in the unknown regions north and west of it, slums do exist which once brewed larrikin gangs, St Patrick's Day riots, gaunt axe-faced footballers, and the bitter machinery of the labour movement. They still brew most of Melbourne's beer. They now accommodate an older population of natives, and many clusters of immigrants. The natives especially have not much cause to love the public authorities that neglect them, and even less the authorities that threaten to 'renew' them. Their local government is always dusty, sometimes venal, rarely productive – if you ever have the rare good fortune to find a Richmond councillor drunk, ask him about steamrollers.

Nobody expects much action of public authority. Robin Boyd, appreciating his native city in *The Australian* of 5 March 1969, forecast another appreciation of it in the year 2001: 'Another mile and a half of freeway has been built ... Mobility has been maintained by a steady increase in the number of trams, some streets having four or six lines down the middle.' A new metal now keeps the tram wheels reliably octagonal. 'Increased parking space has been achieved by bitumenising the Bay beaches as far as Rosebud ... Two more test holes for the underground railway have been sunk ...' Melbourne's physical fabric attracts pained, affectionate reminiscence from a surprising number of its best writers. Perhaps its unchanging face keeps reminding them accurately of how it used to be when they were young. Contemporary impressions read just like memories of the 1930s, Hal Porter, the Florentino, trams, footy, Rosella and all.

Nothing changes, any Melburnian will tell you, because *they* never do anything. That leaves them rusty, so when rarely they *do* try something ambitious, they blunder. The fear nowadays is that they are bent on bulldozing the old town to put something worse in its place. Why? Because they don't *know* anything, your Melburnian will tell you.

Not to know anything should be an achievement in that city. Its educational arrangements, whatever criticism they merit, are probably the country's best. It brings up and holds an outstanding concentration of business, administrative, technical and professional talent. Fixing up a slum, thinking out a housing policy – such things should be easier there than anywhere. But they are not. Why are almost all of the best of those rich skills in private, corporate, academic or federal service, while the state's huge enterprises roll dully on without them?

Sydney as the Magic Place

SYDNEY IS BOXED IN ON THREE SIDES BY THE SEA AND two rugged coastal plateaus. Within the box, fifteen or eighteen miles square, the rich have the beautiful land north of the harbour and along as much of its southern shore and ocean coast as is not needed for merchant and naval uses. Out of sight to the south and upriver to the west there is duller land for industries, rail networks and so on, with slums and suburbs for the workers and clerks. (Of course there are exceptions – some inner slums, and some happy and attractive patches and mixtures of rich and poor in various places, especially along the rivers and in the southern suburbs.) All the sectors meet in the middle at that magic meeting place where new flats and old terraces, parks and gaunt dockland warehouses, the great bridge and the great ships and the opera sails crowd close enough to touch hands around the city sky-scrapers. The rich will never willingly move far from that magic, and who can blame them? The life within it may be ordinary and arduous, but seen from afar, from any of the rich land around the harbour, its beauty has few rivals outside Rio and Manhattan.

There is room altogether for a couple of million, including per-haps half a million succeeders in sight of the harbour or north of it. For any more the only way out of the box is inland, away from the good things and the good weather, where the Cumberland Plain fans out north and south behind the plateaus in a long oval, forty miles by twenty, hotter and colder than Sydney, drier but prone to flood. Any number of workers and clerks can be housed out there, and indus-try can spread there; but Sydney's *urgent* trouble is that the old city on the harbour has run out of suitable land for easy extensions of its centre, and for private gardens for its rich and middle classes. The childless ones are already taking over the inner slums or stacking up eight, twenty, forty storeys high; but too often that increases the luxury and the car parking rather than the actual density of people. Soon those with children will have to pack tighter – they're begin-ning to outnumber the tolerably located private gardens – or else they will have to take over the nearer of the drearier western and southern suburbs. In Melbourne it's different: there's no magic to hold the middle classes so they follow the good land further and further east, while some of the poor get stacked into the old city's sky instead. According to surveys, the Sydney poor think much the same about being twenty miles out as the Melbourne poor think about being twenty floors up. But there remains a critical difference of physical and social geography. Both centres stand where the rich half of the metropolis meets the poor half. Melbourne's direction of natural growth was out beyond its rich half, over good land. Rich and poor would both like to go there, and some of both already mix there. With proper development good centres could therefore prosper there. E.F. Borrie's 1954 Metropolitan Planning Scheme and R.D.L. Fraser's and George Clarke's 1968 proposals would have made the best of those wholesome opportunities. To rule them out, and to turn the workers back to the basalt, the Victorian government and the Victorian rich now have to intervene with strong action *against* the pull of the market. But Sydney had no such wholesome option. Its growth has to go out beyond its poor half onto (comparatively) poorer land. Except for some patches around the fringe, only the workers will go there, so no amount of encouragement could make very good centres or new cities thrive there.

Any metropolis growing past its second million is nearly certain to increase the inequalities of its people. In Sydney the land itself intensifies those effects. So what should Sydney do? It should try to slow its growth and conserve as much as possible of its central structure and variety. To achieve that, there need to be better urban alternatives for its overflowing numbers – new cities elsewhere, and some new independence for parts of the metropolis itself. By 1975 plenty of people agreed with that: the national government, and by then most of its opposition; most of the state's own planners, when they were here to speak their minds; many local governments; large numbers of Sydney's citizens; and a vital branch of organised labour. In their various ways all those people did what they could to reverse the destructive policies of the 1960s. But the real author of those policies – the Liberal and Country Party state government – was still there, and through the 1970s its urban policies became stupider and more destructive than before. The policy of over-centralising Sydney also gets some support from other sources – from some office-builders, property gamblers and other winners from the process of over-centralisation. Because the policy is still alive and active, it is worth pausing to explore its long-term implications for the city.

There was room around the harbour for a wonderful port and commercial city, and industry, and an administrative capital, to serve a state population of two or three million. But for the central activities needed by a state population of seven or ten million, Sydney simply hasn't room. Its land offers no workable direction for ports, commerce, business, industry, government and culture all to extend with rich and poor together giving life and power to a series of linked centres. So new cities should be launched independently, elsewhere. Government commands quite enough portable activities to launch them. There is a unique, double case for such a policy in New South Wales. It has the most people and some of the best sites and economic prospects for new cities. For any million new people it will be cheaper in the long run to construct a new centre than to reconstruct Sydney's. Any billion of public investment can connect more people to better services and give them easier access to real city life in a new city than it can now do in Sydney, where so much of it has to be wasted on demolition and replacement. Most of any billion of investment can probably do more good to Sydney itself by staying away from it.

But compassion for the workers and clerks won't induce many of the Sydney rich to move themselves or their public or private investments away from the magic. They will first have to learn what the magic costs rising numbers of the rich themselves; and how much of the magic must be dulled if they all stay with it. The nature of these costs can be indicated in a simple theoretical way. Besides the mounting proportion of investment which has to go to destruction and replacement before it buys any additional transport or floor space, there are also the following effects if unlimited growth continues around a centre of limited area: (1) each central activity expands, trying to impose its own monotony on a higher share of the centre; (2) fewer and fewer types of activity which can pay the rising rents force out more and more activities which can't; (3) though some of the winners are those who can use central locations most economically, too many others are not – they are those whose directors happen to be able to spend shareholders' or taxpayers' money most irresponsibly; (4) separation reduces the efficiency of many winners and losers alike, because the winners lose quick, cheap access to so many of their ancillaries; and (5) as the number of central employments increases, there is a corresponding fall in the proportion of employees who can live on good land in easy reach of the centre, with real family use of the central attractions and services. In Sydney this doesn't only aggravate inequalities, sending more poor further out west to allow more of their masters to work at Circular Quay, and live on the land in reach of it. It steadily lowers the proportion who are 'rich' at all in any urban sense, changing more and more of the middle ranks from urban 'haves' to over-rented or outer-suburban 'have nots'. To be rich – to enjoy full and workable family membership of Sydney – you have to be richer every year.

None of this need trouble the very rich. They will still make most of the centralising decisions, and direct public investment to provide whatever new bridges, expressways and car parks they need to connect their private gardens comfortably to the centre. As they monopolise more of the centre, the rising rents must drive out more and more of the artistic, squalid, surprising, wayward, intellectual, picturesque, marginal and shoestring activities which are a main part of a good city's attraction and diversity. In some cities these merely move along the line; in Sydney there is less and less 'cheap city' on central public transport for them to go to. They have to disperse to the suburbs, and some of the results of that – especially around the harborside – are locally very attractive. But removal from the centre extinguishes some of them altogether; the rest lose their central locations and the centre loses *them*. In their place it gets more jewellers and fur shops, galleries for established painters only, and expense account hotels and entertainments. Or chiefly, it just gets more offices; and inside them, not much further diversification of activity, but more and more of the same activities, and people not more but less diversified than before.

So although many of the effective centralisers are philistines, it is surprising that they get support and applause from professional men and intellectuals, lovers of diversity and sources of some of it, who will surely be among the losers – and losses – as the central rents rise. They seem slow to notice the steep decline in romantic appreciations of life in New York. The public and private costs, the complexity and savagery of that city now outrun the most talented and expensive efforts at control. Various kinds of power, marketing and entertainment still concentrate there but invention doesn't. Invention comes from middle-sized, middle-western industrial cities. Discovery comes from the outskirts of smaller or more sprawling cities in New England and California. The best novels by New Yorkers are written in Paris, Tangiers or the New England woods, and New York is their word for hell. *No* New York authority would now build anything like that desperate centre, if the chance came over again; but once built, the interests committed to it are unbeatable, as they already seem to be in Sydney.

The Sydney citizens who nevertheless long for a Manhattan may not even have noticed what seems – though of course the impression may be wrong – to be happening to the more creative productivities in their own city. Already the rents around Kings Cross make sure that the sale and consumption of urban goods drive out the distilling. Most of the novels discussed and pictures sold there are nowadays written and painted in Sarsaparillan suburbs, or the bush. The little theatres play five miles away, in different directions. The dwindling number of picturesque characters now have an angle, or a pusher. More women are brought in than brought up there – more bought than honestly made, perhaps. When students make a cafe culture it will be somewhere else – if they make it at all, from their suburban campuses. Bohemian life and adventurous taste are already driven over the hill to Paddington, and somewhat monotonised even there by the rents that will soon drive them from 'city' altogether. An ambling hippie culture may settle here and there for short sojourns; but there will be very little hope of any old-style Chelsea or Bloomsbury or Left Bank or Greenwich Village: no central place with cheap land and cheap old buildings on a main skein of good passenger transport and with plenty of cheap beds of its own, where the young and the arts and the ideas can rely on meeting one another. In Sydney the elements of diversity must probably be fragmented and scattered to a dozen places in a dozen ill-connected suburbs, to become less valuable and accessible to each other or to their customers.

But even these, artists and thinkers and students, will be modest losers compared with larger numbers of plainer folk. More workers must sweat without city at all on the western plains. More of the middle classes will be squeezed harder, will see less of the magic, will spend rising proportions of their money and time on drearier travelling to more distant or expensive housing. It seems sad that those who see the best of the city, and doubtless love it best, should do most to raise its costs and cruelties, and disperse its magic, by using as many of our loans and taxes and insurances as they can get their hands on, to pull down much of the very best city we have. Why? To clear a site. For what? For a smooth-skinned office centre with expense-account amusements and car stack: a hive which could be built as well for less, and function more efficiently, somewhere else. Good money after bad. I liked the Quay and the Cross better twenty-five years ago.

If any critic wants one, that is the clue to the sour temper of this chapter. I loved the Cross as a sailor, when it still had poets and novelists and amateurs. That was between loving Melbourne when a boy could still ride out of it, and South Kensington and Greenwich Village when a student could still afford *them*. This isn't a small-town recoil from big Sydney. It's a lover's howl of pain as big Sydney's heart grows more heartless and remote, too full of glossy spenders, less and less accessible to lovers.

4

AUSTRALIA AS A SUBURB (1970)

Australian intellectuals had long looked down on the suburbs. 'Suburban' signified all that was mediocre, conformist and philistine in Australian society. This was despite the fact that, as Stretton observes here, the prejudice was itself a conformist echo of English ones, and that many Australian intellectuals actually lived in the suburbs. Stretton was one of the first Australian writers to confront this paradox, and to appreciate the real benefits Australians derived from their suburban houses and gardens. Rather than turning their backs on the suburbs, he argued, democrats should ask how they could improve them and spread their benefits more widely.

How much of the Australian way of life is worth having?

Most Australians choose to live in suburbs, in reach of city centres and also of beaches or countryside. Many writers condemn this choice; and with especial anger or gloom they condemn the suburbs. Planners' debates often concentrate their disagreements on the same issues: the question of urban density, and the quality of suburban life.

Especially for Australians, residential density presents a true dilemma. It seems to have contradictory effects on life at home and life away from it. If we had to consider only our journeys from home and the quality of the destinations they lead to, then we could easily agree to live as closely as possible together. We could then walk more journeys, make more of the rest by better public transport, and save our cars for the social, impulsive and off-track outings to which they give such marvellous freedom. Cities could save land and money by building shorter lengths of everything. Shorter rails, roads, parking lots, pipes, wires and service distances could all save public and private resources for better uses. Most transport and utility industries are basically dull, for their workers and customers alike. Yet they use what seems an absurd proportion of Australian productivity, a higher proportion than in almost any other country in the world. It would be wonderful to shift some of it back to freer, more interesting uses. Besides money, it would be good to save time. Some of the compulsory travelling and delivering and bury-your-own-garbage time could be distributed to each man's choice of work or play, real privacy or real company; and the shorter routes should bring more varieties of work and play and company within everybody's reach.

The money economies claimed for this scheme are probably illusory – dense housing is likely to save $1000 per house on transport and services by spending an extra $2000 to hoist each house into the sky. But believers in high density think the expense would be worth it: home life itself would be improved by crowding it. Some say that living close encourages community with neighbours. Others claim that it improves privacy – the city apartment can have a solid door, no fences to peep over, and utterly anonymous neighbours. Its tenants don't have to do much maintenance, and they can share public parks and gardens very sociably. Some Scandinavians crowd into skyscrapers with forest and mountain landscapes all around them. The crowded quarters of other cities are further from the countryside, but often rich in life and urbanity. The culture of assembly and conspiracy, of theatre and gallery and cafe, of great newspapers and little magazines, of chance encounters and intellectual colonies, is rarely strong in a commuters' city. Once there, such a culture does attract commuters, as well as tourists and various roving international communities. But it needs a residential base. You rarely find it in quarters which empty at night. The great cities are the ones the people live in.

It does often happen that the rich and the writers live there because they want to, and the poor only because they have to. The rich, the volunteers for crowded life, include those who locate the jobs which crowd the rest. But the rich themselves usually have plenty of relief from the crowding: a large share of the city's open spaces, a scatter of yachts or country houses, a seasonal round of holiday retreats; country boarding schools or large town parks or private terrace gardens for their children. Rich or not, the writers and painters have often been footloose, disappearing to farms or Mediterranean islands for their most creative work. Or nowadays, to suburbs.

It has generally been where crowds of the willing and unwilling happened to mix that the artists have celebrated the dense kind of city life, noticing the faces in the street tense, each unique, all various as the variety of man. But even in the famous cities' famous quarters' famous times (which is not a lot of historical city life) the faces have sometimes been tense like hunter and hunted, various as the diseases and childhood servitudes that variegated them. In the Latin Quarter's famous days, what its artists caught were the many faces of suffering and the transience of most delights, the bloom and the beautiful accidental textures of decay. Most of them were angry about the suffering, however they celebrated the survivors. But many of the best of both were not brought up in Paris; they were products of quieter places. They came to watch, and enrich, the passing parade of Parisian faces: on those, all sorts of experience is printed, but too much 'rich humanity' has been carelessly discerned in what were chiefly raddled, desperate faces with bad teeth. With our better diets and dentistry, our sidewalks will never present a really pleasing range of pain and loss to delight arty tourists. Neither the workers' battery-housing outside Omsk nor the high-rise apartments over Kirribilli are likely to incubate a classical city mixture. They'll more likely bulldoze and segregate and monotonise any interesting Carlton or Paddington that was there before.

For most urban excitements and fertilities it is the people themselves you have to diversify – which means diversifying their origins and upbringings and life chances. It's no good merely crowding more similars closer together. Numbers and density are not really the key to urban excitements. London and New York and Tokyo attract some exciting mixtures. Most other monster cities don't. Plenty of the same excitement flourished in Athens and Rome, Berlin and Vienna, Boston and San Francisco and Sydney, when they had many less people than Melbourne and Sydney have now, and housed them much less densely than Manhattan does now.

✳

There is a contrasting parody of the chief alternative to crowding, in the urban intellectual's stereotype of suburban non-life.

Suburban vegetation is well damned in song and story. Barry Humphreys' Moonee Ponds; Graham McInnes' East Malvern; with only a little misunderstanding by the reader, Patrick White's Sarsaparilla. Less compassionate critics depict dreary dormitories where life shrivels, festers, taps its foot in family prisons. All relations oppress; any love is greedy to own or devour the loved one; conversations if any are boring; neighbours pry. Mum does the dishes, dad potters and mows, the kids pick their acne between homework and the telly. For relief (they talk a lot about 'relief' and 'satisfaction'), Dad has the RSL booze and poker machines, Mum has the *Women's Weekly*, the young who used to cycle to tennis and become engaged now make use of used birds on the back seats of their used Cortinas.

What these clichés about suburbs call for is really a rejoinder about life. Plenty of dreary lives are indeed lived in suburbs. But most of them might well be worse in other surroundings: duller in country towns, more desperate in high-rise apartments. Intelligent critics don't blame the suburbs for the empty aspirations: the aspirations are what corrupt the suburbs. The car is washed on Sunday mornings because its owner has been brought up to think of nothing better to do, not because suburbs prohibit better thought.

As a matter of fact, high-fenced, overgrown quarter-acre gardens can be as free, private and self-expressive as any other private property. With or without the fences, you can find in some of them the most creative arts, non-conformist squalor, fertile bohemia, funny eccentricity, busy business – and, sometimes, beauty. Most accusations of 'mindless conformity' pick on raw new income-segregated suburbs. Sometimes the accusations are just. More often, I suspect, they're ritual – conformist imitation is itself a strongish feature of suburban intellectuals' familiar manifestos about suburban life. They often cloud the meaning of 'conformism', which isn't a sin until it includes some element of reluctant or stupid imitation. There have been few serious efforts to sort out the suburban similarities. How many signify independent free choices, how many are coerced, how many are imitative, and why is that necessarily wrong, or unfree? The accusers themselves are quite inconsistent in thinking it's the monotony that matters. They don't complain of good monotonies – health, Georgian houses, Paris boulevards, monotonously high incomes or abilities. The similarity of tastes and choices is all right if they are good tastes and choices. Even if not, the similarity is often and above all a sign of *freedom*: more and more people are at last getting what all of them have always freely, independently, identically wanted. Before we all got the same houses, the contrasts of mansion and slum did not signify individual differences of desire, nor a tenth of the free choices we have now.

At the heart of the trouble is a tension inherent in identical human desires to be individually significant. You and I, similar creatures, want too many of the same things; one of the same things we want is to be different from each other. We seldom achieve it by innocent difference of taste. But there is one difference which is consistent with identical tastes: the difference of better and worse, more and less. The quest for individuality loses its innocence in competition and politics. I get more money and buy some difference for me. I get more power and force some difference on you. Any decent intellectual despises the difference of more and less, and reveres the difference of originality. His own sameness to a thousand other people is hard to bear: so he will sometimes pretend to have unique potentialities, which are however imprisoned by the other people – by the prohibitions of a mindless, conformist society which punishes creators. Creative ambition lacking talent; the desire to be different from a million others identically desiring it; the desire to excel a million others identically competing – these are part of the human condition, not just the suburbs. They spur and frustrate desire in every sort of house and street, not just in suburbs. Suburbia is merely one arena for them in life, and in literature one well-worn symbol for them.

✳

Why *do* so many Australians choose to live in a way so unfashionable with intellectual urbanists – twelve or twenty to the acre, halfway between real bush and real city?

49

It's no problem why they prefer the suburbs to the bush. The cities offer most of the jobs, and most services – not only the deep drainage and garbage removal which are easier to get in many country towns than in most outer suburbs, but also specialised services of every trade and professional kind; the greatest variety of public and private entertainments and social opportunities; the greatest variety of girls to marry, and goods in the shops. A recent survey for the New South Wales Department of Decentralisation and Industrial Development suggests that what people in country towns now miss most of all is higher education that their children can get without leaving home.

But why do so many live sparsely in suburbia instead of densely in real city?

Some don't have much choice. There are only small and diminishing quantities of *cheap* dense accommodation, mostly with bad reputations and worse schools. Law and building economics combine to prevent such slums from expanding either sideways or upwards. Most cheap new housing, public and private, goes to the cheap outer-suburban land, where another mixture of law and economics dictates five-roomed houses on fifty-foot frontages. Many new industrial employments go there too. Within reach of them, most of the annual increase of working-class families have to accept the outer-suburban houses because there is no large quantity of anything else they can afford.

But of the majority who *can* still choose freely, why do most still choose the suburbs?

A cottage on its own land is at present the cheapest way to build ten or twenty squares of accommodation. The space around it (though too often badly designed) can be the best and cheapest source of light, air and insulation against sight and sound. The bungalow's insides can be got into the closest relation with the widest variety of private outdoor spaces. It can be close to its own and visitors' vehicles, for easy or private delivery and loading. Its suburban street carries vehicles, walkers, services and plenty of parking; however unsafe or unattractive its traffic, it economises land and pavement very efficiently.

The 'dilemma of diversity' appears between residential units. Maximum diversity between them may mean maximum monotony within each. With good design, that allegedly monotonous and repetitive suburban quarter-acre can include an infinite variety of indoor and outdoor spaces, further increased if some of the partitions are flexible. Large or small, private or open, sunny or cool, paved or overgrown, efficient or romantic, the rooms in the house and the quarters of its garden can offer real variety of colour, use and mood. Suburb-haters, thinking of people *without* personal resources in *ill*-designed houses and gardens, too often undervalue the free and satisfying self-expression, the mixtures of community and privacy, fond familiarity and quick change and escape, which this miniscule subdivision and diversification of the quarter-acre's spaces can offer to the lives it houses. Compared with it, the private realm of the city apartment is internally monotonous, and its owner more restricted in what he can make of it. He loses a whole field for self-expression, and many chances to adapt his environment to idiosyncratic needs. He has only one escape. That one may be into the crowded city's full and valuable diversity, but he can't go there undressed. The escape is to nowhere quiet or private, to nothing he can kick, dig up, replan, encourage to grow or hang a wet shirt on. In many cities the landless city apartment is where the rich get most neuroses, and the poor get most delinquents.

Above all, the house-in-garden is the most freely and cheaply flexible of all housing forms. Tents are its only competitors. It can be altered and extended in more ways and directions, with less hindrance from laws or neighbours, to meet more changes of need, than any denser housing can be. Each owner has considerable freedom to choose his own degree of privacy, publicity or neighbourliness. This freedom to alter his house without changing his address is an underrated one. Many people like gardens, and gardening. Nobody knows, but I guess that those who do what they like with their gardens, and like doing it, probably outnumber the reluctant conformists. And many more things than gardening go on behind those fences – there's no need to catalogue the hobbies and small trades and storages, all the arts and crafts and mercifully private disasters that clutter people's backyards. Children's uses of them are probably the most valuable of all – and not only to the children. Home allows the widest variety of outdoor activities and constructions, especially the complicated, continuing, accumulating ones. The players can build their own scenery and sets, and keep them intact for serials. Collectors can house their zoos. Parents, children and visitors, and the relations between them, all share in the benefits. In some urban circumstances (or social classes) children can't 'go out' without due notice, a change of clothes and a minder. But private suburban gardens let them go in and out of doors as they please. Minders can mostly mind their own business, much of which (like writing some of this chapter) is consistent with keeping an intermittent eye or ear on children moving freely about the resources of their own and neighbouring children's houses and gardens.

Where on the other hand children can 'go out' freely, but only to the streets because their mates don't have private gardens either, all parties may lose a good deal. Whether this matters depends on many things. Two extremes of family relation are nowadays under attack. Some parents become their children's slaves, enter incessantly into their games, curry favour (or 'mateship') with them, chauffeur them about. (One ten-year-old is alleged to have said, 'I'm wholesome-choked.') At the other extreme, working or slum-cramped parents have to abandon their children to the streets of the built-up cities to be socialised entirely by their peers – to the horrors of *Lord of the Flies* reset in Harlem.

Over-dispersed suburbia may help the first extreme, urban density the second. Australia's 60-foot x 150-foot suburbia – sparser than much English suburbia, closer than much American – does at least permit three societies to coexist. Child, family and adult life can use overlapping territories without too often getting in each other's hair. There can be subtle gains in the generations' consciousness of each other. They are not imprisoned together inside a city apartment, forced into too many direct, irksome and conflicting relations until one or the other 'goes out' to rejoin its own generation, out of sight or understanding by the other. The house-and-garden gains can include more independence and escape for both, but also more un-interfering observations and understandings by each of the other's world, and frequent but brief invitations into it. Not many activities – least of all children's – can do without ten-minute breaks every hour, and busy streets are not always the best places for such excursions. There are also ranges of perfectly tolerable behaviour (child and adult), which however can't be tolerated either indoors or on public land: building, carpentering, metalworking, digging, hosing, basking, horsing about. There are innumerable games and skills – amusing, educational, utilitarian – which adults and children can't teach each other either indoors or on public land. Altogether the suburbs allow people, if they want and know how to, to enjoy the unoppressive community of generations which many of the English rich shed when they consigned their children to servants and boarding schools a century ago, and which some of the city poor lost when they lost their children to the streets about the same time.

✳

Some tough planners object to all this soft stuff. After all, they say, children and adults are the same people. If cities are planned chiefly for the adults, the children will all grow up and get their turn.

But childhood and child rearing together occupy as much as half of a majority of lives. If you undervalue that half because of its lower economic productivity, you have a funny notion of productivity. It's a matter of opinion how far childhood is 'preparatory', and adult life the real thing. I think each year of both has the same value and deserves the same attention, whatever 'mature opinion' says – like most city planning and government, mature opinion tends to come from well-off adult males. It is of course absurd to think that parents have 110 other roles. But intelligent 'mother-and-child-centred' planning aims to emancipate parents and children from *needless* dependence, and to make it easier for mothers to continue as adults.

One unspoken valuation is concealed in almost all arguments in favour of dense city life. It is that human relations between adult strangers are generally more stimulating and valuable than are relations within families, or within stable neighbourly communities, or between people where they work. Certainly the great value of cities lies in the variety of company they offer; but it is worth looking twice at the common assumption that all intimate, durable relations are 'dull' or 'stifling', while all casual relations are 'exciting'. The 'strange encounter' cult has been rightly ridiculed in its sexual manifestations, only to reappear in more general form in the writings of those who use cities basically as rich consumers' playgrounds. The eternal hope that new faces will bring new revelations does sometimes deserve to be understood as a Casanova complex: a chronic incapacity to give or get much from whatever relationships the sufferer has already. In fact, happy or helpful or creative human relations are not confined to any type. Good and bad relations appear within the closest families, and equally in the busiest open markets. Everyone has an individual pattern of need and response, in relations of both kinds. It is not hard for good cities – especially urban-suburban cities – to offer their members wide and compatible opportunities for relationships of every kind. But any planning theory is silly if it systematically overvalues the strange encounters and undervalues the family and neighbourly and working relationships. The oddest idea of all is the illusion that the strange encounters are always more 'creative'. Life as a long cocktail party is usually for consumers, not creators. Most of the creators I know – poets, organisers, discoverers and other originals – draw inspiration from the depth of a few relationships, not from an incessant pursuit of first nights. They also use a lot of free solitude. If Australian cities developed more of Melbourne's rather private, ruminant character, that might not necessarily be bad, depending on the quality of love and thought that flourished behind the high fences; even if the quality of life there were poor, it wouldn't necessarily be improved by pouring the people out to mix in public places. People need city centres, crowded with opportunities for fun and profit; but as long as they are there within forty minutes' travel, people will be freer and happier in proportion as they also have a generous tract of privacy at home, and steady friends at work.

So – to sum up – you don't have to be a mindless conformist to choose suburban life. Most of the best poets and painters and inventors and protesters choose it too. It reconciles access to work and city with private, adaptable, self-expressive living space at home. Plenty of adults love that living space, and subdivide it ingeniously. For children it really has no rivals. At home it can allow them space, freedom and community with their elders; they can still reach bush and beach in one direction and in the other, schools to educate them and cities to sophisticate them. About half the lives of most of us are spent growing up and then bringing others up. Suburbs are good places to do it, precisely because they let the generations coexist, with some continuing independence for each. These are the gains our transport costs buy for us.

5

WHO IS MY NEIGHBOUR? (1970)

In 1966 Stretton spent a sabbatical year at the Australian National University. Halfway through the year he had completed the manuscript of The Political Sciences. *The Strettons were living in Hughes, a new suburb in Canberra's Woden Valley, with Hugh working at home and the children attending local schools. Interest in urban planning among Canberra's academics and bureaucrats was high, and during the remaining months of his leave Stretton began to look more intently at his own neighbourhood. What were the principles and values that shaped it? How were neighbourhoods structured to mix and separate the people who lived there? 'Neighbourhood', for Stretton, was an ethical ideal, as well as a sociological concept. In this chapter from* Ideas for Australian Cities, *he argues, drawing on his Canberra experience, that socially mixed neighbourhoods are 'one of the simplest, cheapest and least oppressive ways of reducing the effects of other inequalities'.*

HAT SORT OF GOODS ARE NEIGHBOURS? Some citizens try to live among one sort or avoid some other sort. They may get what they want by any combination of paying for it, covenanting

for it or rigging the law. What should public authorities do about these facts of life?

The problem has many forms, and scales. Who should have to put up with me over my side fence? Who should be allowed to share the public places and services of my neighbourhood, or city? There is no end to the protections that different people sometimes want. They may want segregation by race, religion, occupation, education. Some can't stand the noise of children. But in Australia, apart from some voluntary clustering by migrant groups, the phenomenon appears chiefly as segregation by income – *appears*, because that effect by no means always represents the purposes of those concerned.

The scale of the problem runs from Canberra's segregated streets to the nation's immigration policies, and not as a simple increase in the scale of evil – some segregations are defended as good in themselves, others can be defended as avoiding the need for worse ones. For example, if rich people can have plenty of private land behind high fences, they may be more willing to live in mixed streets. If you give them segregated streets and schools, they may be readier to tolerate mixed neighbourhoods. Racial immigration policies are sometimes thought to preserve some internal racial tolerance and willingness to mix.

On any scale, it is most important to notice that there are two different problems. Segregators have an interest in muddling the two together, but everyone else ought to distinguish them sharply. One: in already-segregated cities, what should the individual rights and freedoms be? Two: is it good or bad – and is it necessary – for cities to be segregated in the first place? Where public authorities have any choice about it, what pattern should they try for? If you are stuck with an exclusive Toorak and a slummy Collingwood, a practical case can be argued for letting the rich outbid the poor for Toorak, and the poor put up with Collingwood without any chance to vote about it. But that practical case for the status quo should never be allowed to masquerade as a practical, moral or democratic case for *creating* such segregations. How people behave perforce in segregated cities is no guide at all to the pattern of segregation or mixture they are *capable* of living with, or would *like* their cities to have.

How they vote may not be the best guide either. Segregation is like any other democratic paradox – opinions help to construct societies, which however have already helped to construct the opinions. People in well-mixed districts don't usually want to start segregating them. The few who do may not understand what the result would be. They may imagine the same rich people and the same poor people, living apart for a change. But in practice the poor (or the Jews or the blacks) are neither the same if they live in ghettos, and neither are the rich. The unskilled imagination of alternatives is just as common in the opposite case. Where cities are sharply segregated, the exclusive minorities rarely want to desegregate them. They have no experience of what a mixture would be like. Instead of imagining a colourful city mixture, or a quiet suburb with all sorts concealed behind its fences, or a comfortable country town, they can only think of being 'sent to the slums', or of their 'nice' areas being invaded by slum-dwellers with slum-bred habits. Either way, they are not entirely wrong. Active desegregation is usually traumatic. But it tells you nothing whatever about the quite different life and atmosphere and property values of 'natural-grown' residential mixtures.

What mixtures *will* work? Even in comparatively comfortable Australian society there is no simple answer. It depends on many more things than the range of the people's incomes. (Some of the worst social relations are in segregated districts where the people are all 'the same'.) It depends on innumerable, complicated aspects of the people's social needs and values and experience. It depends on the general state of the nation's class relations, and on the particular reputation of the mixed district. It depends on sources of optimism or anxiety that have nothing to do with the residential mixture itself – on the people's roots, their jobs, their marriages, their interests and tastes, on what brought them to the district in the first place. New districts can depend heavily, and permanently, on the nature of their first pioneers. Mixtures are certainly affected by density and privacy – how closely are the people crowded? How high are the fences? Overcrowding usually breeds extremes – either unusual intimacy, or a cold hostility to any communication at all. Limited, amiable neighbourliness is commoner where there are private gardens. Mixtures may also depend on the proportions of families, couples and solitaries, young and old, native and immigrant; on the quality of the local schools; on the alternatives which other parts of the city offer; and on dozens of other facts in the people's natures, feelings, social structures and government. *All* those confident generalisations – to the effect that all or none of the people simply 'can' or 'can't' mix – are false.

Nor are residential and social mixtures the same things. Residential mixtures can include any amount of social mixture, or none. Even with no social relations, or bad ones, residential mixtures may still be valuable for reasons of justice or economy, or to avoid worse alternatives.

So there is no simple answer. But there is certainly a range of possibilities. In Australia, the existing patterns of mixture and segregation suggest it is a wide range. Even the existing segregations don't all arise from social feelings and choices. Many arise from independent causes like travel distances, and the physical attractions of good residential land. Without these non-social pressures on the market, Australians might well enjoy – or tolerate – many more mixtures than they have at present. They could presumably also tolerate more segregations than they have at present. So the workable range – the field for choice – is wide.

Within the workable range, public authorities already exert influence, and they could develop more. What should their policies be?

Residential policies affect conflicting interests. They call for social and moral choices. There *ought* to be political disagreement about them. Among alternative political policies, here is one candidate: public influence on residential patterns should be increased; it should always be used to encourage mixtures; it should absolutely prohibit large-scale low-income segregations; with skilled attention to the local facts of each case, it should generally try for the best mixture that can survive without self-defeating backlash.

Why recommend such a policy? Three minor reasons and a major one are worth mentioning. First, taste – mixed districts are generally more interesting, and so as a rule are people who like or tolerate them. Obsessive segregators – those who want segregation even when no real social dangers or financial penalties drive them into it – are usually unpleasant or dull. Second, as a corrective. Some of the old cities are heavily segregated; even if you don't want them one-class all over, there is a case for expanding the mixed areas for the numbers who do like them. Third, there is the direct social value of mixtures for many of the people in them. Where they exist already, neighbourly relations are quite common. (Not everybody joins in them; those who don't tend to deny that the others do.) Besides taking each other's children to the speed-car track and the theatre, there are more important rich-and-poor exchanges of ambition, compassion, and the learning and initiative required to use whatever social services are in theory offering. From poorer neighbours, affluent children may pick up better politics, mechanical skills and social capacities than their snobbish schools offer them. There are also, of course, more opportunities for recoil. Even then, when better understanding increases people's dislike of each other, it may not all be social loss. Relations within the many mixtures that exist seem to me to leave no doubt that some balance of good for most of their members arises from all sorts seeing further into each other's values, afflictions and corruptions, and exchanging each other's inimitable services. However limited, such effects should be compared with the harm ghettos do to many of the people in them. In different ways, rich segregations are often as unpleasant as poor ones.

A fourth reason is more important: the local conditions of residence have reciprocal relations with the general quality and structure of society, and with its distribution of public burdens and benefits. The class structures and relations of mixed societies are not *necessarily* better than those of segregated societies, but they are usually better, and they are always different. Financially, segregation invariably increases inequalities – 'separate is never equal'.

For various reasons, a rich man may have a clear financial interest in segregation. When he does, he often thinks of it as one of his basic property rights: nobody should interfere with his freedom to live as he likes. (Usually, nobody is trying to interfere with it. *He* is trying to restrict *other* people's opportunities to live near *him*.) His rich ancestors once claimed similar 'rights' to be 'free' from income and company taxes, from death duties, from the regulation of their businesses and houses and land uses, and (often by paying for exemption) from compulsory military service. The 'right' to residential segregation is exactly like those other rich men's rights to the unlimited enjoyment of the fruits of inequality. And just as they did, it develops its ideological defences.

Among planners, the segregationists love to talk of freedom and democracy: 'people should have what they want'. They always mean rich people should. They never, never mean poor people should. What the rich want to buy, the law should provide; indeed, the law should help them to get it below cost. What the poor might vote for the law should not ask. If the rich use their money to segregate the poor, that is democratic freedom. If the poor use their votes to desegregate the rich, that is tyranny.

When it isn't 'freedom', the segregationist philosophy is usually a racket called 'realism'. Realists say planners should provide segregation because the motives that produce it are universal. Some of the motives may be – so are some motives for theft and rape, but we· don't ask our planners to help them along. In any case, it is simply false to say that either the facts of segregation, or the motives for it, are the same everywhere. They vary widely from person to person and place to place. Many segregations don't arise from social motives at all.

But insofar as segregation does have social motives, what are they?

Nobody wants the cash value of his property to fall. In mixed areas, changing neighbours are unlikely to affect it; in thoroughly segregated areas, one negro in the street can devastate it. Some Australians think one truck driver can.

Nobody wants a neighbourhood unsafe to walk about in. Whether the safety of the rich or the whites requires segregation depends on the society. In Johannesburg or Chicago it may; in Australia it mostly doesn't.

Some people want their housing to assert some personal superiority. But not all of these want segregation. Some of them clutch at the edge of the richest district they can. Others like a 'good' street of houses just like their own. Others lord it in the biggest establishment in a street of poorer ones. Some want their servants' and tradesmen's quarters near their own. Others want to segregate occupations, or housing styles, regardless of income. Some want their houses to overstate their wealth; others to understate it. Not all selfish or antisocial motives demand income-segregation; many demand mixtures of one sort or another.

Many Australians seem unusually concerned with the broad and solid appearances of 'good' streets. When asked about mixture and segregation, they give more answers about streets and houses than about people. Some of these answers may be merely tactful or hypocritical but obviously many are not. In citizens' chatter and land salesmen's patter, lovely homes crop up at least as often as exclusive areas, with the lovely (or hideous) people omitted from both. The appearances of streets and houses seem to be connected to segregation more by municipal logistics than by social feeling. Regulated frontages and house values present high-class facades and foliage (and exclude the poor). 'Good' districts plant broad streets with trees (and raise easy rates for good public services).

Indeed, it would be worth questioning, by real research, most of the popular notions of the relation of physical segregation to social feeling, even though the answers from old cities won't prove anything about the mixing capacities of new cities. Researchers have studied how – in what order – people rank the suburbs. They have not so far asked whether the people would like to live in a city of diverse but equal suburbs which couldn't be ranked. Nor have they usually asked how many of those who do rank the suburbs want to climb that *particular* ladder of rank and how many don't; or why, in each case. Some people do seem to fit the stereotype of snobbish social climbers pining to get with the top people, and to give their children an inside run at the richest jobs and spouses. In my own acquaintance, those are heavily outnumbered by people who do not fit that stereotype. Many who could afford to move 'up' to a more exclusive suburb don't. Many who could afford to move out of a mixed suburb don't. Increasing numbers, especially of the childless, now leave exclusive suburbs to move into denser, slummier mixtures nearer town. Of those who do move 'up', many don't want the segregation they incidentally get. Why else do they move? As a good speculation where the fastest-rising land values are; or for a particular house, or garden, or view, or business; or for easy journeys to work or city or schools; or to be nearer to mum or further from mum-in-law – and so on. How many in total move or stay for which reasons I do not know. All those cynical, knowing folk to whom the answer is obvious – they do not know either.

For example, Melbourne's segregations would be much the same if there had never been any conscious desire for them at all. For a century, almost all employments were in the city and its surrounding two or three miles of flat central district. In reach of those employments, the physically best residential land was an eastern arc across the river. If the buyers had competed for nothing whatever except the nearest attractive land, that alone would have segregated the metropolis much as it is segregated now. It quite likely did so, without much help from segregationist intentions – it certainly had no help, when it began, from segregationist covenants or by-laws. Most of the earlier settlers came from places which had acute inequalities, but comparatively little segregation. Their snobberies still attached to land, house, wealth and acquaintance rather than to particular suburban addresses. So the land market probably did more to breed segregationist feeling than vice versa, and the horrors of flat industrial suburbs – the horrors that *follow* segregation – soon reinforced the feelings.

In the same old suburbs a hundred years later, there was continuing evidence for this view. The *Melbourne Metropolitan Planning Scheme 1954: Surveys and Analysis* reports how many people in each suburb dreamed of moving, and where to, and why. As might be expected, plenty from the old inner slums wanted to move out. Plenty from the outer suburbs wanted to move in. Plenty, therefore, wanted to converge on that middle-distance arc which includes the richest eastern suburbs: but not on the rich ones only, and not apparently for 'social' reasons. They wanted the same old combination of space, fresh air, good houses and short work journeys. They said nothing whatever about the human society in either the old or the new locations. This might merely mean that they concealed snobbish feelings from the interviewers, if it were not for another piece of evidence in the same report: a map of the destinations the people wanted to move to. The middle distance looked equally good in *all*

directions. The northern and north-western middle-distance suburbs are dull lower-middle and working-class areas with no social
cachet whatever. But they do have standard-sized homes-in-gardens,
some undulating land, and short journeys to the centre. They seemed
just as satisfactory as the fashionable east did, both to their existing
residents who wanted to stay, and to people elsewhere who wanted
to move. On this evidence, some of the Melbourne rich and most of
the poor are neither segregationist nor anti-segregationist. The private quarter-acre itself is what they think about.

For this impression, there is some indirect support in David Scott
and Robert U'Ren's *Leisure: A social enquiry into leisure activities
and needs in an Australian housing estate* (F.W. Cheshire, 1962). In a
Melbourne suburb of segregated low-income public housing, what do
people do when they're not at work, at school, or travelling? Answer:
they stay at home. They tend the property, watch television, read a
little; the men just as much as the women and children. When rarely
they go out, it is seldom to meet anyone outside the family. Most of
them don't go out at all from Monday to Friday. Their weekend outings are visits to relations, or family drives, or family visits to drive-in
cinemas. Less than a fifth (in each case) regularly visit friends, or go
to town, or play or watch sport, or go to church. Away from work and
school, *family* is their society; *home* is their place. Home ends at the
fence. So it is rational to choose the home for its price, its internal
space, its work and shopping journeys, and nothing else.

If some of the workers thus seem indifferent to segregation, some
of the lower-middles are popularly supposed to be obsessed by it. One
incident in Canberra in 1966 exposed some social feelings, though of
so few people they support no generalisations. The people may also
have been quite unrepresentative of the rest of the community – they
had chosen to live in a most unusual street. The road planners had
treated a round hill with uncommon formality, drawing concentric,

circular streets around its contours. Thus they made a pyramid, rare in Canberra. It was a low hill, a small pyramid, or the rich would have had it. As it was, its top provided a few modest, middle-priced blocks which were not halfway up someone else's hill, but crowing on top of their own. The outer side of the smallest circle at the summit served fourteen residential blocks. Inside it, the sale map showed a plain green circular acre of public open space. At the auction of the blocks, the buyers paid lower-middle prices and complied with covenants to build houses of lower-middle value.

Soon after the buyers had built and moved in, the commission announced a plan to fill the central circle with an imaginative playground. Besides gymnastic equipment, there were to be forts and earthworks for cowboys and war games, and banked trike tracks which could double at night as amphitheatres for drama and bonfires. A majority of the householders in the top circle objected. People from the other streets welcomed the playground and objected to the objectors. All relevant politicians were appealed to. The local paper published several letters, and officers of the commission interviewed the residents of several streets.

The characters in the top circle were too few for their opinions to support any generalisations at all. But their petty statistics and a few of their pettier thoughts supported some cherished Australian prejudices in a heartwarming manner. Seven of the nine Australians accepted an amended plan with less gravel and earthworks; it may also be that they moderated their opposition when it was accused of being snobbish. Anyway, they had never mentioned any but the 'hard' factors: their resale values, and the way the gravel would blow about in summer. They either had, or disclosed, no class attitudes. The only German also worried about the values and the gravel, but didn't appear to understand what a class attitude was. Three English, with one of their two ex-Sydney allies, did have social opinions. They'd paid, they repeated incessantly, the highest prices on the hill for 'their' park at the top. People 'below', 'down below us', 'lower down' and 'in the lower bracket' are the sort that use playgrounds. The children 'up here' have gardens of their own. (The gardens down the hill were identical sizes.) 'Back in England,' one said, 'if you played in the street you weren't a nice sort of person.' (The playground was meant to keep children *off* the streets.) The English were the most indignant when the commission polled the 'other' people down below, getting a predictable majority for the play-ground, and when the whole district's Progress Association endorsed it too. Why should 'other' people either use 'our' street or be consulted about it? 'We have private enterprise houses.' (Half the 'yes' voters in the street below had identical project houses.)

The folk in the top street mostly had modest jobs and incomes. The government houses in the mixture 'below' probably contained a wider range of incomes, including higher ones. They certainly included some higher educations. Nobody in the top street could match the prose style of the European schoolchild who wrote to the paper for (he said) forty children in one low street: 'I commend the action of the National Capital Development Commission in plan-ning a suitable area for our recreation, and assure those who oppose the project that we will cause no fall in values ... It would be much better for all concerned if we had our own playground, because quite often irate motorists interrupt our games. The street is quite crowded at times, and traffic frequent. However, we have raised no protest (officially) against the motorists or nearby residents using the traf-fic way so we fail to see why they should object to a clean swap – the street for a playground ...'

The whole incident is still the worst recorded in a valley with (now) seven years' experience of income mixtures, including the mixture of most of its incomes in common schools. This record scarcely condemns any of the incomes as incapable of mixing.

Children and schools are at the heart of many conflicts about segregation: once segregated, it is practically impossible to integrate them. But the connection between segregation at school and at home is not simple. The differences between state and Catholic parish schools don't seem to have much effect on choice of suburb, and even if they do, they don't segregate incomes. Criticism concentrates more often on the small minority of children – Catholic and other – who go to fee-paying, independent, income-segregated schools. This segregation of schooling may in itself be a worse thing than segregated residence, but it doesn't *cause* segregated residence; if anything, two opposite relations hold. The fee-paying schools locate near the rich. If the rich later spread, their children simply travel longer distances; surprising, tiring distances sometimes. Thus, residential mixtures can be positively helped, because their schools don't deter the rich from living there.

The school segregation is very hard on the majorities left in state and parish schools. They lose a disproportionate number of bright, ambitious children; their learning climate and social experience are that much poorer. They also lose those children's parents, as critics and helpers. So nothing but the conscience of a few of them keeps the influential classes interested in the primary and secondary schools their children don't use. (For the tertiary institutions, which they *do* use, they have worked a federal financial revolution. As also for the teachers' colleges, from which their private schools increasingly draw staff. As likewise for the Canberra state schools, which they do use. Their discriminations are too precise to be accidental, though of course they may be 'unconscious'.)

All this makes sure that the state and parish schools will rarely be very good. It only requires the addition of some residential segregation to ensure that many of them will be very bad. State and parish schools derive as much of their character as private schools do from the character of their catchments. Many innocents – including educational reformers – think the slum schools could be made equal by special services and expenditures. But no educational expenditures can give equal educational chances to segregated children. Neither dull nor bright children develop best in schools with *predominantly* dull, poor or foreign-language catchments. This is true whether fee-paying or residential arrangements segregate the schools. Through most Australian cities there is a final discrimination which really pins the poor to their ghettos. Wherever the rich live, they can send their children to private schools as far away as they like, at concession rates on public transport. But more and more state secondary schools are *zoned*. If your parents live in the ghetto, you won't get cheap fares out of it, because of all the schools your limited means can afford, only the ghetto school is allowed by law to admit you.

So it is not for the real rich, but chiefly for the poor and middling, that the schools can help to accelerate segregation once it starts. If not too many Australians fear contamination across their side fences, plenty do have strong and correct fears of bad schools. Their motives are rarely studied because friends and enemies already, passion-ately, *know* them. But as with residence, so with schools: how people behave in a segregated system may tell you very little about their motives and nothing whatever about their opinion of segregation itself. There are certainly plenty of exceptions to all the stereotypes. On the one hand, some parents of private-school children dislike their privilege and segregation, vote against their subsidies and work actively to raise the state schools to competitive standards; while on the other hand, some parents of state-school children are snobs and segregationists. Some well-heeled radicals make it a point of socialist principle to spend their money on themselves, rather than on good education for their children. Rather more and nicer radicals find good state schools for their children by living in carefully chosen mixed or middle-class suburbs – or in Canberra.

Above all, parents are driven to the privileged schools – private or segregated public – because they love their children and want a humane and technically good education for them. How many actually do value the privileged schools' religion, social segregation, affluent atmosphere and privileged run at a few lines of employment? How many are more interested in the exam results? How many are more interested in the real intellectual services than in the exam results? How many value chiefly the gentler manners, the safer virginities? How many value especially the children's better chances to act, paint, play in orchestras, edit newspapers and magazines, and publish poems? How many simply count the class sizes and teacher turnover in state schools, and avoid them at whatever cost? How many buyers of each of these advantages genuinely dislike some of the others? No friend or enemy of educational segregation is entitled to assert (as many do) the predominance of any one of these motives. Their distribution is not known.

Whatever their causes, residential segregations are steady and potent enemies of all equalities – including the most sacred and official equalities. Mixed suburbs can distribute municipal services equally to unequal ratepayers, but segregated suburbs make sure the poor get only what they pay for – including, sometimes, the municipal councillors. Segregation usually unequalises people's access to open spaces – to parks, views, well-kept playgrounds and playing fields, sometimes rivers and beaches. It can often unequalise peace and quiet and fresh air – the poorest districts often need the most but get the least protection from noise and pollution. Segregation sometimes unequalises the safety of the streets, always their beauty and cleanliness. In some of the big cities it is now unequalising – in the wrong direction – the cost of journeys to work. There are also a number of services which plenty of the poor can pay to use individually, but which exclusively poor areas can't collectively attract (commercially) or finance (municipally).

What if the segregated poor don't miss what they don't get? This, a poor argument at the best of times, collapses for anyone prepared to think of the poor and their children as different people. The Melbourne suburb surveyed in *Leisure* had poor community services, and the parents scarcely knew or used the few it had. They scarcely noticed, or minded, how poor its schools were. They couldn't see – or imagine – anything very interesting for its teenagers to do. There was nobody but a transient teaching staff to encourage children to stay at school. The parents presumably didn't read sociological reports or financial abstracts to discover what stimulating company, common benefits and redistributions were available in rich or mixed districts. But 'what they don't know they'll never miss' was never a good argument against compulsory education or public health for the children of the poor; it is not a good argument for segregation either.

Mixture, on the other hand, is one of the simplest, cheapest and least oppressive ways of reducing the effects of other inequalities. If every fourth household is tough and able, that will serve to defend and improve a neighbourhood almost as effectively as if the successful occupy all of it. This is a service the rich can do for the rest quite painlessly, without there necessarily being any direct neighbourly relations at all. Not as charity, either. A rising proportion of the skills of the rich are developed at heavy public expense: there is a conventional moral case for demanding that the rest of the taxpaying community should get some shares of the services they thus finance. The public expenditure that produces a doctor, lawyer or architect doesn't only produce those specific skills; unavoidably it also produces some more general and diffuse capacity for self-defence and public influence. Residential mixture is one effective way of returning some share of those endowments to the taxpayers who helped to bestow them.

Whatever the strength of that morality, there can be no doubt of the interest which the poorer half of society has in mixing with the richer half. Any district can use a thick sprinkling of able, obstinate succeeders, helping to keep the local councillors honest, resisting pressurised rezonings and philistine road-builders, chaining themselves to menaced trees, paying for planning appeals and hectoring the local MP; organising local branches of the political parties; agitating for kindergartens, parks, playgrounds and libraries, and showing how to use and criticise and improve them; paying good rates for these good things. The same sprinkling of affluence can make a critical difference to the quality and variety of service and social activity that the district can support communally or attract commercially: sporting clubs, squash and tennis courts, swimming pools, sailing and walking and pony and dog clubs; better shops with a wider range of goods and a greater readiness to deliver them; marginally more doctors, dentists, solicitors, vets, beauty parlours, and services of all sorts. Such better services enlarge everybody's choices. They also help to equalise opportunities. As a minor example, a mixed catchment makes a great difference to the paperback books stocked by delicatessens and newsagents. A majority of working-class customers may scarcely notice the difference, but some of their bright members and youngsters, and quiet wives, will find enlightenment which wouldn't be worth stocking in the shops of a working-class ghetto. As a more important example, mixtures – as argued above – raise the infectious proportion of ambitious learners and stayers in the schools, increase the local resources *and demands* for school improvements, and improve the general standards of parental cooperation and vigilance.

Segregation reverses all these tendencies. Inequality, once entrenched, perpetuates and increases itself; the relations of rich and poor suburbs grow more like those of rich and poor countries. Once segregated, most of the inequalities are irreversible, even by the best-intentioned aid programs. In Australia we don't even have those.

6

—

IDEOLOGIES (1970)

In Ideas for Australian Cities *Stretton brought the lessons of his first book,* The Political Sciences, *home to Australia. Urban planning, he argues, is no more 'value-free' than any other social science. 'Since planners can't in fact be neutral, they might as well work for whatever they believe to be right and good.' His brilliant analysis of the metaphors that shape the thinking of urban planners, and the values that underlie them, he would later develop into a user's guide to urban planning,* Urban Planning in Rich and Poor Countries *(1978).*

SHOULD PLANNERS BE REFORMERS, OR SHOULD THEY be politically neutral technicians? Scientifically neutral, perhaps? How democratic can they be? How is it likely to affect their policies if they think metaphorically of a city as an organism, a system, a marketplace, an arena? What is 'a progressive attitude to change' and how does it mix with 'a progressive attitude to conservation'? What politics may be concealed in notions of 'urban efficiency', 'community need' or 'common good', and 'functional design'?

Obviously a planner must be some mixture of master and servant, never purely one or the other. He can't impose unpopular plans dictatorially. On the other hand, he could be a neutral servant only for

74

a city whose people had no disagreements. Politicians are supposed to look after the disagreements. But governments depend on expert information and advice, often choosing between options already chosen for them by the experts. They are prodded or cautioned about reforms by their own servants as well as by public pressures. They sometimes confide whole classes of contentious issues to planning authorities and tribunals; and even when they don't do that, their political directives are often broad enough to leave many discretions to their servants. Whenever planners are asked to propose something complex, like a metropolitan outline or a transport program or a new town project, it is safe to say that no political directive can ever specify all the values to be weighed. The planners' own values will matter, whether by act or omission, whether they follow their personal convictions or choose which other opinions to follow instead. In connection with any such large new project, they usually have to do plenty of public education and propaganda. The particular persuasions they attempt, the particular aims and advantages of planning which they advertise, are all contributions to the public stock of social and political ideas; no contribution to that stock can be neutral. Most planning also includes an element of design. Every designer differs from every other. Each will lay out a unique pattern of economies, restraints, facilities and beauties; no plan for a city or a transport system or a neighbourhood can be optimal for every user of it. Wherever there is room for art or choice in design, there is usually room for politics too.

Some urban planners nevertheless insist on posing as neutral, technical, unbiased servants of the people. Some American planning schools (and a few Australian imitators) actively urge them to do so. These contrast themselves with a British tradition, which they belittle as utopian, directive, 'paternal' and generally undemocratic – though the governments in charge of British planning are more democratic than most. The critics profess instead a philosophy of 'adaptive' or 'non-directive' planning, with strictly objective science as its basis: find out what the citizens want to pay for and plan it for them.

In practice there is usually a contradiction within this abstinent philosophy. Planners may think of themselves as obedient servants of government, but they also advise it and are one arm of its power. So the abstinent philosophy tends to issue in advice *to government* to treat its citizens in a certain way: to plan what the buyers are offering to pay for, and to avoid 'directive', 'ideological' planning – that is, to avoid using town planning as a method of social reform. Whether it is urged on governments voters or students in planning school, this right-wing ideology should be allowed no false pretences of neutrality.

The adaptive philosophy also tends to go with a view of planning as an objective science: anything you can't measure and prove as a cold fact is 'subjective', probably 'ideological', and certainly an unscientific basis for technical advice to governments. 'Planning should get all its values from the citizens, and keep all its facts objective.' Ironically, the effect of combining these two anti-ideological beliefs can be very biased indeed. This happens for two reasons. First, rich people and organisations are generally better equipped and organised to import ideas, hire advisers and present demands in more effective ways than the poor can. This is likely to give a bias to any planning which sits passively waiting and listening for the citizens' initiatives. Who will invent or import planning ideas for the poor's advantage, or propose such things to the poor's politicians, if the public planners don't?

Second, the preference for scientific objectivity reinforces this effect. What can be measured objectively? The market demand for land; investments and their direct returns; traffic flows and congestions; car parking; rateable values; money transactions of every kind; conventional measures of economic growth. What can *not* be measured objectively? Women's and children's rights; the need for education or recreation; the beauty or humanity of the urban environment; the happiness or creativity of the people the city brings up; the quality of their relations with each other; the equality of their access to the city's good things; the social costs of economic growth. Money and physical movements and structures are 'objective'; justice and social health and the quality of life are not. Thus a desire for scientific neutrality begets its very opposite: a strictly political preference for satisfying one type of demand at the expense of others.

Adaptive planning philosophy is not always so silly, or so plutocratic. It originated as an intelligent reaction against unduly static, utopian or tyrannical planning. At its best, it identifies the public planner quite correctly, as one contender in the political arena – one among many, doing what he can. It is right to advise him to adapt to the people and pressures and realities around him. He must attempt 'the politics of the possible'. But that does not always have to mean the politics of the rich. Planning for nothing but traffic flows and property values and investment returns doesn't merely adapt to existing banalities and inequalities, it actively increases them. It offers expert services to those who will prosper in any circumstances, while denying those who need help and protection most. Not surprisingly, it has coloured the planning of some of North America's most unequal, savage and uncontrollable city life.

Since planners can't in fact be neutral, they might as well work for whatever they believe to be right and good. They should also obey necessities and politicians, and patiently accept the best compromises they can get. There need be nothing arrogant or dictatorial in a planner's own values and convictions. The best public servants have long understood the proper relations between their own aspirations for good government and their duties of obedient service to public and politicians. But if educators had not cared about enlightenment, if public health officers had not cared to define health, if welfare administrators had felt neutral about neglect or starvation, if economists had been personally indifferent to employment or productivity, then the world would now be even nastier than it is. A high proportion of its most effective reformers have been public servants under public-service discipline. For planners as for others, public service does not absolve the servant's social conscience. It often makes high demands on it.

*

Anybody's social conscience owes something to his understanding of what society is and how it works. Society is so complicated that any general understanding of it must simplify it. That is what most general social and political theories try to do. Many of them can be grouped according to metaphors they use for society. It is as well to remember the political tendency of each type.

Among recent theories, there is a boom in 'systems analyses'. In practical form these are mathematical methods of analysing things like traffic, specific organisations and some of the more measurable services that a city uses. They can be very useful, and as long as their limitations are understood there need be nothing contentious about them. But some enthusiasts would extend the method to comprehend most social (or urban) research. If that happens, political implications follow. From all the irregular complexity of social activities, systems analysts will generally pick out patterns of regular, mutually sustaining activities. If the analysts want to be scientific, they may prefer activities they can measure and relationships they can prove. There is thus likely to be plenty of bias in their choice of *what* to isolate and attend to as the city's 'basic' or 'essential' systems. Markets, transport and some other services have measurable inputs and outputs. Educational or family systems can expect less attention because their outputs are so vague. Plenty of valuable social activities can expect no attention at all.

Some theorists go as far as to use 'system' as a selective or metaphorical model for cities as wholes. Others do much the same with 'functional analysis', which typically defines as 'basic functions' some very few activities or characteristics of a society. If you meet one of these, he may for example say: 'What is a city? A city is essentially an intense interaction system.' What does that scientific-sounding abstraction tell you about *him*? Usually, that his political bias is all the stronger because he does not know it is there. His theory directs attention to interaction as more important than the other activities that occur in cities. Cities do allow plenty of interaction, and planning should facilitate plenty of it. But to prefer it to other activities is a judgement just as personal as any preference for parks and gardens or black-glass skyscrapers. It is however a specially unhelpful judgement because it usually tries to value the quantity of interactions without noticing what the interactions are. Making love is an interaction; so is a business deal or a visit to the doctor or a sparkling conversation about art in somebody's salon; so is every jostle on a crowded pavement, every bit of unwanted commercial soliciting, every exchange of complaints about the noise or pollution or segregation of the city; so is every eviction, extortion, blackmail threat, sale of dope, or crime of violence in the city. Indeed, the only thoroughly uninteresting qualities of interactions, which are generally not worth valuing at all, are their number and frequency.

As a way of regarding cities, a systemic-interactionist view is as selective, value-structured and political as any other. In practice it usually goes with a preference for high-density, public concourses rather than private retreats, commerce rather than manufactures, and the consumption rather than the production of cultural goods.

It typically doesn't think about the production of people; it is likely to plan for the wants of well-off educated childless adults, rather than for the home-keeping, book-reading, telly-watching or lower-paid ranks in general, and children and family life in particular.

If 'system' is the newest metaphor for human society, the oldest is 'family'. This can emphasise the bonds of love and membership, of mutual aid and protection and nourishment which ought to knit society. It can also recommend very authoritarian and unequal arrangements. In the days when father monopolised whatever there was of power, authority and property, family metaphors for society appealed to many monarchs, aristocrats, hierarchic churches and authoritarian personalities. But there has lately been some reverse imitation. Families nowadays go some way towards imitating democratic societies. Perhaps familial theories of society, less paternal than they were, may revive: they emphasise that the citizens are stuck with one another and had better make the best of it, they recommend love and duty as useful relations, and they are more realistic than most liberal theories are about some hard social facts of dependence and unequal individual capacity.

Among other metaphors, 'market' and 'arena' remain the classical favourites. A society or a city can be understood as a marketplace, and most social relations as transactions or contracts. This emphasises many rights and freedoms of individuals, and the voluntary aspect of their relations with one another. It is also a way of relating conflicts to common interests, while acknowledging the full importance of both. Buyers and sellers have opposite interests, which however give them a common interest in keeping the peace and striking a bargain. But in treating all bargains and contracts (and social and political relations) as free and voluntary, such theories tend to assume that all the people have equal bargaining powers. In fact they don't, so in practice many of their relations are neither fair nor voluntary. Market and contract and other libertarian theories rarely explain how wealth and bargaining power get distributed in the first place. They politely ignore most public and private frauds and coercions. Applied to society, they often express an old-fashioned liberalism grossly favourable to the rich. Applied to cities, they fit well with 'adaptive' planning philosophies: follow the private enterprises; plan for those who can invest and pay, rather than for those who want to vote themselves some collective or 'uneconomic' help. This is the constitutional theory of earlier centuries, when votes belonged to property rather than people.

A radical rival of that philosophy, which however allows the same individuality to individuals, uses the metaphor of conflict: men are mostly engaged in battling with each other for shares of scarce resources. Where market theories see the citizens pooling their pennies to buy some big thing they can all use (like an underground railway), conflict theories have them plotting and making alliances to outgun each other, the winners taking most of the loot (like collaring the underground railway money for Melbourne before Sydney gets it, or before the schools or the pensioners get it). This harsh view of life recognises that many so-called 'community' uses of 'common' resources are really factional captures of other people's money. It need not see society as a jungle – it can recognise common interests, and contests within agreed rules. It is as value-structured as other theories, choosing to regard distributions of power and goods as more important than other qualities of society. Politically, it is common left of centre, and it commonly underlies arguments for greater equality. But winners as well as losers can use it – for example, when the winners say 'what we have, we hold', or when they protect rich values or segregations by zoning.

In extreme contrast to conflict theories are those which assume that society need have no conflicts at all. Some conservative and some consensual theories concentrate on understanding society's rules and shared values and habits of behaviour. If you see the rules themselves, rather than the people and interests who make and break them, as the essence of society, then it becomes easy to define efforts to break or change the rules as 'breakdowns', 'deviations' or 'dysfunctions'. If patterns of agreement and rule and habit are thus nominated as society's 'essential structure', they may soon also be dignified as 'normal'. Change 'normal' to 'natural' and you are well on the way to being an organic theorist. Organic theories have taken such thrashings from modern political philosophers as to be scarcely worth another attack; but they do appeal to a few planners, and for all their faults they do pose interesting questions about urban growth and change, and about some qualities of city life.

Organic *language* need not be metaphorical at all. People are a species of organic life. Their health depends on their environment. They need fresh food and air and water, sunlight and regular darkness. Their nervous systems can suffer from too many quick-changing stimuli, from buffetings and confusions and anxieties. They may be wise to keep some touch with plant and animal life, with wind and rain and seasons. Cities should meet these needs of their organic inhabitants; but that doesn't make the cities organisms too.

Even as a metaphor, 'organism' has some harmless uses. A city is complex and many of its people's activities are interdependent. One way of emphasising this is to compare a city to a person. Like a person, it has physical structure and functions, cellular decay and replacement, and mental life. The health of the whole depends on the efficient working of transport 'arteries', administrative 'brains', rubbish and drainage 'bowels'. If you remove any essential organ from the city, the whole may suffer like a body that loses an essential organ. The whole may adjust to changes in particular parts of it, as a living body does.

It is in these two senses that urban philosophers like Lewis Mumford make liberal use of organic language. Mumford seems also to include in his thought an idea sometimes called 'the human fallacy'. Small towns are built 'on human scale' and house 'human' relations. Big cities have 'inhuman scale' and their complex organisation makes their people's relations 'inhuman'. In fact, of course, Manhattan – and rockets to the moon – are artefacts as human as any grass hut. Complex organisations are built and run by people as human as the village squire and parson ever were. Loneliness, anonymity and alienation are qualities of relations between humans, just as love is. Those who say human and inhuman when they mean good and bad are assuming that goodness is natural to humans but evil is not. All the cruelties of the big cities are done by humans, most of them deliberately enough. Plenty of face-to-face relations in smaller communities are also selfish and unloving. Personally I agree with Mumford that, on balance, in societies like ours, direct relations probably do allow more good relations, while the indirect relations and manipulations characteristic of complex organisations do tend to make selfishness easier to commit and harder to combat: stand-off bombing is easier on the conscience than face-to-face bayoneting. But all the parties are equally human. Even when complex machinery makes for impersonal mistakes, and for effects beyond the mechanics' intentions, those errors are as human as any others.

These various uses of organic language – to emphasise man's organic nature, or the complexity of cities, or the value of small groups and face-to-face relations – are common usages in everybody's language. They have scarcely any connection with formal theories of organic society.

From Plato to Mussolini there is a tradition of social theory which likens the people and classes of society to the organs of a body. The intent of such theories is usually that people and classes should specialise more exclusively, then exchange their specialised services to make the social organism function more harmoniously as a whole, and best for each of its parts. In Plato's famous formulation, governors should do nothing but govern, shoemakers should do nothing but cobble; that way, each will get the best boots and the best government. What is wrong with specialisation and harmonious interdependence as social ideals? For most people in most economic systems, specialisation is a regrettable necessity. To push it to extremes and idealise it contradicts every aspiration for the whole and versatile personality, and for the full life that can be led by the many-sided creature man is capable of being. Organic theorists usually expect the enjoyable specialisations (like governing, or writing social theory) for themselves. 'My brain being *slightly* better than yours or his, I will be the *only* brain; you can be the belly, he can be the anus.' As far as I know, no organic theory has been written by an invoice clerk, a coalminer or a member of the strategic reserve of unemployed.

Organic theory may be absurd, but organic theorists in practice include some fine planners and critics of planning. That is because they apply the theory (if at all) with unconscious but systematic discriminations between good diversities and the other sort. Why profess an irrelevant theory while applying a good one? Organic complexity, growth, health and harmony are analogies which can do nothing good to illuminate a city's mixtures of common and conflicting interests, or to improve planners' choices between alternative goods, alternative evils, alternative complexities and alternative directions of change. For debating changes, plain language is usually safer than any metaphor.

A GOOD AUSTRALIAN CITY (1972)

In 1972 Stretton contributed to an ABC radio series on 'The Science of Cities'. Broadcaster John Challis began by asking him to imagine a good Australian city.

A PRACTICAL WAY TO DO THAT WOULD BE TO LOOK at the good bits of city we've got already. You could put together a fine composite city. Think of a city that had Sydney Cove and the top end of Collins Street. The Rocks and Battery Point. There are busy places: Martin Place, Rundle Street, your favourite arcades. There are odd, interesting places – the city markets, the Greek and Italian quarters. You'd have to have same essential services – choose your favourite docks and noxious trades districts. For transport, perhaps the Melbourne suburban railways and the Sydney ferries.

Then you could think about all the good places Australians have built to live in. Start with some of the classical, quiet, tree-lined suburbs, with private houses in very private gardens, where plenty of Australian families live very satisfying lives. This has sometimes been stereotyped as the only way Australians live in cities, which of course it isn't. A lot of them live in rooms and lodgings, and we build thousands more flats every year. There's terrace housing left from the last century – Paddington is one of the best collections of Victorian row housing left in the world. We've also had attractive commuter villages – places like Eltham or the Adelaide hill towns, or the beach towns along the coast from Sydney or Melbourne. Put all these historical bits together and they'd make a very good city indeed.

But only in imagination. In real life, there's a problem. Most of the best things we ever built we've made it illegal to build now. Terrace houses were banned for half a century. We can't make many more private gardens like the ones in Camberwell or Turramurra, because in most new suburbs we've banned front fences. A lot of mixed land uses have been forbidden. With good intentions – trying to see that respectable folk don't wake up to find someone has built a crash repair shop next door – we've fixed it so you can hardly mix anything. In a lot of suburbs you can't build a granny flat onto your house. You can't mix brick and timber. An architect can't build his house behind his office. A residential neighbourhood can't have a corner shop, even if the residents and the shopkeeper both want it there. One way or another, we've legislated against the worst things in a way that also bans many of the best things. We've done it chiefly by insisting that the things, the streets and block sizes and zoning regulations and so on, have to be much the same all over.

There are still a few exceptions to the new monotony. For example, there's a back street built since the war on a flat bit of land behind Victor Harbour, an old seaside holiday town in South Australia. A few dozen cheap houses were put up there twenty or thirty years ago. There must have been no law, or no surveyors, because the property lines seem quite muddled – the front fences are set forward and backward of each other so that the street itself is an irregular sort of common, covered with rough grass, which the residents occasionally mow. A few trees grow out of it, and a narrow gravel roadway wanders through it. This is efficient. It was cheap to make; it imposes a natural speed limit; the gravel is all the pavement that's needed for about two cars an hour; when there are visitors they park on the grass, and when there aren't the kids play on it. The whole effect is practical, peaceful and beautiful – and of course, if you tried to build it now, strictly against the law.

There's another patch of freedom at Point Avenue, Beaumaris, a seaside suburb of Melbourne. Point Avenue used to be a sand track through ti-tree, serving a couple of cottages on a private estate. Then the scrub was subdivided for proper suburban development, so Point Avenue had to get straight sides and regulation-width footpaths, curbs and roadway. But the citizens at one end of the avenue decided to hang on to their sand track and ti-tree. They battled and negotiated for years to keep it as it was, and they won: it's there still. But they're about the only citizens of greater Melbourne who have won in the last ten years, against the spread of regular municipal monotony.

Why do we ban the things we love? Why do we fix it so we can never again build houses onto narrow streets and back lanes in the old cities, or onto quiet gravel drives through the bush in new suburbs? I think this is a more important problem than most city planners realise. If more planning control is just going to mean more standardisation in every detail of our new towns and suburbs, the control won't be worth having. If it isn't worth having, people will eventually get rid of it. It wouldn't be the first time that elaborate planning controls had been found too oppressive, and repealed. If we don't want that to happen, we have got to restore some flexibility to the controls – without of course restoring freedom for unserviced subdivisions, or for the crash repairer to set up next door to the old folks' home.

Besides freedom and variety, what else does a good city need? Its general qualities could be summed up as efficiency, security and equality. To work efficiently, it needs cheap land, short journeys, good centres on an efficient transport network. For security, people need to feel that they're protected against the unwanted kind of change in their neighbourhoods – against drastic clearances or changes of character. For equity, a city ought to distribute its costs and favours fairly. Ideally, the poorest citizens should pay the lowest taxes, have the shortest journeys and live near the cheapest shopping and the free recreation like parks and beaches.

But it's easy enough to go on like this, imagining the good details a city ought to have. The problem is to get the good things built, and connected with each other, in a whole city that works.

At this stage, experts will tell you that you need traffic and economic research, urban systems analyses and growth models, and so on. They're half right – there are uses for some of those approaches. But if you were to go instead to one of this country's biggest suburban developers, he'd tell you to start thinking about the problem the way he does: start by thinking of the people concerned, and think of them at home, finished breakfast, figuring how they're going to reach whatever they want to enjoy in their city in the course of the day.

If I think about the city in this way, I know what I want. I want what I've got. A house of my own, where I can sit under a vine in my own backyard; a park somewhere near, where kids can kick a football; a short walk to Tom the Cheap and a local pub; an easy trip to work in the city; half an hour's drive maybe to a beach or some open country.

That suits me, but it's not the style of life everybody wants. More than half of all Australians don't drive cars. Quite a number of them don't want gardens. I know one couple who live in a city flat because they're out, and busy, from breakfast time to midnight; and another family who bring up children in a suburban flat because from Friday to Monday morning they're in tents, bushwalking, and they don't want to waste their weekends at home gardening. A good city should have options for everybody. Some of the most important options, often neglected by governments, are places where people without much money can live near the centre: students, deserted wives with families and city jobs; single people who are lonely and like the life of the centre; and the populations which all cities have of homeless old men. People without enough money in fact are lucky if they live in cities which still have slums.

Besides all these particular things that different people want, there's also the general kind of home that a city offers: its image or collective personality as a whole. This may look very different to the eyes of different inhabitants, and it's hard to pin down, or plan for. But for many people it can be the most important quality of all. It is made up of all sorts of things – landforms, architecture, districts with special life and colour, memories of love or childhood. Nowhere in Australia can rival Sydney – old Sydney, the Sydney of the first million – the most beautiful and surprising city to move around, with intricate steep old streets, urban villages, marvellous building forms tumbling down harboursides to the waterfront, great ships right in town – and, even if you're not after any of it for yourself, an impression that the trendiest sins are keeping jetsetters occupied around the clock in Kings Cross.

That's my image of it. But others have different selective vision. Someone less interested in the look of the place, more conscious perhaps of ideas, or politics, or business opportunities, might see Sydney differently: a lively, rackety place but hard, cynical: a city of knockers and disbelievers; critics and traders rather than thinkers and builders. Someone else again – perhaps a worker in a western suburb – may have a plainer image altogether of his city as a whole. He may see chiefly a network of roads and bus routes, to get to work and visit relations, to get kids to doctors and groceries home from shops – a ragged, ordinary place, and a bit expensive.

Really a city doesn't have one collective personality, it has a lot of them. It shows quite different faces to differently placed people. This isn't an idle poetic thought, it's very important in city planning and government. Good leaders need some vision. But a single-minded vision of what a city ought to be can sometimes be a narrow-minded vision, a selfish service of a single taste or class. When we're electing people to local government or appointing planners and administrators, we need to look for more than skills. We need skilled people who also have broad education or experience and broad sympathies – people who know the many faces that a city presents to its people, and who will want to improve all of them.

This isn't a romantic idea either. Five or ten years ago it might have sounded romantic. In those days it did not seem possible to hope for much change in the natural sprawl of the cities. The difficulties were too great. Local government was stodgy. Property rights were entrenched. The public utility engineers would never listen. The people themselves were apathetic.

But suddenly, some of these have turned out to be paper tigers. Both political parties have developed quite promising urban policies. In local planning there's more care for the environment. Some of the old mixtures of people, and mixtures of land uses, are back in fashion. One or two new towns, for example, are planning to mix education and housing and recreations right into the town centre with the shopping and offices. A few new suburbs are getting continuous systems of pedestrian ways to connect all their schools and playgrounds, and the local shops, into a safe green realm for walkers and children. One public authority is building 500 or 600 row houses in a pedestrian park, between a boating lake and a beach. There are some creative ideas in the new central-city plans. And there's some very cautious rethinking about urban freeways. Bulldozing gets harder every year. Following the example of Paddington, residents' associations are springing up all over. They've taken control of a number of local governments, and some state and federal politicians are taking some notice of them. Urban land prices – which have been the death of a lot of planners' good intentions – look as if they may at last come under effective control, in some states at last. In two remarkable reversals of form, South Australia has actually turned away an industrial investor, and Victoria has actually proposed some urban renewal that doesn't bulldoze anybody.

So there's hope. But there are still tough technical problems. Even if we adopted policies of zero population growth tomorrow, the population would still double once more, more or less, before it levelled off. It will be very destructive if these doubled numbers have no option except to sprawl onto the outskirts of the existing cities. This country started new city centres freely through its first hundred years – it's absurd to lose the art through the second hundred years, when we need it most. We must learn how to build new centres within reach of all these new people.

They still won't be very good new centres if they're built under present rules and regulations. That's the second tough problem: how to free our designers, and adapt our laws, to allow some individuality in the new urban places we have to build in the next thirty or forty years. The people and the politicians have really gone a long way in the last year or two to create a climate for change. Now we need new kinds of expertise to get new city centres started, and to give us back some difference in our neighbourhoods.

8
———

ADVICE TO ACTIVISTS (1972)

In the early 1970s Stretton became a staunch but not uncritical supporter of the residents' associations springing up in response to citizen interest in planning issues in Adelaide. His own suburb was the home of the first of these, the North Adelaide Society, founded in 1970. With the publication of Ideas for Australian Cities *and his appointment as deputy chairman of the South Australian Housing Trust, Stretton was soon regarded as an oracle on local as well as national planning matters. The following extracts from speeches given to their first annual meetings offer encouragement and shrewd tactical advice to the newly formed Adelaide Residents' Society and the Residents' Association of Dulwich, Rose Park and Toorak Gardens.*

SINCE I THINK THAT RESIDENTS' ASSOCIATIONS ARE A good thing and that all sorts of good flows from having them, strong and vigorous, I have often thought that it would be good policy for a city to have a portable six-lane highway and point it, as a threat, at neighbourhood after neighbourhood. You only have to point it at them for six months and the neighbourhood is politically organised, socially aware; they know each other like they never did before; they have taken control of their local government and all good things are in store for them. Then you can take the highway away because they have had their first victory.

I take it that this association is perhaps in a halfway position – you are not under threat of bulldozing development, but I understand that you are disturbed about your zoning regulations and about the slower kinds of processes of change that you have to expect if you don't do anything about it. That is a halfway atmosphere in which to found an association.

I think you will have both gains and losses from being founded in that way. The one loss is that you won't have that instant rush of membership that you can get by hawking the threat around the district by saying, 'Do you want a highway to go through your home tomorrow?' This is the quickest way to build up a big membership. If you are ever in that danger you will get the numbers to withstand it, don't worry. You might get a lot of gains, though, from being founded in a more deliberate and less combative way.

Different associations, differently placed and with different kinds of territory and population, obviously develop different roles.

It is sensible to talk about some of the hazards and pitfalls. Associations like this sometimes start off all too buoyant and sanguine, so here are a few warnings about the kinds of troubles you are likely to strike – not with your enemies but within yourselves.

Because you have come together as residents bound together by that common interest, it is a great mistake to suppose that you will agree about everything. You are almost bound to find that just as any political society is divided by differences of view and differences of interest, so you are likely to be. So I wouldn't start off imagining that on all the issues that concern you, you are likely to get a broad consensus. On some you will and on plenty I hope you will. But there are bound to be some divisive issues. A lot depends on how you handle those. To take an example, the North Adelaide Society has an almost official list of quite important local issues on which it does not have a policy and does not intend to have a policy, because it knows that they are deeply divisive within its own membership; this is perhaps likelier with that association than with yours because it is not a residents' association – it is the whole area association, and it has some few but severe conflicts of interests between its residents and its shopkeepers and its commercial investors. To hold together, it finds it expedient (even though it is a bit disappointing to some) to leave some issues out of the range of action.

As an association, you are a dead duck if you get identified as belonging to one and not the other of the political parties. It is almost essential, if you want to be politically effective in this situation, to see that you don't become a Labor captive or a Liberal captive, or become suspected of being the voice of just one party rather than the other. You need to keep a free-swinging liberty to abuse either when it is in office without getting too identified with the other, because you will want your freedom to support or attack it the minute it gets into office in turn. This is what is called special interest politics rather than broad class or party politics, and you have to pay a price for it, I think. You will find some divisive issues and you will have to cope with them in some kind of compromising, gentle way if you want to stay together.

You could say that an association like this is strong in proportion as it is big in both senses – that it runs over a wide area and represents everybody and every kind of interest in the area. The more all-embracing it is, the more it will impress state politicians, and the more effective it will be in picking off council wards at election time.

On the other hand, the more all-embracing it is, the more internal conflict it is bound to have, and the more issues you will find on which it is prudent not to have a policy or on which you are in danger of splitting.

The sins you may be tempted to commit are chiefly those that arise from thinking you own your own patch to such an exclusive degree that you can break the general rules of society. The moment you start thinking that because you are in the majority of residents on this area you can say: 'In this area we will have no workers, no public housing, no blacks, no Greeks, no Italians, no industries and no shopkeepers' – with every one of those phrases you will break one of the broadest and one of the most fundamental civil liberties on which our whole society runs. Even if those are the ends you want to achieve, I recommend without much sympathy that you translate them into other terms – at the very least, say 'no house worth less than $20,000' – or something like that. You still won't fool anybody.

If you are composed of mainly rich people, there is a danger that they will assume a rather frozen conservatism that says nothing must change in this neighbourhood – every vacant lot is sacred and every decaying house that we have grown up with we would like to keep there. There is seldom much future in a frozen refusal of all change. Sometimes it takes the worse form of trying to kick out whatever remains of the Aborigines or the poor or any other 'undesirable' group that the neighbourhood finds within itself. This is the natural form of the neighbourhood society over most of North America. Where you find a neighbourhood society in North America, you know that there are covenants to keep Negroes out; these societies are very largely for selfish, segregationist purposes.

A choice that any association of this kind must face is how far to work on its grassroots strength and its amateur status, and how far to resort to professional services. If you want fundraising, sometimes it is most efficient to get professional fundraisers. If you want to get free space in the media and free time on the TV by presenting interesting issues, then – at least in the short run – professionals in the advertising and publicity business can often get it for you more effectively than you can. My advice is that anything you can possibly do with your own resources, it is best in the long run to do it that way. It is more plausible and believable. Politicians, state and local, are not fools; they recognise the hand of the professional publicity agent, and they make enormous discounts for it. The honest intention and perhaps the technically bumbling methods of a lot of amateurs are recognised as more authentic – this is the real voice of people who don't ordinarily stir themselves. If they are stirring themselves on this issue, if they are doing real legwork around the electorate, if they are producing deputations and long lists of signatures on petitions and so on, then real politicians take real notice and you are halfway to victory.

In practically all of your politics, in organising around the district to get up your membership, to visit every street, to distribute membership literature and newsletters, if you can run on your own leg power and amateur energy, I think you will be more effective; as with all of your writing and publishing.

There are two areas where it probably is more sensible to reach for professional help. One is law. An association like this in a district like this will have many lawyer members, and it is likely that you will get a good deal of help from them; there is nothing wrong with that – in general advice, committee membership, dreaming up strategies and that sort of thing. But if you ever need legal services, it is usually prudent to pay for them, and I think the lawyers here will probably agree with this. No service from lawyers, if what you require is a professional performance, is likely to be quite as reliable and quite as satisfactory if it isn't paid for. There is an instance that contradicts this: the model of Australian residents' associations, the Paddington one, has a remarkable collection of talent living in Paddington – it has a leading conservationist-architect, a leading professional consultant town planner and an eminent local government and planning QC for legal services. But unless you happen to have not just lawyers, but appropriate ones with a practice in local government law and planning law, it is as well to buy your legal services. And you may well need help from time to time from professional planners.

One of the most fundamental services an association like this provides is simply to make machinery – to provide a place to meet and communicate with each other – both to find out how much consensus and agreement you have among yourselves, and to provide a voice to the outside world, approaches to local government, state government or public utilities. So merely in existing, as long as you can keep alive enough interest, find enough interesting things to meet and talk about and do, you are already performing a kind of social service that gives an extra social interest and social dimension to the place where you live.

Next I recommend that you should not underrate the power of local government. Residents' associations started because most Australians had completely lost faith in the effectiveness of the formal machinery of local government. You remember the kind of extreme pessimism and apathy about local government that we all felt – I certainly did – five years ago. What residents' associations have done is to reactivate local government and to make it extraordinarily effective, to make it reverse many of its courses. I think that many of the associations have been surprised to find how much they get done by using the formal machinery of local government, where they perhaps expected that they would have to get things done by bypassing it or getting the minister to clobber it, or by direct action of their own.

If you ever do have to go into battle with public authorities, you need to have certain resources. The first thing you need is as massive a membership as you can get; nobody will take much notice of a society of 100 purporting to represent 5000 or 7000 residents. The North

Adelaide Society, in its combative phase, which didn't last very long, found that nothing was as important as the credibility it could get from the number of its membership.

You need good research; try to know more about your neighbourhood, and more about the implications to it of any hostile proposals, than the authorities themselves know.

I don't think you will need physical force in the streets, but peaceful forms of it can be effective if used with care and with sufficient numbers. Demonstrations are successful in proportion to the number of middle-aged mothers with small children in conservative dress who can be put up the front in demonstrations. The longhaired radical demonstrator is not likely to be effective in local politics.

In any case, it is always worth beginning with pleasant, civil approaches, because you find out from those what proportion of the public authorities are willing to be on your side and to disclose, to listen and to inform on all the things you may want them to. Don't start abusing them needlessly until they act as if they deserve it.

Direct and indirect gains come from serious political organisation at local election time. The outstanding example here in Adelaide is the North Adelaide Society, which has existed for about two years and has taken nearly half of the residential ward seats in the city and can clearly take the rest. It hasn't got working on aldermanic elections yet; already some aldermen are scared of the day when it does. Some of them are not scared, because they have spent a year assiduously listening to the association. It is very hard to imagine the Adelaide City Council doing anything in its residential areas contrary to the wishes of the North Adelaide and South Adelaide societies.

The sort of policy issues that are likely to be important to you are, for example, the nature of your zoning arrangements for the area, and the provision of facilities in your area. You have to decide whether you want basically a high-service arrangement – that is to say, a local authority that does a lot for you and charges high rates for it – or whether you want a low-rate, low-service kind of local government. Not a lot of government money gets wasted. Not much change, either in rating levels or in the level of services, has ever been achieved by economies that could be made at the Town Hall; there may sometimes be possible economies but they will be found to be marginal. If you want trees down every street, rubbish twice a week, land bought for playgrounds and kindergartens and that sort of thing, then you have got to pay for it.

Local planning matters constitute another of the large matters that associations like this are centrally concerned with. I think you have been most concerned with statutory planning – that is to say, with a set of laws that tell the private landowner what he can and what he can't do with his land – zoning plans, and zoning regulations and aesthetic controls, if you have them. Here again I would say, 'Don't be negative.' I don't mean by that that you should not be conservative. I don't see any reason myself why a neighbourhood with an established residential character should not have it as its aim to minimise change. You have got a very nice place to live. You probably have a fairly high majority of those in it who want to keep it that way; so I do not think there is anything wrong with being negative in the sense of saying, 'We don't want our neighbourhood mucked around with.'

On the other hand, if you are presented with schemes you don't like, you get nowhere if you are purely negative, saying, 'We don't like them.' The obvious tactic in all cases is to generate as quickly as you can a viable alternative and run it as your policy.

I might elaborate one point here, because it is worth saying that most of the reasons alleged by councillors, with the best intentions, for permitting intensified residential building for flats and apartment houses and so on, are technically untrue. It does not mean that their policies are wrong – flats may be good things to have in themselves. It does not mean that there is anything wrong with the attitude that says our conception of land ownership means that a man ought to be able to develop his land as he wants to – I am not going to argue on that issue. But where it is alleged that building more flats will increase the number of people living in your area and the value on the land, so that the level of rates won't have to rise and you will get better service for less money – that is, from beginning to end, in every particular, bunk in Australia. Its applications are only true on such a tiny scale that they don't make sense for the district as whole.

Throughout Australia, where single-family housing is replaced by flats or towers there is never any change in the residential density if you look at it over any significant area. If you have a block with two houses on it, and you pull them down and put up a tower block with fifty flats, you may increase the density on that pair of two blocks. But if you stand back and look at your neighbourhood as a whole, you will generally not have increased the number of people living in it. Kirribilli was the first and is the most spectacular example of this – that's what you see straight across from Sydney Cove, below the north end of the bridge. It was all made over from two storeys to ten storeys. Exactly the same number of people live there. They are just five times more affluent in the amount of floor space and car space they are using. This is modernising – but it is not increasing density, and it is not hard to see the reason why. What happens is that you have an old family house and garden – perhaps with five people in it – and somebody buys it and the one next door that has five or six people in it, and there go twelve people from two houses. This makes room to build say ten walk-up flats, which have an average of 1.2 residents in them, and you have the same twelve people as you had before, except before you had twelve people and two cars and now you've got twelve people and thirteen cars. That means, quite seriously, that where before you had twelve trees, you have now got one or none. All these projects that purport to increase living density in inner suburbs in Australia over broad areas are having the simple effect of replacing children by adults, and trees by cars – they are quite neutral as to the number of people on the land.

The only way known to man of increasing the amount of rates you can get out of a district without actually raising the rate – so that with the rate struck at a certain level there will be more money flowing in – is to replace poorer people by richer people. This does work, and if you want to be as callous as that, off you go – I think you are a fair way along that track already. But density of residences is not by itself a rate-raiser in most Australian circumstances, where the legally required space for a motor car is larger than the legally required space for a person. All you do by these replacements is make a bit more space for the people with motor cars without increasing the people's numbers.

9

PLANNING TO BREAK THE RULES (1972)

Stretton insisted that Ideas for Australian Cities *was an 'amateur' book: a political tract written by an interested citizen, not a manual for professionals. Among professional planners it had a mixed reception. It was, some admitted, perceptive and very attractively written. Where it was right, said critics, it was unoriginal; where it was original, it was wrong. Yet such was the book's popularity and intellectual class that its author could not be ignored. Soon he was speaking to professional planning bodies as well as residents' associations and state bureaucrats. Good planning, he insisted in this address to the Royal Australian Planning Institute, requires a critical balance between innovation and conservation, regulation and improvisation.*

THIS PAPER IS ABOUT ORIGINALITY IN URBAN planning and government, and the whole unhappy relation between desirable controls and undesirable standardisation.

In urban affairs, 'originality' is a word with many meanings. It is used variously of inventing, innovating, copying or being unique.

Here, for example, are four common meanings of it:

- When the rest of the world is changing, don't. Go on as you were. Conservatism can be original. Think what an unusual city we would have now if we had continued for the last seventy years to build chiefly terrace housing, and to rely chiefly on foot, pedal and public transport.

- When the rest of the world changes, copy it quickly. This is quite unoriginal but it is the commonest method of innovation, which often passes as originality. Copying is a sensible mode of innovation, though two general warnings apply to it: (1) copying other people's techniques often means accepting some of their social and political values as well, sometimes without realising it; and (2) it is often better to copy late rather than early. For example, it may be no bad thing that most Australian cities have lagged twenty years behind the world's leaders in things like urban freeways, comprehensive and compulsory clearances for residential redevelopment, and factory fabricated and transportable housing. We are now better placed to judge the costs and benefits of those novelties than their original innovators were.

- Forget the past. Ignore the foreigners. Use your unaided native wits to solve your problems. This may be blinkered arrogance, but it's the method in use at the two extremes of the urban spectrum. It is the method of the sleepiest local councils, and of the leading innovators – of New York and Los Angeles, Stockholm and Milton Keynes.

- Educated independence. By all means learn whatever the past, and foreign theory and experience, have to offer. But then apply your own values and imagination to your own problems. This is obviously the best approach of the four. But notice that it has no necessary connection with originality. Depending on the case, your own people's values may prompt you to *invent* something original, or copy a foreign model or go on as you were, or even turn the clock back to your own past. (For example, some of the radical urban programs of the 1970s were proposing, though they may not have known it, to revive roughly the coherent central controls and the conservationist values that were last practised in Australian cities by a few colonial governors before 1851.)

Besides that four-way classification, there are other ways of distinguishing originality from unoriginality. If you want to be *un-*inventive, one way is to analyse and predict current trends, then adapt to them and plan within them. This has lately been regarded as the trendy way to plan. Even where choices and reference to values are inescapable, you can still pretend they are technical. Never say 'We ought to do this' or 'Your electors demand that you do that.' Speak instead of 'elucidating' aims, 'identifying' goals and 'charting the political parameters'.

If on the other hand you do want to be original, it may be necessary to bring your techniques under the command of an opposite style of thought – political or historical thought – which hunts for opportunities to bring more processes under deliberate democratic control, to intervene, to modify or reverse trends.

Plenty of current trends are really paper tigers. But a fully sophisticated urban social scientist, trained to believe only what he can extrapolate, sometimes can't tell a paper tiger from a rock of Gibraltar. The people who do know which is which are the residents' associations. For example, there has *never* been a more inevitable-looking trend than the tendency of fast-growing single-centred cities to force destructive transformations of their inner suburbs. Every economic, traffic and locational use analysis showed conclusively why that had to happen – until the citizens of Paddington, North Adelaide, Carlton, then Cremorne and Mosman converted it from a matter for scientific prediction to a matter for political choice.

In doing that, they drew attention to a basic misdirection of our attempts at originality. For a generation after the war we allowed the suburban sprawl to proceed in a most conventional, unoriginal way, while *various* professional and state authorities dreamed of radical reconstructions of the old cities and inner suburbs. That was in many ways irrational. The old Victorian fabric, and its old-established social networks, are what we should conserve. The practical opportunities for originality lie out in the paddocks, where new suburbs and cities must be built. This has always been the view of the inner-suburban residents, and the old-style planners of the New-Town and Garden-City tradition. Both were disregarded for too long; but then the residents brought us forcibly back to our senses.

The main thing to remember about all these things – scientific analysis, up-to-dateness, participant planning – is not to be snobbish or doctrinaire about any of them. Each can be serviceable or useless, rightly or wrongly employed. Planning does depend increasingly on information and the understanding of complex systems. But technique should be the servant of policy, and more and more planners are coming to agree that most professional planning is a necessary mix of techniques, public education and active politics.

To sum up: originality is neutral. Planning proposals should never be judged by their originality, their up-to-dateness, or their scientific or unscientific appearances. They should be judged solely according to the good and the harm they will do to the people they will affect. Knowing what their effects will be usually calls for both scientific and political understanding. With complex urban problems, the best solutions usually include some of everything: a bit of copying, a bit of conserving, a bit of inventing. That is certainly true of the main subject of this paper: the problem of the undesirable effects of uniformity or standardisation which may result from the operation of well-intentioned planning controls.

If they speak in sufficiently general terms, most architects and planners and citizens can agree about the unities and diversities a city should have. We want cities different from one another; within them, precincts diversified to all tastes, with the widest possible choice of housing, workplaces, recreational opportunities and lifestyles. These are the diversities we want. The unities we want are the casual unities expressed in classical villages, townscapes and city quarters: relaxed, organic unities rather than monotonous uniformities.

We are not succeeding in building many casual unities. Instead, we are building uniformities, or else a sort of confetti diversity. This is true of the effects of our regulatory controls, and it is also true of much of what we do in the way of comprehensive design.

The constraints which produce too much monotony or uniformity are familiar. First, there is a political asymmetry. Electors don't mind a dozen missed opportunities as angrily as they mind a single visible offence to the townscape or to their land values. So our controls have a bias towards preventing offences, even at the cost of preventing valuable diversities.

Second, there are some genuine economies of scale which make for repetitions.

Third, there are uniformities of taste and demand, though most of them are compatible with 'casual unity' rather than repetitive uniformity.

Fourth, and chiefly, there are the imperatives of social organisation. Our division of labour is complex, and it is further complicated by the pattern of overlapping areas within which the labourers perform their respective functions. The role of each has to be defined so that his work will fit into the work of all the others. A house has to be designed to fit compatibly with the property rights of its immediate neighbours, with the zoning regulations for its locality, with the lending habits of its city bankers, with service connections standardised for the whole state and with a building act which some would like to see uniform throughout the Commonwealth.

Running throughout this complex division of labour there is a general relation – too often, an adversary relationship – between the rule-maker and the performer. This may be between client and designer, or between the law and the developer. In both cases one person has made the rules and another must design within them. The one who makes the rules has in mind a list of offences which are to be prevented, but does not have in mind the whole, infinite list of inventive possibilities which it might be desirable to allow. This relation between lawmaker and designer is the heart of the problem, and it is important to remember both its elements: the rules are there to prevent undesirable developments: but they are also there to ensure efficient integration of roles in the complex division of labour.

In practice, in order to integrate roles in the complex division of labour, there have to be not one set of rules but dozens of sets, usually drawn by different people at different times with different purposes. The rules – and the roles they define for all the labourers – have been built up and made to fit with one another by long historical processes of adaptation. It becomes difficult to suspend one rule in a particular case, because there would then have to be accommodating variations in a dozen others. Even if an inventive variation in the design of a building or a street would be entirely good and do no harm whatever, it is often impractical to think of persuading half a dozen independent authorities to bend their rules in order to permit one small variation or grace in one local environment. So everybody sticks to the rules, even though nobody would defend the result as the best solution.

To improve this oppressive system, it may be best to try to operate on two features of it. First, more of the rules should be designed so that on particular jobs there can be dialogue between the designers and the controllers, and between the labourers in the division of labour. Second, there needs to be some reform of the pattern of areas within which rules apply, and dialogues and variations are possible.

The value of any such machinery must depend on the spirit with which it is worked. This is especially true of performance requirements. With one bias they can become so precedent- and rule-ridden that they lose what they were intended to provide; alternatively they can become capricious and unpredictable, as government by laws is to some degree replaced by government by persons. These difficulties are so well known that it is worth remembering the counterbalancing advantages of well-administered performance requirements: (1) They escape the dead hand of out-of-date regulations and by-laws. The interpretation of performance requirements can adapt to changing techniques and community values. (2) Projects can be exempted from requirements that are irrelevant or harmful on the unique facts of the case. (3) Advantages can be traded for each other. (4) Any general requirement to maximise environmental quality is in practice impossible to express in strict regulations which will apply intelligently to all cases. Performance requirements really offer the *only* method of encouraging, or enforcing, any greater concern for environmental quality than we are achieving now.

10

LETTER FROM AUSTRALIA (1976)

In 1976, in the bitter aftermath of the dismissal of the Whitlam government, Stretton pondered the state of his country in a letter to the Annual Record *of his old Oxford College, Balliol. It is addressed to its editor, political philosopher Steven Lukes. The allusions to the Balliol historian A.B. Rodger and to contemporary British and American events were for the benefit of his readers among Balliol's wide diaspora. There was mixed pride and disappointment in the intellectuals' contribution to the urban reforms of the Whitlam years, but, significantly, Stretton's sharpest barbs were reserved for two Oxford-educated Australians: 'Lord' Rupert Murdoch, and the third-class philosophy, politics and economics student Malcolm Fraser – now the Australian prime minister.*

DEAR STEVEN,

In this country we have been enjoying what A.B. Rodger would have called stirring times. Radical hopes, then a lurch to the Right – in politics as well as on television, we spend our time rerunning old British and American movies. Gore Vidal visited us the other day and went home saying, 'I have seen the past, and it works.' He meant it kindly – in America 1946 had been a vintage year. But we are really more up-to-date than that. You will remember how John F. Kennedy won his 1960 election with a swinging young image; Lyndon Johnson conservatised it in 1964; Richard Nixon led America right back to hard work and strict old-fashioned morality in 1968. You will also remember how Harold Wilson was swept in by the white heat of technology in 1964, acknowledged those austere economic realities in 1967, and lost to Ted Heath's real Right in 1970. Just so did Gough Whitlam adopt a Kennedy hairstyle in 1971, put an end to twenty-three years of Tory misrule when he took our wildest hopes into office with him in 1972; then adopted conservative budgeting in 1975, and lost to the real Right of Malcolm soon afterwards. Whether our 1973 coal strike and/or Watergate will come punctually in 1977 remains to be seen. Being myself the remains of a historian rather than a seer, I shall devote this letter to the historical origins of our poor imitations of such poor originals.

Academics see life in miniature in the universities. Two or three years late, we had our gentler version of the militant events of 1968. Some universities survived unchanged. In others, including mine, the one enduring effect has been to transfer power from professors to the rank and file of academics – which here tends to mean from the young to the old. Australian academics already enjoy a very comfortable combination of British tenure and teaching, American salaries and uniquely Australian rights to plenty of well-paid study leave. To those blessings is now added self-government by the academic staff, with some token presence of students. All ranks elect the policy-makers and departmental chairpersons, and control what they do. The change is not regretted because the former oligarchy was often worse. But nothing in Oxford is quite as crustacean-conservative – as proof against change or innovation – as a provincial university of stable size governed by its senior lecturers. The future of classical studies was never safer; the curriculum was never designed with such an exclusive eye to the comfort of teachers; consideration for the students' intellectual experience is confined to the wrangles about examining it; even the blue jeans are disappearing. These are the ironical achievements of five years of grassroots militancy.

We have also done our best to follow the example of British and American academics out in the marketplace. If we have not exactly repeated the American Camelot scandal, or the sanguine British expenditures on cost-benefit analyses of rival airport sites or channel crossings, it has not been for want of trying. Through the 1960s there was a mushroom growth of social sciences. Many of them were extensively mechanised, Americanised, sterilised and dressed-up for sale to politicians and public departments. That hopeful Labor government of 1972–75 then hired a lot of keen young scholars, and commissioned research from a lot more. Some of it was good and effective – usually where it was done by old-fashioned, committed, social-reforming folk of all ages who investigated social evils, denounced them in language learned from Beveridge and Tawney, and designed practical reforms to get rid of them. But rather more of those sudden intellectual works were of the other kind: expensive pseudo-objective studies which concluded by calling for further studies. When they recommended anything practical, it tended to embody the welfare ideology of Professor Moynihan (replace welfare services by doles) or the economic ideology of Professor Friedman (of all the ways of reducing real wages and increasing unemployment, prefer the monetary ways). My prejudices are showing – but it really was tough for Mr Whitlam to shower so much money and opportunity on professions so inept, pretentious and hostile to most of what he stood for. Not even in Chile have the economic ideas of the Chicago school conquered as completely as they seem to have occurred in what is jokingly termed the mind of the Australian Treasury.

Under the Labor government, that made for some irresolution in national economic policy. The path to hell is clearer now that the same experts have more congenial political masters in Mr Fraser's Right-of-Right coalition. But it has been the politicians rather than their policies that have chiefly entertained us through the past year.

Under the Australian Constitution, a government with a majority in the lower house may often face a hostile Senate, and the powers of the Senate are, on paper, much greater than those of the modern House of Lords. The Senate has often blocked government legislation, but before 1974 it had never felled a government by blocking its money bills. The Australian Senate dropped that convention and sent Mr Whitlam back to the electors twice in three years. The first time, he won. This time, he lost – but in a specially spectacular and newsworthy way.

When the governor-general decided to dismiss the majority government, install a minority government for long enough to get the Senate to pass the money bill, then dissolve the parliament, he had to do it quickly and secretly – otherwise the same few hours would have seen him sacked instead. There still seems (to the romantics in us) to be fleeting, half-hour chances to relive the historic moments of Elizabeth's or Charles I's parliaments: for the lower house to sit fast, and try the allegiances of officials, judges, soldiers. Whatever else, that would have opened an assured growth industry for generations of Australian historians.

But no Peter Wentworth or Hampden rose to the hour – instead of a revolution, we had a coup. The bonanza has therefore provided not reef-gold for historians, but a field of alluvial paydirt for quick fossickers in a gold rush of the Ballarat or Californian kind. The first seven books are already out, all by journalists. Some Whitlam ministers had been trying to raise huge public loans with dubious legality from dubious Arabs, through intermediaries who couldn't even be dignified as dubious. There had also been mistresses, CIA plots, curious party funds, and dilemmas when Rupert Murdoch wanted a mining lease or a diplomatic appointment in return for services to the party. (The party may well regret renouncing imperial honours: a barony that levelled Lord Murdoch with Lord Thomson might have saved everyone trouble.)

Impartially, the conservative dirt was just as payable. Like Mr Heath in 1970, Mr Fraser promised the electors that he would abolish the prices tribunal, slash the budget deficit, reduce the public sector and stiffen the laws against trade union leaders. Unlike Mr Heath, he has broken all those promises in his first six months. He is also accused of voting himself a lot of subsidised manure (perhaps as the bucolic equivalent of Mr Heath's return of supertax) and of unmentionable personal scandals in Singapore. (To saner minds it seems much more scandalous that we are governed by a man with a third in PPE.) Meanwhile, the governor-general is accused of contriving a quickie divorce to hurry on his own remarriage, and of having performed his coup under pressure from his bride, the General Staff, the CIA, Rupert Murdoch, Catholic renegades from the Labor Party, and other likely and unlikely sources too numerous to mention but all newsworthy.

Some of the abuse from both sides is so actionable it circulates only by word of mouth. Some gets into print in dark, oblique ways. But a great deal of it hits the front pages after being libel-proofed in one or another of the dozen houses of parliament with which our Federation is blessed. The State of Queensland (our Alabama) runs a regular commercial service in libel-proofing. Punctually one week before each national election, its premier uses his state parliamentary privilege to accuse the national leaders of the Labor Party of taking or soliciting enormous bribes and commissions. (That actually seems to be the only kind of indiscretion of which they have been wholly innocent.) Reciprocally, Mr Whitlam is now accusing a dead Liberal of taking Lockheed money. This week the prime minister has decided that the last two parliament's financial agreements with the states are invalid, so he can repudiate them. Half the states have decided to take him to the High Court. A convicted twenty-year-old has accused yet another minister of sleeping with her.

I suppose what we are really suffering from is too much news. Beneath all those trivia, serious life goes on. Even serious government – the Whitlam government did plenty of enduring reconstruction, and the Fraser government is already improving on some of it. But with so many symptoms on the surface, it's still hard not to believe in the disease, and there are many rival diagnoses of it. One of the simplest comes from Donald Horne, an able journalist who twelve years ago published a bestselling book called *The Lucky Country*. 'I had in mind,' he says, 'Australia as a derived society whose prosperity in the great age of manufacturing came mainly from the luck of its historical origin. It was sufficiently like the innovative industrial societies of the West to prosper from their innovations; it didn't have to think up much in the way of techniques of design or organization ... Nor, more widely, did it show much originality in general social and political changes or world views.' A second-rate elite merely copied the work of foreigners, but then took full credit for it. So, having posed as the authors of innovation through the prosperous 1950s and '60s, they couldn't avoid the blame for the very different imports of the '70s. What really hit the country in the '70s was a universal capitalist disease which hit all countries like it. But – Horne suggests in the first of the quick books about the coup – the local Right was able to convince the local voters that those troubles were the single-handed creation of the villainy and extravagance of Mr Whitlam's government.

This year a very old and eminent novelist [Xavier Herbert] has published the biggest-ever Australian novel: nearly a million words entitled *Poor Fellow My Country*.

11

DEMOCRACY AND HOME OWNERSHIP (1976)

At the heart of Stretton's democratic vision was his belief in the importance of the family and household unit. All his experience and observation persuaded him that the good of society depended on the good of its constituent households. So, against some other socialists, he defended individual home ownership, arguing that governments should help to spread its benefits more equally. And against most economists, he insisted that households were part of the real economy. Soon after the publication of Ideas for Australian Cities, *he was appointed Deputy Chairman of the South Australian Housing Trust, the state's public housing authority, and in 1974 he delivered the ABC's Boyer Lectures, advocating progressive housing policies to match the radical urban policies of the Whitlam government. If we took the role of the household seriously, he argued in this chapter from his next book,* Capitalism, Socialism and the Environment *(1976), we would have to think about economics in a different way.*

I N AFFLUENT SOCIETIES (AS IN MOST OTHERS) MUCH more than half of all waking time is spent at home or near it. More than a third of capital is invested there. More than a third of work is done there. Depending on what you choose to count as goods, some high proportion of all goods are produced there, and even more are enjoyed there. More than three-quarters of all subsistence, social life, leisure and recreation happen there. Above all, people are produced there, and endowed there with the values and capacities which will determine most of the quality of their social life and government away from home. So the resources of home and neighbourhood have commanding importance. Home may be the scene of some general exploitation of women by men and children, but those relations tend to improve as the resources improve, and most other uses of domestic capital are capable of being wholesome. It is in the activities of home, neighbourhood and voluntary association that there is least money exchange, least division of labour, least bureaucracy, least distinction between production and consumption, least occasion for oppressive or exploitive or competitive uses of ownership, and most of the best opportunities for cooperative, generous, self-expressive, *unalienated* work and life. Anyone interested in building a more cooperative, affectionate or equal society should therefore look first, and centrally, to the resources of home and neighbourhood.

But that whole domestic economy – a third or more of every developed economic system, and two-thirds or more of every social system – tends to be systematically undervalued and consequently starved of resources by the orthodox economic thinking of both Left and Right.

What should Left theorists think instead? Instead of finding domestic ownership guilty by association with commercial ownership, they should recognise it as potentially the benign opposite of commercial ownership. They should stop thinking of private corporate ownership and state ownership as the basic alternatives for productive capital. For most purposes those two should be lumped together as institutional ownership. Whoever the shareholders are – whether public or private or cooperative, capitalist or socialist, equal or unequal – institutional organisation must necessarily divide and specialise and alienate a lot of the labour it uses. We nevertheless need a good deal of it for productive purposes. It can be half-civilised in various ways; and it need not occupy more than a third of anybody's week, or between a sixth and an eighth of conscious life, if you count everybody's waking hours from birth to death.

Institutional ownership characterises most of both of what are commonly called the public and private sectors of the money-exchange economy. Together with private small-business ownership, it uses perhaps three-fifths of a developed economy's capital, and about the same proportion of its labour. The domestic economy, using chiefly home capital and free labour, accounts for the other two-fifths. *Those two should be perceived as the basic divisions of the economic system.* Allocating resources between the two, and between households within the domestic economy, should be the subject of the most careful economic policymaking that any government does.

This chapter argues that it should be socialist policy to shift more resources into the domestic sector, and as far as possible to equalise household capital. The likely effects of that are widely desired by the masses, and widely misunderstood by their economists and ideologues. It need not lead to the 'private affluence and public squalor' condemned by J.K. Galbraith, if resources in both sectors are distributed with productive intent, environmental care and proper equality. A more generous and equal provision of domestic resources is what can now do most not only for the private life of affluent societies, but for their public and social life as well. It can probably assist their real economic growth, in environmentally tolerable directions. It can do most to reduce alienation and replace it by more self-expressive and cooperative activity, and by more of the living unities which the critics of alienation dream of. And it offers the most effective single strategy of equality for capitalist *or* socialist societies; whereas without it, more equal distributions of money and services (which are anyway harder to achieve) will be much less valuable in their effects.

✳

The subject can be approached by understanding the history of changing relations between commercial and domestic resources, or more directly by observing how people in developed societies use space and time.

Before the coal-and-steam revolution, most of the people who were able to live in settled households at all lived close to land and home. They farmed, or worked at other trades as close to home as farmers do. Most members of most households helped to produce any goods that were produced for market, as well as goods for their own subsistence. So however poor or exploited they were, families were often cooperative producers with some control of their tasks, their timetables and some at least of the goods they produced.

The first industrial revolution broke up that co-op. Work moved out of the family and into the factory. Labour still had to live in walking distance of it, so millions moved into the crowded slum housing of the early industrial cities, where they found neither space nor spare time to do much more than eat and sleep. Members of the family went off singly to long hours of low-paid wage labour. At home they had to live on what their wages would buy. They were slaves of the commercial economy right around the clock. Scarcely any work was done except for money; almost everything produced was sold for money; so to a modern economic science which counts *only* work and output which exchange for money, that era's statistics of economic growth still look wonderful. Even housework was commercialised – the practice wasn't new but the scale soon was. With the primitive equipment of those times, it took long hours of labour to keep home up to any genteel standard; so to look after the rapidly rising numbers in affluent upper and middle classes, domestic service became the biggest single occupation in the commercial economy. But there wasn't much housekeeping in the warrens the labouring classes lived in. Child rearing was short. Children went to work young, and learned most of the little they needed to learn on the job. Many of their mothers as well as their fathers worked long hours for wages. Off work, without time or space or opportunity to do anything constructive, personal skills and versatilities didn't develop. Housing was merely shelter. The family wasn't together much, and didn't do or produce much. It was at its most degraded and unimportant as an institution.

Then came the second industrial revolution: mass-produced household goods, network water and gas and electricity, ubiquitous transport; and another great shift of productive resources. The first industrial revolution had moved production out of the family into the factory; the second industrial revolution moved a lot of it back again. By 1970 the British housewife was using the horsepower the British factory worker had used in 1910. Households could *make* and *do* things: a steadily increasing number and variety of things. With equipment and materials supplied by the commercial economy, they were soon producing a good deal of the twentieth-century standard of living for themselves.

Productivity in one sector bred productivity in the other. As the factory economy grew more efficient, it used less labour for shorter hours, so it did the double service of giving people more domestic capital and more free time to use it. We think of washing machines and vacuum cleaners and do-it-yourself tools and materials. But the thing people wanted most, for itself and as a condition of most other blessings, was space: bigger and better houses, with more rooms for more diverse activities, with working and storage and garden space around them, and with space for schools and parks and community services in local neighbourhoods. Affluent minorities may value modern transport as a means of personal mobility and busier, wider-ranging communications. But to most people the richest gift of powered transport has been private space: the enlargement of home. Since the first railway, London's population has multiplied fivefold, and also increased its private space per head several times over, so that the metropolis has sprawled over twenty or thirty times its old area. But the average time it takes a Londoner to get to work or city has scarcely varied through all those years. People have converted each improvement of transport into an increase of private space.

All this suggests that the flow of consumer goods has been over-rated as the characteristic product of industrialisation. The most profound achievement of modern industry – of the forty-hour week of organised, alienated labour – has been to give people at home energy, equipment, materials and communications, and time and space and freedom, to produce for themselves: to make and do what they want, when and where and how they want, working together or apart as they feel inclined, and enriching their time and social experience in all sorts of ways freely chosen by themselves.

*

Most of the new freedom and productivity depends on (among other things) distributions of private space. Distributions of space don't follow at all automatically from distributions of income, and their effects are scarcely noticed in most contemporary economic and urban theory. Five kinds of effect are specially important: effects on life at home, on public and social life away from home, on environmental policies and possibilities, on economic growth, and on equality.

The effects on life at home are dramatic enough to generate universal desires for better rather than worse home space and resources. More people than ever now choose to live in family households, and they want private housing on private ground if they can get it. The middle classes get it everywhere. Whether the urban working classes get it depends very little on their market preferences or capacities to pay, and almost entirely on public policy. In most English-speaking countries and in Norway, a good many of them do. Through the rest of continental Europe, most of them don't.

Whether or not people are getting it, their desire for the small house and garden is fully intelligent. For most people under eighteen or over thirty, private housing on the ground is incomparably more resourceful and adaptable than landless apartments can ever be. If land prices are under control, small houses are usually as cheap as other housing forms to build and service. As time goes by, they can be replaced, altered, enlarged or modernised according to individual need, without the wasteful private and social costs which usually go with the mass demolition and replacement of apartment housing. They can be shaped and grouped to meet diverse tastes, as free-standing houses, pair, rows, clusters. Compared with most modern 'landscaped apartment suburbs', they can often house people almost as densely on the land and almost as conveniently to services. They can generally allow more freedom from 'house rules' and other constraints by landlords or neighbours, and their occupiers are freer than most apartment-dwellers to control and vary their privacy or publicity in relation to neighbours and visitors and strangers; and to allow individuals similar options of privacy and community within households. Many small housing forms can be built in stages, and most can be altered – often cheaply, by do-it-yourself methods – to adapt to changing tastes, means, family numbers and interests (or injuries and handicaps) through households' lifecycles. Their indoor, outdoor and outhouse spaces can be adapted to allow a marvellous variety of sociable or solitary activities, productive or enjoyable and often both, including a very large number that are not possible either indoors or in public places and are therefore denied altogether to apartment-dwellers. All sorts of payable part-time and full-time trades flourish in backyards, especially where the working classes are allowed to have backyards. (Those are often the *only* opportunities for underaged, overaged and part-time tradesmen.) People of every age and class can grow flowers and fruit and vegetables and green shade; they can keep birds and animals; they can work with wood and clay and metal and chemistry sets; they can make more noise and more mistakes; they can dismember cars and cycles and other machinery, and make toys and build kennels and hutches and boats and dolls' houses and walk-in cubbyhouses – all with more freedom than any communal workshop or public park can ever allow. And a wide range of social possibilities goes with those private freedoms.

Those resources are used. Most of the hostile stereotypes of house-and-garden life are unresearched. There are some unhappy and some inactive people in every kind of housing; but 'suburban apathy and isolation' predominate only in limited and atypical circumstances. (Those attract most of the researchers.) Whenever they are fairly sampled, most urban and suburban people don't think of good housing either as convenient shelter, or as something chiefly to display in a competitive or conformist way. They think of it as ample, versatile, *usable* private space, indoor and outdoor: their own bit of the world where they can live as privately or sociably as they like, and do as many and varied and interesting things as possible. They perceive their houses and gardens as resource centres, use them accordingly and very often use them well. And although the material things which people make and do and enjoy in their private time and space are a large fraction of all economic activity, they are often less important than some other effects: the human relations which develop in resourceful households; the scope which their intricate, alterable, home-designed indoor and outdoor spaces offer for art, self-expression, fantasy and imagination; and the skills, capacities and values that people develop in the course of using them.

*

Those skills and capacities and values also have powerful effects on life away from home. That is one of many reciprocal relations between private, commercial and public resources. An understanding of those relations ought to be at the heart of almost any general social or economic theory; but in most contemporary theory they are neglected or falsified.

Two mistakes are very common. One simplifies (and perhaps misrepresents) the argument of J.K. Galbraith's *The Affluent Society* (New York, 1958) to assert that capitalist societies oversupply people with private property and undersupply their public services. Some public services are indeed undersupplied, in the USA and elsewhere, but doubling their budgets doesn't usually get them used by the people who need them most. The main cause of that, and of the other effects Galbraith complained of, is not an excess of private resources but their unequal and unproductive distribution. An absurd extravagance of private space and superfluous equipment for some people contrasts with the crowded and unproductive squalor of big-city slums and out-of-town shanty towns, and the caravans and prefabricated 'mobiles' in which a sixth of all Americans have to live. The same mal-distribution of private resources helps to account for the mal-distribution of public services which was first noticed by Richard Titmuss: resourceful middle-class households are able to seek out and use more services than ever find their way to the land-less, barely equipped shelters of the poor.

The second mistake, common in older orthodoxies of Left and Right alike, is to see private and public resources as alternatives. 'You don't need private gardens if you have public parks' (or laundries, or kitchens, or creches, or workshops, or libraries). That is about as sensible as seeing husband and wife, or bolt and nut, as alternatives. The real need is to understand the reciprocal, mutually necessary relations of domestic, commercial and public resources, and to allo-cate resources in the way that allows each to do most to nourish the use and productivity *of the others*. The fertility of each does not depend chiefly on its getting more than its share of the available cap-ital; it depends at least as much on its exchange of services with the other two. Homesteads – however affluent – are underused if they are starved of public and commercial services. Commercial capital is unproductive unless a developed domestic culture supplies it with highly developed human capacities. Many public services are under-used, and some are quite unusable, if they are offered to people who do not have appropriate domestic resources.

The interdependences between home, neighbourhood, public and commercial resources run all the way from the rooms inside a house to the most central services of cities and nations. Inside the house, diversity of activity depends on stimulus from outside, *and* on space and storage at home. People cooperate more, and usually like each other better, if they can escape each other sometimes. Gardens help them to do that; so do separate indoor and outdoor spaces, which allow different activities to go on at the same time. People with resourceful rooms of their own are often the best contributors to common family life. In the garden, children with plots of their own take more interest in the garden as a whole. People who work urban land of their own take more knowledgeable interest in public gardens and parks, and they go (more often than people without land of their own) to enjoy any accessible wilderness. Community workshops and trades and crafts get used where people have space to practise the crafts at home: people practise the crafts at home where there are community workshops to attract them to meet, learn, use common equipment and compare work. Similar relations hold between neighbourhood and central city services. There tend to be good local libraries where there are good central library services. Local craft centres do best where there are central craft markets and training schools. There is most amateur and local theatre where good professional theatre and training are within reach. Reciprocally, the first-class central and professional activities do best where there is plenty of home and local activity to generate interest and custom and recruits for them.

Home is where most people now hear most music, read most books, watch most drama, read and see and hear most of the world's news and most analysis and commentary on it. If the 'alternative' theory of resource allocation were true, public and community life should have dwindled correspondingly. But the theory is not true, and the 'isolation of home' is not happening. Since young people got tapes and transistors, they play more instruments of their own and go out to more live pop gatherings. The people with most gramophone records at home tend to go to most live concerts. The people who have most books at home make most use of libraries and educational services. The people with room to play most games at home also play most away from home. These relations are general. It is where home space and resources are *poorest* that poor people spend most time at home, but do least there, and watch most of the poorest television. There is no truth in the theory that it is possible to fill the streets with sociable life by stacking the people into lower flats. The ground around tower flats is usually the most arid, unsociable and unused of all urban space. There is no way to nourish public social life by starving and overcrowding private life. On the contrary, the better the resources and opportunities are at home, the more versatile the inhabitants are likely to become, and the more active and sociable and interesting to one another they will be away from home. Reciprocally, diverse experience away from home stimulates more interesting and creative activities at home, as long as there is space for them there.

So even if the enrichment of leisure were the only purpose, there would be two good reasons for distributing private space generously and equally. In all the places sampled in the international time studies reported in *The Use of Time*, people spent at least three-quarters of their purely social time with kin rather than with other acquaintances or strangers. That by itself would justify a generous and equal distribution of private space and resources. But the same policy will usually also do most to nourish the use of commercial, communal and public social places and resources. As long as the away-from-home resources exist and are reasonably accessible, they in turn will stimulate the fullest use of the domestic resources. Life may still be arid in new outer suburbs and new lawns before their public services arrive and their community networks and activities develop. Studies of those pathological situations account for some of the professional dislike of house-and-garden forms and low residential densities. But the cure is to develop the support and stimulus that will get the private resources used; it is not to turn the clock back a hundred years by taking the private resources away.

*

There are similar relations between domestic resources and environmental values. Environmentalists should stop thinking of cities and suburbs as enemies of the countryside, or as worse land uses than farming. It wouldn't enhance human happiness or improve anyone's diet if the people of Paris were housed in one cubic kilometre (as they could be), while the rest of the town was ploughed under to grow maize instead of people. People are the richest of all crops, yielding much the highest value per hectare: but, as with other products, the quality may decline if the land is sown or grazed too densely. Instead of complaining about suburban sprawl, its critics should get it better planned, better centred, better served. Instead of wanting less room for private gardening in town, they should try for more. Generous private houses and gardens *can* degrade the environment if people fill the houses with machinery and drench the gardens with chemicals. But the same relaxed housing forms also allow the best scope for *good* environmental behaviour. It is in private houses with storage space and some land around them that it is easiest to use more human energy in satisfying ways, and to manage with less-powered commercial services. It is also easier to adapt to many kinds of environmental and industrial breakdown. People in landless apartments suffer most when the rubbish truck doesn't come, pipes burst, the lift and clothes dryer stop; and at other times, especially if they are affluent, they tend to make the most insistent demands for powered commercial services, including passive entertainments. And they are likely to bring up children like themselves.

That points to the most important relation between home resources and environmental values. Environmental policies will always be determined chiefly by people's values; and urban houses and gardens are the nursery of most of the best environmental values. People who live in town but grow some foliage of their own, and keep a cat to deter mice, are the mainstay of all the movements which work to protect larger landscapes and ecosystems. Private residential land is both an environmental good which ought to be fairly shared, and a vital educator: a classroom for work skills, play skills, nature study and environmental values which an environmentally careful society would be mad to deny to any of its people.

*

Though they are rarely noticed in orthodox accounting, there are obvious relations between domestic resources and economic growth. Through the first industrial revolution the organised use of paid labour contributed most to the growth of productivity. Now that the factory and transport revolutions have transformed about as much of daily life as they can, commercial growth is slower because more and more of it has to be in labour-intensive services. With full employment and a limited working week, those services cannot grow much more except by attracting people back from domestic activity to work for wages. But a great deal of commercial output has meanwhile gone to build and equip houses and connect them to services and communications. That equips people to do more for themselves. With the domestic economy as well capitalised, as many commercial services are, it can often contribute more than they can to growth, especially because it can draw on reserves of underused labour. Plenty of that is not hard labour but quite welcome activity, with the double value that the work and its output are both enjoyable and both deserve to count as goods. But the domestic growth is necessarily slow. It depends on the development of skills and interests and incentives, and on the distributions of space that arise from the slow growth and reconstruction of cities. Plenty of European and some American city building is still designed to give ample private land to middle-class households but none – and also less indoor space – to poorer households. That restricts national productivity, distributes its output more unequally than conventional accounts will ever show and confines the poor to forty hours of alienated work for others (often by one member only of the household) and very little for themselves.

That is only one of the relations between housing and equality which tend to be ignored by experts of almost every persuasion. Left experts dislike the private ownership of productive property. Right experts treat housing as a consumer good and expect people to buy as much as they want of it out of income. Both are obsessed by money flows, and by the money-exchange transactions, which are the only things their one-eyed accounting systems are designed to record. Both – if they think about it at all – suppose that distributions of income determine distributions of private space just as they determine distributions of other goods.

In practice, present capacities to pay have comparatively little effect on distributions of private space. Most subdivisions, houses and apartments are indivisible and last for several generations. *Past* capacities to pay, *past* politics and *past* uses of landowners' class advantages have constructed most of the present housing stock; rich and poor now occupy respectively the best and the worst of it, and have to accept whatever equalities or inequalities are built into it. Grossly unequal capacities to pay could not now house the New Zealanders very unequally, because they inherit a stock of very equal houses. Perfectly equal capacities to pay could not now house the Swedes equally, because a third of their stock of urban housing has private land and two-thirds doesn't.

If private urban space were subdivided and distributed freely in open markets, it would usually be distributed (in cities of any size) with extreme inequality. That would happen because land ownership is somewhat monopolist; because suppliers have many bargaining advantages over buyers and tenants; and because for various reasons the mass of would-be house-buyers have very little chance of borrowing the price of a house if they must bid for money in open capital markets. So all affluent societies rig and regulate the business to some degree – though not always in the interest of equality. Government everywhere fixes or influences, the type, size, land allowance, safety, sanitation and general quality of the new housing that may be built; supplies some public housing; taxes owners and tenants differently; and controls or influences mortgage-lending in various ways. It thus determines much of the basic distribution of new capital between the domestic and commercial economies, and by its influence on the distribution of private urban space it does a good deal to determine domestic productivity. Over most of the affluent world government does this in substantial ignorance of many of the effects of its policies. In most European cities a few dollars' difference of household income allows one household to rent an apartment, another to buy one, and a third to buy a capacious house and garden. Differences of domestic productivity then act as a powerful multiplier to increase the original inequalities of real income. Meanwhile, in many English-speaking cities different policies give the poorer household as much space as the richer; the same multiplier then works to reduce their real inequalities – but painlessly, at little or no cost to the richer.

Domestic investment probably has an up-and-down curve of marginal return. Varying with local values and circumstances, people generally identify a level of housing which allows them to do most of the things they are likely to want to do. Beyond that level, they don't typically use additional income to move house or buy more space, they spend it on other things. If a house can give each of its inhabitants a room big enough for some work and hobbies and storage as well as a bed; if a house for more than two or three people has common spaces to allow more than one common activity to go on at once; if it has some each of covered and open outdoor space for work, storage and gardening; and if it is insulated and equipped to heat water, cook food, wash clothes and keep people at tolerable temperatures – then it can accommodate most of what most people of ordinary means are likely to demand of it. Bringing it up to that standard is likely to be productive investment. Expenditure beyond that is likely to be more like expenditure on consumer goods – it buys margins of comfort or luxury or display which may increase the pleasure with which people use the house, but won't usually extend the *range* of activities they can use it *for*. A principle of very rough justice might define investment up to the sufficient level as mostly productive, and above that level as mostly for consumption, or anyway of less marginal value. There is some alternative support for that principle in Michael Young and Peter Willmott's book *The Symmetrical Family* (1973). They think that many high-income households try, both at home and away from home, to do too much for their own good. Individuals suffer strain, uses of time and space conflict, cooperation deteriorates. So even if extravagant housing does extend the range of household activity, the marginal output may not be worth its personal and social costs.

In summary: private indoor and outdoor space is not quite like any of the three conventional categories of goods we are accustomed to distributing and accounting for. It is not like commercial capital, whose output can be measured by its money returns – though it usually has to bid against commercial uses for its resources. It is not public goods like roads – though in equipping people with productive capacities, it is a little like education. It is not ordinary consumption goods – though it is an enjoyable possession whose owners should contribute to paying for it. It is best understood as productive capital, whose output can never be fully accountable because it ranges from measurable economic goods to quite unmeasurable social and personal goods and qualities of life. The distribution of existing stock will generally be ordered by inequalities of wealth and income; but the equality or inequality of the stock itself is everywhere determined (directly or indirectly) chiefly by government. That stock is a large and fertile part of any developed society's capital, but its fertility depends almost entirely on its degree of built-in equality. It can be most productive only if it is distributed in sufficient shares to all households. We are quite accustomed to insisting on commercial full employment: a job and a basic wage for everyone willing to work. Since almost as much investment and output are at stake, we should learn to insist in the same way on domestic full employment: on sufficient private space and opportunity for every household willing to use them.

*

When houses and gardens and local neighbourhoods are perceived in this way as 'resource centres', and their inhabitants as producers, it becomes obvious that land and housing policies can be potent equalisers or unequalisers. That is true of relations within households, between households, between classes and between nations. Within families, traditional housing reformers have probably been right to see housing as an asset more likely than most to be shared well. Unlike money income, it can't easily be monopolised, lost, gambled, misspent, overcommitted to the hire-purchase of oversized cars, or taken away altogether by absconding husbands. Like the housing stock as a whole, it can have physical equalities built into it, for example in the form of labour-saving equipment for housewives or generous space and storage and privacy for children. Between households and classes with unequal money income, a stock of physically equal housing can be a specially practical equaliser. Unlike most other distributions of wealth or income, distributions of space can be arranged so that the rich don't have to lose nearly as much as the poor have to gain. Good housing and land policies don't merely transfer income or services from one consumer to another. They give otherwise-poorer people usable capital: the means of producing for themselves goods and satisfactions which would otherwise never be produced at all to be enjoyed by rich *or* poor.

Once again, there are reciprocities. Over time, unequal capacities to pay do exaggerate inequalities in the housing stock if government allows them to do so. In turn, the terms on which private space is occupied will usually increase inequalities of wealth and income if government allows them to do so – it usually happens that private tenants pay most for the use of private space, public tenants pay less, and (over time) owners pay least and gain most: effects which are compounded by most countries' tax systems. So every consideration of national productivity and personal and class equality converges to support the conclusion that private space should be distributed very generously and very equally, and should wherever possible be owned by its occupiers.

The first industrial revolution allowed its town workers scarcely any private space or time or equipment at all. They lived like twentieth-century battery chickens, for the same reason as the chickens do: a ruling class owned all the means of production, including the bare tenements the workers slept in. Instead of the twin economic systems we have now, there was only one, and the masters owned it. So in the world Marx knew, scarcely any ownership was innocent.

That miserable phase didn't last long, but it lasted long enough to beget. One true socialist insight and one fatal socialist mistake. Marx developed a perceptive and compassionate theory of alienation. It described the condition of workers who did not own or control their land or tools of trade or their time or anything their labour produced, and who could express nothing and see nothing of themselves in what they produced. They were denied the means of developing and enjoying most of the potentialities that humans are born with. They were fragmented and denatured: kept alive like animals to serve a single purpose of somebody else's. The institution which enslaved them seemed to be the institution of property. So Marx and his heirs identified ownership itself – instead of its wrong distribution – as the root of evil. That may have been under-standable at the time, but it was about as sensible as attacking the mal-distribution of food by abolishing food.

The mistake was the more remarkable because Marx and some of his contemporaries understood very well what those suffering masses needed. They needed to replace unequal, impersonal, exploi-tive relations of production by more equal, affectionate, cooperative and voluntary relations. They needed the living unities they had lost or never had: to live whole lives as whole men and women, digni-fied and many-sided, able to work at tasks and by timetables and with companions of their own choosing, making and doing things for themselves and one another – things which expressed their own intentions and satisfied their own tastes and needs. *They needed precisely the unities and freedoms which the domestic economy now allows to the more fortunate of their great grandchildren.*

*

At the heart of the critique of alienation was the idea that the worker ought to control his resources: his capital and labour, his time and his product. His work lacked meaning and his life lacked fullness and unity because he did not own those things. Why didn't the early socialists therefore decide that he *ought to* own them? Some utopian socialists did. But in their programs Marx could see only the sacrifice of industrial productivity and a reactionary retreat to the poverty and 'rural idiocy' of peasant smallholding. The prom-ising technology of his time could be made productive only by the institutional organisation of divided and alienated labour. Max Weber thought that complex organisation, under *any* ownership, must unequalise men and degrade their lives to some degree. So did Marx, often enough; but like Weber, he couldn't think how to civi-lise the monster so he designed his practical proposals to correct its other sins, especially its distributions of money and power. About the problems of alienation under socialist organisation he was usually evasive.

It was a technical misstep to expect that the new technology would go on reducing the amount and importance of domestic production. In fact, it soon began to do the opposite: to equip the new domestic economy. In that economy, which among other things produces every society's supply of labour, independent smallholding is technically efficient. Free choice and voluntary cooperation come naturally. So can the dreamed-of unities. And productivity does not depend on competitive motivation, 'incentive inequalities', institutional ownership or bureaucratic organisation. It depends instead on the most equal possible distribution of domestic land and capital into private ownership. So the new domestic economy (complemented by appropriate communal and public services) offers socialism a historic opportunity to resolve most of its internal dilemmas and contradictions, to reconcile productivity and freedom and equality, to be truly popular – and even perhaps to get elected.

Institutional production must obviously continue. Much of it needs to be reorganised, often by traditional socialist methods for traditional socialist reasons. But whoever owns its capital, it also needs to be 'humanised'. A lot of that has been done already, and more is in hand here and there – job enrichment, workers' participation in management, the organisation of smaller and more stable working teams. But that sort of improvement does not depend only on institutional arrangements at work. It also depends on the cooperative or uncooperative capacities and values which people bring to work. Most of those capacities are built into people by their upbringing, which in turn can depend a good deal on the resources with which they are brought up – a good domestic economy is a necessary condition for civilising the institutional economy. By no means all institutional work has to be soul-destroying. Some of it will always be challenging, inventive, absorbing. A lot of it can be tolerably interesting and sociable. The worst of it can at least have fair pay and short hours. But for all that, it must always be heavily regulated and only half-civilised: the institutional economy can rarely offer the best or most important scope for either the freedom or the brotherhood of man. It needs to be tamed and deprived of as much as possible of its power to corrupt and unnerve and unequalise people. It should then cease to be the centre of socialist attention. It should become a service: a banal but necessary supplier of goods and services, mostly to that other economy in which men *can* be their own masters. Its necessities need occupy less than a third of the week of most workers, less than a sixth of conscious human time. Socialists should concentrate on equalising and improving the other five-sixths.

✳

That is not what most socialist leaders and experts and ideologues have concentrated on. They have concentrated on the institutional economy and the distribution of money. They are rightly obsessed by the task of getting institutional capital out of unequal private ownership. But too many of them have been wrong about nearly everything else, and intolerant of any women or liberals or utopians who tried to put them right. In most of the liberating and potentially equalising growth of the domestic economy which Young and Willmott trace, 'hard' socialists can see only a monstrous historical mistake: a capitalist victory and a class betrayal: a worthless and corrupting *embourgeoisement* of the masses.

Seeing the masses seduced by capitalism, 'hard' socialists respond by doubling their distrust of ownership. It does not occur to them that the house and garden and car turn people away from the party of equality chiefly because the party of equality officially despises the house and garden and car, and the life they allow. The heart of the trouble is this: most Left ideologists have never worked out what they should do with the institutional economy when they *do* capture it. What should it produce, what should it enable the ordinary worker and his family to *do* with the five-sixths of life that are, or ought to be, their own? A good test of any ideology is to insist that it answer that question *in detail* – minute by minute, hour by day by year: what should ordinary people be able to do with their time, and what are they likely to want to do with it? Most of them do not wish to divide most of their time between cocktail parties and *avant-garde* theatre; nor between watching television in a landless apartment and socialising in strictly public places. They want a much more complicated pattern of diverse activities, private and familial and social and public, including a great many active, productive, creative activities. They also know, as Left ideologues don't, that their outgoing social lives will be better in proportion as their home resources are individual and good, *not* standardised and poor. They want to *have* things so that they can *do* things, including many of the things they do socially with other people – as Marx in his wiser moments understood.

Besides the general distrust of ownership, socialists are prevented from understanding this chiefly by the Marxist theory of class. I believe that the least misleading way to understand modern inequalities is to see them as continuous from richest to poorest. Values and attitudes are also distributed continuously, though lumped and layered and clustered in patterns more complicated than patterns of income and occupation can (by themselves) explain. Some of the richest and most reactionary people are employees; some of the poorest (and some of the most radical) are dependent tradesmen or proprietors. Parties of equality have the difficult task of persuading majorities of middle and poor to act together. The 'natural' working class, for which Marxists see a natural common interest and political role, is no longer distinguished by the fact of wage labour. It is distinguished in practice by low pay, blue collars and (very often) mean rental housing; and it has long been a minority class. Its 'lost' numbers – skilled or white-collared or otherwise prosperous – are enjoying their possession of houses and gardens and cars and are unlikely to vote for anyone who wants them to trade all those for a standardised apartment near a jolly public park. But neither on the other hand do most of them love their employers much. They'll vote socialist again when socialist policy offers them what they correctly recognise as the material conditions for equal, cooperative, unalienated work and life. If the leaders of the Left can't learn that from the obvious sources – from the evidence of their own eyes, and from the living experience and aspirations of the masses they are supposed to represent – but must learn it from books instead, they should begin with Michael Young and Peter Willmott's book.

With economic growth, whole classes cross thresholds of income. When workers can afford education, cars and resourceful housing, they use them much as middle-class people do. But because Rightist minorities had those resources first, Marxists call the resulting culture 'bourgeois' and identify it with class-exploitive politics. (Because aristocrats installed the first water closets, it should follow that every modern WC endows its user with aristocratic values.) That kind of determinism is absurd. Even on Marxist assumptions, political values relate to class position, not material culture. In most countries the spread of common lifestyle *increases* the vote for more equality. And not only for class equality – Young and Willmott notice that as household resources improve, men and women grow more alike, exchange more tasks, do more together and share more fairly. Given equal resources, productive households promise to reduce both class and sexist exploitation.

Meanwhile, ideology continues to determine policy. Attitudes to private ownership determine which socialist policies can be good and which cannot. Industrial income and tax policies can be good. Many public, welfare and personal services can be good in themselves because they can run on public capital and wage labour. But they cannot be fully fruitful if they are offered to people with very unequal domestic resources (which are chiefly human, but depend in various ways on material resources); and because it runs best on private ownership, the domestic economy (and therefore a large fraction of national productivity) has generally done poorly wherever 'real' socialists have governed. Communist governments do their best to confine productive work to the institutional economy and to prohibit production outside it. Socialist housing is the affluent world's worst. Socialist cities (including Swedish cities) give private land to the lowest proportion (and exclusively to the richest) of their people. Pathetically, Russian town-dwellers go out and comb the countryside for patches of neglected land they can plant, visit, enjoy, 'make their own', however tenuously. Their masters, who own everything just as the masters did in Marx's day, discourage this petty bourgeois practice. In that and other ways, they do their best to build for twenty-first-century Russia the urban fabric of nineteenth-century Manchester. Plenty of Left as well as Right technocrats are doing the same for the working-class quarters of western European cities. The hard Left – Marxist and technocratic – thus works as hard as any capitalist to kill the most promising of all socialist opportunities, and to perpetuate the alienation which Marx condemned as the worst effect of primitive industrial capitalism.

Voters know this. Women know it all too well. 'Next thing, they'll confiscate hearth and home.' Not many of the democratic people who vote against socialist parties are in love with big capitalism, or in fear of revolutionary bloodshed. They are in love with private life, and afraid of *any* contempt for it; and even in the milder parties of the Left they see some contempt for the furniture and security of the private space and time in which all people are born and formed, and ordinary people then suffer or enjoy the greater part of their experience of life. The ideologues are wrong, the people are right, and more than any other single cause it seems probable that this explains why most democratic-socialist parties have got fewer votes from women than from men, and have spent most of the twentieth century out of office.

That has allowed the Right to get most of the credit for the imperfect but nevertheless prolific distribution of the new domestic resources. Right governments and capitalist markets distribute them very unequally. To extract profit from the domestic economy, they do their best to infect it with commercial values and competitive anxieties, and to persuade households to see themselves as consumer-cooperatives rather than producer-cooperatives. But however they try to corrupt the domestic economy, they do not threaten to starve or abolish it. Right rhetoric celebrates the family, promises to nourish and protect it, and recommends that it *own* all the private space and resources it can. When Right leaders say that people want to be equipped to do things for themselves, rather than 'expecting everything from the state', they may often be hypocritical but they are nearly always right. And besides prudent politicians, the Right has its share of honest and generous reformers. When they want to reduce inequalities their traditional philosophies positively encourage them to do it by improving the distribution of do-it-yourself resources by redistributing domestic rather than commercial capital ownership. Good housing policies (though seldom *very* good) have come more often from the Right than from the Left. For all its faults, the Right approach to the domestic economy has generally been more intelligent, productive, egalitarian and popular than the usual approach of the Left.

So the Right has deserved its victories, and the Left its defeats. But the suffering citizens haven't really deserved either. Wrong options face them at election time. If they want good private resources they have to vote also for the rapacities of commercial capitalism. If on the other hand they want that monster reformed, they have to vote for parties which appear to threaten their private resources. The options need to be reconstructed. Social-democratic parties should be radical at work and liberal at home. The main purpose of the radical reconstruction of the institutional economy should be to put it to work to enrich and equalise the domestic economy and its complementary public services. The domestic share of social capital could well be raised to half, and distributed with physical as well as financial equality.

Not much of that will be achieved merely by tinkering with housing and town-planning policies. It needs a fundamental change of socialist philosophy; new symbols of what the Left stands for; changes and replacements within the industrial and party machines; and decades of persuasion and public commitment to convince the citizens that the change of heart is real, and based at last on true instead of false understandings of the economics of freedom, equality and productivity.

*

In summary: institutional and domestic ownership should be perceived as the basic alternatives for productive capital. Much of the institutional economy needs to be taken out of unequal private ownership, and civilised as far as possible. But that may never be very far: elements of alienation and bureaucratic inequality are bound to go with any complex division of labour and coordination of effort. That will matter less as institutional production occupies less of life, and loses its power to unequalise the rest of life. Much of its output should go to equip, serve and complement the domestic economy, more equally than happens now. The distinguishing purpose of socialism should not be to reduce private and increase public ownership. It should be to tame institutional and increase domestic ownership: to attack inequality and alienation by giving to every household (as far as scarcity and environmental prudence allow) the fullest control of the most versatile resources it can use.

Nothing in that need make any household – or any society – more settled or suburban than it wants to be. It is consistent with a society as footloose, sociable, crowded, adventurous and away-from-home as any other. But lifestyles and the habitations they need should be open to choice by poor as well as rich, so that urban densities and diversities don't have to mean a free choice of private pastures for most of my life, and a box in a battery for most of yours.

Most capacities for love develop (or don't) in childhood; the largest quantity of willing human cooperation occurs within and between households; cooperation there is the pattern, and has to be the continuing basis, for cooperation anywhere else. To put it in the most shocking possible language, socialism should cease to be the factory-floor and chicken-battery party, and become the hearth-and-home, do-it-yourself party.

12

CITIES AS DISTRIBUTORS (1976)

How do cities shape the lives of those who live in them? In the late 1960s, the eruption of violent protest in Paris, Chicago and Los Angeles alerted social scientists and politicians to the unequal distribution of resources, from housing and schooling to medical services and open space, between and within urban communities. The Marxist geographer David Harvey's Social Justice and the City *(1974) offered the most radical diagnosis of the problem. Stretton's, influenced by the milder tone of Australian debate, as well as by his social-democratic inclinations, was characteristically subtle and attentive to historical contingency.*

THE GOVERNMENT OF CITIES IS AS COMPLICATED and conflict-ridden as the government of whole societies. People in cities have both common interests and conflicting interests. Town planners and urban theorists have a chronic tendency to talk only about the common interests – or about conflicts between vehicles and pedestrians, or between rival land uses – as if conflicts of class interest were not their business. In fact, the structure of cities distributes costs and benefits as drastically as the structure of incomes does. It is chiefly as distributors that cities ought to be understood and governed.

143

By connecting everybody to pipes and wires and standard services, and by allowing some concentrated education and organisation of working classes, modern cities have helped to improve some equalities of income and lifestyle. But in other ways they have been powerful unequalisers. They have often distributed their costs and benefits to increase concentration of wealth and to aggravate inequalities of income. If one family earned twice as much money as another, it could often spend a lower proportion of income to get more than twice as much land, housing, privacy, clean air, urban travel and public goods and services. Having less, the losers could earn and learn and do less, so the differences increased.

Many of these effects continue. They do so for various reasons. The most powerful are the self-interested politics of the winners, but the most intractable are the inequalities which have been built durably into the urban fabric. Plenty of the poor still live in neighbourhoods built to the inequalities of 1870, while in other parts of town the broad streets and ample public and private gardens which the rich could buy or legislate for themselves in 1870 are the shares of space the rich have still. Progress can supply old slums with new services which are not land-hungry: power and sewerage, teachers and social workers, transport and television. But it doesn't give their people private or public space worth having, or room for track and field games – or green shade – at school. Deliberate distributions of urban space are commonly made only once, at the first conversion of open field to urban use. After that, change is piecemeal and (except by thinning the occupation of overcrowded housing) rarely does much for anybody's rations. Physical inequalities persist; and social attitudes are entrenched, by self-perpetuating segregations, to be imposed on new suburbs as well as old.

These iniquities are technically easy to avoid in new urban development if there is political will to avoid them. Plenty of new towns and suburbs have given rich and poor people fairer shares of land and local services than their unequal incomes could have bought in free markets from unregulated subdivisions. But that wholesome will has too often given way to Left, Right, technocratic and environmentalist desires to condense cities by housing their classes at battery densities. As fast as the people vote with their feet to lower the densities of the old slums, misguided governments try to rebuild the old densities vertically.

What should the Left do instead?

All parties should of course try to make city life as efficient, safe, interesting and sociable as possible. Beyond that, the distinctive aims of the Left should include these: Cities should keep their central and local attractions and services in reach of their poorer as well as their richer people. Where that can't be done by locating the people, it should be done by locating the centres. Taxes and services should be distributed to redress differences between richer and poorer neighbourhoods, and there should be persistent efforts to get rid of such segregations. Land should be kept as cheap as possible, and payment for its use should be arranged to reduce, not increase, financial inequalities. The stock of housing and private land should have strong equalities built into it. The stock should also be various, to allow a full and interesting diversity of lifestyles and types of housing and places to live; but the diversity should as far as possible reflect differences of taste rather than capacity to pay. Every household which wants the city's average ration of house and private land should be able to get it, and preferably own it, without too much locational disadvantage.

Most of that is easy to achieve in new urban development. As higher proportions of people get their fair shares of private space, and demand more public space for schools and sports and other activities away from home, many cities will continue to grow even if population numbers don't. Their new parts can be made to distribute benefits equitably. Their old parts are harder to reform. Improvement has to contend with built-in inequalities, and with the politics which defend them. When cities grow too big – i.e. when too many people are forced (by those who locate their jobs and housing) to live and work in reach of a single centre – there are also unavoidable conflicts of locational interest. Cities which are already too big may need some re-centring; and a good deal of their land may need to be taken out of the market, and allocated by other means than competitive bidding.

*

In most industrial societies, except a few which inherit unusually good urban patterns, government should do what it can to limit the size and improve the centring of cities.

There are both common and class reasons for this. When cities grow above a million or so of population (more or less, depending on shape and geography), too many of their problems intensify. They usually cost more to run. They generate more travel, congestion and local pollution per head. They force wasteful rates of demolition and rebuilding on their inner parts. Intense competition for central and accessible locations makes it much harder to solve problems of density, shares of space and – above all – land prices.

These effects may depend as much on the distribution of central activities as on gross metropolitan numbers. London does, and Paris could, do better than some cities with half their numbers, because both have usable land in all directions from their centres. They can be more compact than (for example) lopsided cities with coastal centres. London and Paris afford great pleasure and efficiency to many of their inhabitants. They also exact high prices from others in the cost of services, in money transfers to landowners, and in housing so many of their service populations as battery densities. Most other very big cities do worse, and distribute their costs and benefits with strong class bias.

The size of a city is often of very different interest to different classes of its citizens. The richer people are, the more valuable big city centres usually are to them. They are likelier to work in downtown centres. They have more money to spend, and they spend less of it on necessaries available locally and more of it on the specialised shops and services and entertainments which can only be supported in centres with catchments of many millions – i.e. in catchments which include hundreds of thousands of the comparatively rich, including free-spending visitors and tourists. Poorer people may depend as vitally on their cities, but usually on a narrower range of commoner jobs and goods and services. Most of what most families want can be provided, in an affluent telecommunicating society, by a city of a quarter or half a million. Most ordinary people have comparatively few and minor interests in their cities being bigger than that. But plenty of affluent people like cities to be bigger because they are the chief investors in, and users of, the additional diversities that can be supported as cities grow. The rich are also the chief gainers from the rising land values of big cities. They can usually get whatever they want of private land or central location. And they make the public and private investment decisions which affect cities' growth – and often their overgrowth.

'Strong' decentralisation – not a rural scatter but a pattern of good small cities – should usually be the policy of the Left. Decentralisation isn't easy, but it is one of the fields in which a few early failures have too often led reformers to give up, rather than to improve their methods and try again. It usually takes both push and pull – some restraints (for example, on new office or industrial investment) in overgrown cities, and positive public action to develop good alternative locations. The alternatives need to be attractive, interestingly centred towns or cities. Too many attempts have failed because they concentrated on decentralising industry and very little else. Towns built on the principle that 'jobs attract people' are generally company towns at worst and one-class towns at best. At good locations on attractive land, where investors and managers and professionals as well as captive employees would like to live, people and jobs can usually attract each other about equally. Public efforts to build new towns, or to attract growth to existing towns and small cities, should rely less than they have often done on tax and transport incentives to industrial investors, and more on providing good education, services and housing in naturally attractive places.

At the same time, government should work to improve the distribution of jobs and centres and services through existing metropolitan areas. London works as well as it does partly because even its middle is many-centred, and much of the rest of it houses people at comparatively low densities in districts of distinct character, many with strong centres of their own. Younger metropolitan areas should imitate that as far as they can. 'System cities' and 'new towns in town' can do quite well if they are developed carefully, with attention to where people actually live, work, play and want to travel, and with some refocusing of transport and some redistribution of institutions and services. In North America and Australasia, too many hospitals, universities, technical and teachers' colleges and high schools and trade schools, suburban office developments, supermarkets and filling stations, theatres, cinemas, pool halls, squash courts and other high and low entertainments have been scattered like confetti along main roads through characterless expanses of housing, in the name of decentralisation – or more often in the uncoordinated pursuit of cheap sites. Not houses and gardens, but that formless uncentred litter of facilities on and off public transport routes (which anyway lead only to one dominant downtown centre) is the true and disastrous meaning of 'suburban sprawl'. Policies of *recentralisation* should try to gather those activities to support each other – whereupon they will support other things as well – in strong town centres with their own local transport, local government, day- and night-life, and sense of identity.

For these purposes, public planners have more resources than they have usually been allowed to use. One resource is government itself, which constitutes as much as a third of the office work in many cities. It often clusters into metropolitan centres because the public servants rather than the citizens want it there. Nor is the location of private investment always as profit-seeking as it pretends to be: it goes where it suits its directors to live or work, often enough. Without much loss of public or private efficiency, government (if skilful) could be more forceful in directing both kinds of investment to the places where they will do most good for the pattern of urban growth.

Old commitments are obstinate; change is necessarily slow; it shouldn't be hurried by bulldozing houses or people, or forcing mass migrations (even of public servants). But wherever a big metropolis goes on growing, whether by increasing its population or by shaking out its densities, its new growth at least should be made to take a good town-centred form, so that people can live well locally, and be free to use the larger metropolitan networks and centres as much or as little as they like. Where existing commitments and the lie of the land allow them, linear metropolitan forms may sometimes serve these purposes best. They can help smaller centres to compete with big ones, intercepting custom and economising transport as common routes serve both metropolitan and local travellers; and they can keep most town-dwellers in easy reach of countryside.

∗

Good city shapes and systems and centring *allow* a lot of equities, but don't guarantee them. The detail of the fabric is just as important – and often harder to reform.

Most people like to see interesting new activities appearing in their city and local centres. Most of those who feel cramped like to get more private space, and more public space especially for children. But those are almost the only changes which settled urban communities can be relied on to welcome. Structures of local law and representation should generally be designed to arm rather than disarm people to resist other changes, except where principles of equality dictate otherwise. Local electorates should generally have strong powers to resist compulsory clearances (especially of housing), physical invasion (by motorways and other bulldozers) and some kinds of social invasion (by office developments, industries, supermarkets). The exceptions – when central authorities should sometimes be able to override local opinions – should be for public transport, pipes and wires, and people. People are the likeliest to cause trouble. Government shouldn't force unwilling neighbours on one another; but, subject to the respect which any new building ought to pay to its immediate surroundings, neighbourhoods should not be able to exclude newcomers on grounds of poverty, colour or public housing.

People are one thing, but their numbers may be another. It is scarcely ever true that cities can be made more efficient by subjecting their poorer parts to compulsory redevelopment at high residential density. If that ever does appear to be true of a particular cities, the Left should apply three rules of thumb. One: deliberate residential redevelopment should include the upgrading of schools and services to the standards currently required in new developments. Two: new inner-city housing should, as far as possible, displace old industries, warehouses, railyards, coalyards, etc. (as long as they don't employ many locals), rather than displacing existing housing. Three: if denser housing must displace existing housing, it should do it where the scope for increasing density is greatest. That will usually be where the existing density is lowest and the existing residents are richest.

But increasing density is rarely a sensible aim for government-aided urban renewal. Overall densities are falling in all affluent cities, for good reasons. Public renewal programs should usually have other aims: to replace incurably bad housing; to improve poor neighbourhoods *without* displacing or overcrowding their people; and to improve the general class distribution of residential space, location, work and services. For the first purpose, new housing needs to be patched into old neighbourhoods or built street by street in 'rolling renewals' which allow people whose houses are to be demolished a genuine option of moving directly into new housing already built nearby – with whatever rent aids or other subsidies are required to make that option real. The second aim, in big cities, should be to take more of every kind of living space – dense and less dense, in each of inner and middle and outer suburbs – out of the open market, to be reserved for classes of people who would otherwise be priced out of many of them. Public agencies need to build or buy plenty of all types of housing, at many and various locations, for rent or sale to appropriate occupiers on terms which prevent resale to richer bidders.

That is also the best way to apply public money to the physical rehabilitation of old housing. Since the recoil against the bulldozer, rehabilitation has become fashionable and a number of governments have offered public grants or loans to private owners to do up their own houses. But such policies face a dilemma. If (as for a time in the United Kingdom) the provisions are liberal, they are taken up by affluent owner-occupiers and landlords more freely than by poor ones; and directly or indirectly, they cause a good deal of the upgraded housing to pass from poorer to richer occupiers. So they transfer resources in the wrong direction, and may actually raise the price and reduce the stock of well-placed housing available to low incomes. If on the other hand (as in Norway) the aids are offered on strict conditions, they are not used much. The best way through the dilemma is for the public to *buy* whatever it wants to rehabilitate, do it up, then rent or sell it on terms which prevent its resale into richer hands. This combines rehabilitation with an accumulating low-income share of inner and middle-suburban living space.

Various other things can be done to reduce the built-in, inherited inequalities of existing cities and suburbs.

Many of those inequalities are related in one way or another to residential segregations. The facts and problems of social mixture and segregation can be infinitely complicated. They provoke intricate argument about the definition, 'grain', type and effect of different degrees and kinds of mixture and segregation. But the segregations which affect equalities are chiefly crude, large-scale segregations by income. Though they are attributed to snobbish social feelings, these gross segregations often arise at least as much from market competition for physically attractive land, accessibility or capital gain. Moreover, 'coarse' and 'fine' segregations often arise from different causes and have different effects on equalities. Social, neighbourly, face-to-face relations depend heavily on local facts and feelings; but there can be any amount of petty segregation from street to street, within districts where people with widely different incomes nevertheless share shops, services and local taxation and government. Where there is evidence that rich and poor don't want to be immediate neighbours, that may justify segregation from street to street; it doesn't justify segregation from suburb to suburb or from west side to east side, unless the hatred reaches a New York or Belfast intensity. Ethnic minorities should ideally be able to find options to cluster or disperse; rich and poor should ideally be able to choose between rich, poor and mixed streets; old people should be able to find old or young, quiet or lively neighbours; people of every income should be able to choose between sparse and crowded, quiet and busy, plain and arty quarters; and so on. All those options are compatible with a rule of thumb that the average income in any local government area, and if possible in any primary school catchment, should never be far from the national average income.

There are a number of reasons why that would be a good rule of thumb. First, taste: I observe that many closely mixed districts exist; they are usually the most interesting; it seems to me that people who like them tend to be more interesting and good-natured than people who don't; and some of them nourish more direct and good social relations across class and income lines than most sociologists suspect (or ever go looking for). Second, democracy: it is usually only the winners who *want* major segregations. Poor neighbourhoods sometimes resent rich invasions as they resent other invasions; but wherever poor people have a choice, they tend to prefer public housing in mixed or rich neighbourhoods to the same housing in ghettos. Parents especially prefer it. Meanwhile, one of the most active ambitions in many ghettos is to get out of them, so that the selective emigration of the ablest leaves the rest poorer still. Third, justice: the grosser segregations intensify inequalities of money, land, opportunity, services, local organisation and leadership, and communal self-defence. Fourth, responsibility: large segregations don't just happen, they are contrived or encouraged by private wealth and public power. Anyone who has any influence on the growth and government of cities must use it in favour of one pattern or another. There is no way to be neutral, and the open market certainly isn't neutral. In the present state of social and economic understanding, there are stronger presumptions in favour of encouraging mixtures than of encouraging segregations. Fifth, futures: mixtures are likely to work better as wealth and incomes grow more equal, and they seem likely to make the equalising easier.

Where segregations persist, various things can be done to redress their effects. Rich and poor districts can never have equal (or equalising) schools – but their schools can have equal money, plant and playing fields. Parks and playgrounds can be distributed equally to rich and poor neighbourhoods. Local government is an excellent field for the rule 'from each according to his capacity, to each according to his need'. Local taxation ought to be progressive *both* within *and* between districts. This can be achieved by making transfers from one local government to another, based on the average rateable value per head of population in the area of each. The boundaries and transfers should be designed to put a punitive tax on affluent segregations, so that a rich income or property in a rich district pays higher rates than the same income or property would pay in a mixed district. (At present, opposite relations hold almost everywhere in the capitalist world.) Money should go to districts which need it until their public investment reaches equality with others' and sometimes beyond that – poor districts without much private land need *more* public spaces and resources than do districts full of private houses, cars, gardens, pools, workshops, bookshelves and stereos. Poor districts need positive discrimination in the provision of public services, local outdoor and indoor recreations, consumer protection and tenant protection services. The distribution of social and advisory services should often be biased in favour of populations which need them most, rather than the (often richer) populations which demand and use them most.

Some of these distributions may be improved by means of area surveys and improvement programs. Good area surveys can do more than list local needs. If they are done cooperatively by citizens and voluntary groups, local government, officers of national agencies and some independent professionals brought in to help, they can often generate better ideas than any of the participants would produce by themselves. Somebody looks at the range and accessibility of local shopping and services. Somebody looks at every kind of movement in the area, finding ways to tame or divert noxious or dangerous traffic and to improve pedestrian safety, public transport and delivery services. Somebody looks for underused land, from industrial yards and fouled riverbanks, through underused warehouse and utility land (and any surplus churches), to parks which might be better used and streets which might be closed or narrowed to restrict traffic and provide land for other uses. (It is sometimes enough to mark all the underused land on a slum map for whole new networks of movement, recreation and green landscape to suggest themselves.) Somebody compares surveys of local employment and unemployment – if there are wives wanting work close to home, does the area lack any social or childminding services that might employ them, or private or public employers who might be attracted? If the district needs meeting places or recreations which are not strictly public responsibilities, might they nevertheless be attracted by some public renting or land-dealing? Besides material gains, such surveys can have permanent effects in livelier community organisation, and they can improve the education of all concerned, including the politicians who presently hear imaginative demands for money, land, shopfront services, street closures, and old rope and timber and locomotives for new styles of playground.

These participant methods work for districts and neighbourhoods. On larger scale there are other ways of surveying and redressing inequalities of wealth and opportunity between regions. They have usually concentrated on jobs and welfare services; they should be developed to include direct aids to city centring and services, and to education and housing.

13

TECHNOLOGY AND SOCIETY
(1978)

In the late 1970s, well before the arrival of the personal computer and the internet, Stretton began to think about the social implications of a 'post-industrial' society in which machines would increasingly replace humans in the workforce. Who would control the machines, and what would happen to the people they displaced? Would technology widen existing class disparities? In correspondence with shadow minister Barry Jones, Stretton urged a future Labor government to adopt policies to ensure that work and the new wealth they generated were fairly shared. He was under no illusions about the political challenge: 'When you put together the difficulties of selling novel, long-term prudent or partly unselfish ideas to rip off employers and their politicians; to stand-pat unions and their leadership; and to the brainwashed majority of our complacent, self-serving social scientists – it's easiest to wring your hands and cultivate your garden,' he confided to Jones. Jones would later address these issues in his Sleepers, Wake! Technology and the future of work *(1982). In retrospect, Stretton's analysis seems remarkably prescient, even if the policies he proposed were stillborn.*

WE FACE A WORLD IN WHICH THE MATERIAL goods and material services we really want can be produced by decreasing numbers of us, perhaps imaginably by only three-quarters of our conventional workforce, eventually perhaps by only half of our conventional workforce. That is what defines our problem. Traditionally, our system has distributed income as a reward for work, with only minor additives in the way of pensions or other aids for those minorities whom the productive system did not employ from time to time. So we will need fundamental changes in our methods of distributing income, if the world is going to be that technological world that [we anticipate].

There is one nightmare solution to this problem which I don't want, and which I think ought to be recognised as a nightmare solution. It is the one favoured by most multinationals, and by most United States authorities, and by majorities of those who are in charge of our economic schools and our national treasury, and for the time being our national government. It is that we should go on as before, distributing most income as a reward for work and, of course, heavily over-rewarding many of those who happen to work in capital-intensive industries where productivity is high per head. And we should go on treating the remainder, whom the productive system doesn't want, as social casualties, to be kept from actual physical hardship by sparse doles of one sort of another. It is a two-class system of the employed and the unemployable, the wanted and the unwanted, the productive and unproductive – with the productive taxed to support the unproductive. That system has often worked unfairly or inefficiently in the past. It is worth reminding ourselves how much worse it may become if it is allowed to intensify over the years as the problem of underemployment intensifies. It has perhaps been a tolerable arrangement up to now because such a high proportion of the potential workforce was employed. That high proportion of households have been able to get their income in the traditional work-and-earn way. Most people could feel satisfied and dignified in the way they earned their living and could earn decent livings. The other aspect of the system was also workable, in that the old and unemployed who had to be doled were comparatively few, and the old were comparatively cheap to keep, so that the charge on the earners to provide income for the non-earners was not intolerable. Tolerable levels of tax sufficed to finance tolerable levels of pension. But if we suffer the structural changes which are now forecast, and the proportions shift so that those in employment are more and more productive per head on average (not through any virtue of their own, but because more technology and more accumulated capital is behind each worker) but there are fewer and fewer of them to support more and more 'unwanted' humans, then it is awfully likely that our inequalities will be forced to increase, whether we like it or not.

We bring people up to believe that their earnings are their own, and well-deserved, and taxes should be no higher than may be necessary to provide basic public services. People who have that feeling about 'their own' incomes will not want to see rising wages and productivity matched by steeply rising tax rates, especially if they see their taxes going increasingly as doles to non-working unemployed. As the unemployed demand for income rises as the unemployed numbers increase, the bitterness between the employed and the unemployed is presumably going to intensify. And in that sort of conflict there is not much doubt who is usually going to win. The employed are likely to do better than the unemployed. The difference between their incomes is likely to increase. The difference between their life chances, their sense of identity and self-respect and independence may become even more drastic and destructive.

With shorthand, you might call that whole solution the American solution – though there are many other people in many other countries just as eager for it. I think it ought to be recognised as a dreadful social future. I think we do face it, in some degree at least, if we don't take radical steps to avert it. We certainly face it if we leave the structural problem to solve itself, or if we let it solve itself in what our economists like to call a market way.

So what are the healthier alternatives? There is plenty of thought on the subject, and many of both practical and impractical options are canvassed. All the options have to assume that we do adopt some new and different methods of distributing work, or income, or both. There are many imaginable ways of altering either of these distributions.

Some examples. There is plenty of talk of work sharing. However little work needs to be done in our society – I mean the conventional, paid-for, commercial type of work – why don't we share it out? Why should half or three-quarters of the population have all of it and the rest have none? Since it is so socially important, why don't we share it in a fairly determined and systematic way, even if sharing the work out is not always the most efficient way to get it done? There are, of course, many ways of sharing it – by the day, by the week, by the lifetime. Some unions are already talking of a four-day week or a three-day week. Alternatively, at the other extreme, work can be shared by shortening the working life – people can start work older and retire younger than they do now. That would leave time for more education or recreation or both, and it would generally not have the ill effects on working efficiency which sometimes follow from short working days or weeks, or from part-time or shared jobs.

My own tastes (because of the sort of institution I work in) incline to different modes of work sharing, some of which are under heavy attack at present. Instead of abolishing study leave from the universities, why don't you extend it to the whole working population? Most workers already have modest long-service leave entitlements – why not extend them drastically? If we really have work for only three out of four of our workers, why not have everyone work three years out of every four?

I need not labour the point. If you take the rate of structural unemployment as a percentage of the workforce, and simply translate it into a percentage of the hours worked over a lifetime, then in one way or another the problem should be soluble. If we only need three-quarters as much paid work as we used to need to supply our population with its material needs, let every one of us do three-quarters as many hours of work in a working lifetime. It should also be possible in many trades to let those three-quarters be distributed in interesting, humane, inventive sorts of ways. It need not mean that people have to work as hard as ever for thirty years instead of forty, and then retire comparatively young – unless that happens to be what they *want* to do. Some could perhaps work long, energetic, hard days, but less per week; some could take long-service breaks; some could take retraining breaks so that people could have two or three diverse careers in a lifetime instead of one monotonous one. There are all sorts of ways you could implement that simple theory of sharing the work around, such as it is. And if you succeeded entirely in doing that, which of course would be difficult in practice, you would perhaps have gone a long way to solving the other half of our basic problem, which is how to distribute income sensibly and fruitfully in this new, structurally inconvenient world. Most income could continue to go with work if work could be fairly shared to everyone.

I suppose most of the practical solutions are of that general kind, which can be summed up as work-sharing arrangements. But there are other possibilities, especially for people prepared to raise their sights a bit and look internationally. In an ideal world, the advanced countries might not reduce work at all. Having sufficiently satisfied their own material needs in thirty hours of the week, they might work another ten to produce surpluses to meet the material needs of much poorer countries. And there are other large notions of that kind. But they are not practical probabilities, or not at the local community level. I would rather stick to ideas which might one day be both local and practical in affluent countries like ours. And because I haven't got a lot of time, I thought three general kinds of examples would do. The following three are chosen deliberately as belonging to three different levels of organisation.

The first, which I think is an interesting idea, is also at first sight a fairly scary idea to most people. It seems scary at first sight because of some very unhappy past experience. But properly understood, it need not necessarily be frightening. It is the idea of reintroducing some sort of national service for all young people – but in a form designed to give young people very wide options about the type of service they would like to do. Let everybody stay out of the actual workforce – or anyway out of the normal, orthodox workforce – until (say) the age of twenty-one. Let those who want to serve in the armed forces do their stint in the armed forces, like the national service we commonly have. Let those who want to be students be students. Beyond those two obvious ones, we want to apply some imagination to developing many other interesting, constructive and diverse things for people to do through those years, including tasks for those who want to leave home, and tasks for those who don't. It might be that we could have radically different and better standards of management of our national parks. It might be that we could discover all sorts of tasks of physical and social conservation, tasks which just aren't done now, and won't be done as long as they have to be done with fully paid labour by conventional methods. Such service might or might not be compulsory, but if compulsory at all, it need only be in the negative sense that you would have a very wide choice of ways to occupy these years, except that you would be excluded from the commercial workforce until you turned twenty-one. Those who simply couldn't stand it might find the means to travel abroad. That was common practice through the last period of national service – New Zealand and Canada did very well out of it. I don't think the general idea should be lightly written off. Think of it as a way of rationing work by deferring everybody's 'start work' age.

If that sort of low-paid youth service were acceptable, the same sort of work might perhaps be adapted and extended to other classes of people. One bad feature of our existing system is that we have such a drastic distinction between work and the dole. Indeed, to get a dole at all in most circumstances, including old age, you have to prove that you are doing absolutely nothing – sitting about at home, not working, not learning, not surfing. It has been compared to imprisonment. With proper safeguards, which I think could be devised, it might be good to blur that distinction between full employment and unemployment. It might be possible to say there is a basic dole that you can have if you don't want to work at all, but it is not much (and very few would want it – very few of the unemployed don't want to work).

There is, secondly, an intermediate kind of reward you can have if you are prepared to do some of these do-gooding tasks – cleaning the neighbourhood, helping in the national parks, doing part-time citizen army service, doing useful childminding or home help for people who can't afford full rates for it – all sorts of things one can think of, that simply cannot get done on the basis of a full adult wage. Many such things are done voluntarily now, and could well be done on larger scale for intermediate wages by people who are currently out of conventional work.

What I am basically saying is that we could diversify the dole and attach work to it much more than we do at present. This is, once again, a scary idea if it can be misused to break the monopoly of fully paid labour on fully paid jobs, or to allow regular employers to depress regular wages. But if it were introduced with due thought and care and negotiation, I don't see why we shouldn't do something to break or ameliorate the destructive alternative between work and dole that we have at present.

So there are devices like that which would need to be adopted on a national scale. They are devices to take part of everybody's potential working life, one way or another, and put it to different sort of work, often at lower income and at a time when people either don't need so much income or can't entitle themselves to a normal income by normal methods. It need not mean less wages per lifetime – it could often mean a better distribution of income through the phases of life. But such schemes would usually need to be designed and applied on a national scale.

The second kind of idea that I would like to mention is the kind that would apply at the opposite end – i.e. the domestic end – of the social scale. These are ideas about the different things a private household might do, with or without a private bit of suburban real estate. It has lately been fashionable to depict these possibilities in a backward-looking way. Various writers have looked back to the more complex and extensive functions which are thought by some to have been performed by the nuclear family or the extended family in the distant primitive past. Many of these backward-looking dreams are dreams, rather than good history – the further back in history you go, on the whole, the less functions many families did, the less people lived in families at all, the less intact families there were. But we need not argue about the history. The point is that if we can't employ as many hours of work in the commercial workforce as we used to do, perhaps we can find more and more useful and constructive activities for people to do at home. This already occurs of course on a massive scale. We are a much more do-it-yourself society than we used to be. Many more private homes have workshops than used to have them. They have a much more elaborate array of tools and equipment than they used to have. To quote one well-known statistic, the British housewife (who is significantly poorer than the Australian housewife) had the network energy at her disposal in 1971 that the British factory worker on average had in 1910. In industrial productivity, the housewife was only a generation and a half behind the factory worker! She how has powerful capital equipment to increase her productivity at home. An even more recent and proliferant growth is the gentlemen's capital equipment at home. He used to push a mower for his health. Now everything from his mower through his golf buggy to his toothbrush is being mechanised. Despite the absurdities of golf buggies and electric back-scratchers, there is also a steady increase of home constructions and crafts, and real productivity.

In these and many other ways, the domestic homestead can be elaborated to occupy lots of working time, and to produce many and various goods. Some part of the work of the household is compulsory work, chores that have to be done to maintain the house and feed people. But a steadily increasing proportion of what is done at home is done because people do freely choose and positively value some mixture of the product and the process of producing it. People must like working at home to be doing more and more of it the way they are doing. And it is worth pausing for a moment to dispel some common illusions about the process. It is depicted by many writers as an increasing privatisation of life, a retreat from community. But there have at last been some factual studies, which show that the reverse tends to be true. If you survey the urban and suburban Western world in countries like ours, you find that the more private resources the household has – resources of space like private land and housing and resources of books and arts and gear and equipment – the greater, on average, will be the household's out-reach: the more communal things the people do, the more often they go out, the more hours they spend with other people, and the more non-commercial, voluntary communal activities are done outside the home. The truth is that resources at home for domestic production and employment are not the enemy of communal life. On the contrary, the households with most books make most use of libraries. The households which do more private gardening make most use of national parks. And so on. Many, many kinds of activity thrive best on complementary arrangements like that. The point is worth emphasising because there has been some tendency to think that the elaboration of private productive activities in the household is an enemy of communal life and development. All the relevant research that has been done shows that it ain't. The two are more often aids and stimulants to one another.

*

Those two extremes – national schemes and household possibilities – leave the third, the thing I am really supposed to be talking about, and will now talk about in conclusion. I mean the kind of local, neighbourly and communal activity, which will normally concern community development organisations. That elaboration of domestic life which I just spoke of needs to be complemented by a local communal life. It has rich potential. To show just how rich, perhaps the best introduction is to remember how very poor life is, even in affluent societies like ours, where the level of communal life and service is low. There are raw new outer suburbs around our big cities which have been exposed by more than one piece of sociological research. Their households are typically pushed for income, often including incomplete households without a full commercial income, living wholly or partially on pension or welfare allowances. They typically live in physically adequate housing but with very inadequate access to ordinary urban, suburban and local services, and with bad transport to work and other necessities. There may be many households without motor cars, dependent on inadequate public transport. If you survey the way many of the people spend their time in those poor suburbs, the earners (if any) spend a fair bit of time earning and travelling, often with high transport times and transport costs. Those who are not doing that, when they are also not doing necessary housework, are too often doing as near as humans can get to nothing. They spend long hours at home not doing anything in particular, long hours watching telly, surprisingly long hours lying in bed asleep, or trying to sleep; and when they do walk out from their households into neighbourhoods that don't deserve the name, there is nothing there except a distant corner shop and a distant and infrequent bus. There are no places of communal resort, there is certainly no local pub; the combination of our licensing authorities and our liquor monopolies have made sure that pubs may only be built on an enormous scale two or three miles apart, so you can't get to one without a motor car – you can't drink without driving. That sort of extreme case justifies the stereotypes of the outer suburban desert. It is indeed a human and social desert of a deplorable kind in itself, and there is reason to think it is deplorable in the kind of humans, ill-equipped and unsociable, whom it may all too often bring up to provide the next generation.

So what we want instead is the opposite of that situation. We want a rich and varied communal life, exchanging life and interest with a similarly rich domestic life. There are many good examples, both in literature and in life. In this and many other countries, it is not too hard to find old established urban neighbourhoods with resourceful households, with proliferant gardens, many with workshops, with lots of hobbies and crafts and trades being done by people at appropriate ages and stages of their lifecycles, and with strong local communal resources of many kinds. It is where there are the most well-equipped, resourceful, old-established households that you typically find the best local libraries, the most active local clubs, the likeliest situation for walk-in local pubs. You often also find the most alert and responsive local government. Civic and communal, commercial or voluntary, the sum total of local activity has a tremendous potential for absorbing energy and working time, and for producing goods, services and recreations. And it makes sense to develop this potential use of time and energy, to the extent that the commercial economic system employs less of the people's time and energy.

Of course there are many common sense limits to these lines of development. It is not practical in the modern world to think of households supporting themselves entirely in a local fashion. You have to assume that every household needs some external money income, whether it is a commercially earned income or a government dole or some mixture of the two. But the difference between the employed and the unemployed, the difference between working and being comfortable and paying off the home and the Holden on the one hand, and living as a chronic, suffering, unemployed head of an unemployed household – that dramatic contrast which we suffer from now – could be considerably gentled, and the distinction between those two conditions blurred to everybody's advantage, if we really did think more systematically of a three-part productive system, commercial and communal and domestic.

One of the troubles about our conventional ways of thinking, and about the way in which this structural unemployment problem is typically presented to us by our experts, is that we have thought of work only as commercial paid work, and it is only the product of the commercial paid work that we have thought of as economic goods. People are conscious that there are faults in this view. Above all, every housewife and every women's representative is conscious of the amount of the world's work that gets done without wages, in housework and child rearing particularly. But we have never built that general idea into a more systematic way of looking at how *all* works gets done in our societies. Economics ought to be about all the work, all the useful output, all the income and all the uses of time. People who have done shadow calculations to try to put a wage value or a produce value on housework and what housework produces very easily come to the conclusion that it uses at least a third of our fixed capital, and produces a third or more of the useful goods and services in the society as a whole. And of course it produces a great many things beyond those material products. It produces all sorts of things we forget to put money values on – sociability, temperament, skill, capacities to work, capacities to organise and be organised. All the things that make us a skilful and productive population, which are built into *us* rather than into our fixed capital, have to be produced, mostly by our households and to a lesser extent by our schools.

Once you understand the tremendous potentiality and value and importance of that domestic and local communal productive system, a reduced need for commercial labour does not look so bad. It means that there should be more time and resources to put into the things we do more voluntarily, more among people we love and know, more among people we steadily cooperate with, more in our families and communities. I don't think such a shift from office and factory to home and neighbourhood is to be regretted. If at present we are running something like two-thirds of our activity and production from the commercial economy and one-third or a bit more, perhaps 40 per cent, from the domestic economy, it would not have to be a bad society that managed to change those proportions to fifty-fifty. It could mean that we produced our factory and service needs with less labour, and left ourselves more time and resources to do the things we really like doing, to timetables of our own making in company of our own choosing. All the complaints about alienation tend to connect with the conditions of work in the big, highly organised bureaucratic or industrial areas of life. It seems to me logical to think that the more we can transfer our time to the areas where we are volunteers in every sense – in the use of our time, in our associates, in what we decide to produce – the happier it should be possible to be. Nevertheless, we will regret it if we do not accompany the change with real changes in the distribution of commercial or money income – speeches like this one are hollow if they are merely hot air to comfort the unemployed, or to tell them to get off their arses and do something more useful with their time. It does not make sense unless there is at the same time very serious and fundamental attention to the distribution of money income, or (in real terms) of that part of everyone's material income which does have to come from the commercial economic system.

I think a world in which people made less distinction between these two kinds of work could well be a good world – one in which most people preferred the free kind of work that they did themselves and around the local community, and therefore did only the necessary minimum in the commercial economy, enough to bring in one commercial income to each household. If we built a world like that, it might become easier to solve some other problems too. For example, if we had a guaranteed minimum income which was fairly high, then the effective costs of many community activities might fall – many public enterprises have low practical costs when the gap between wages and the dole is narrow. I don't want to underrate the problem which confronts the economists, or the hard problems of finding a way to distribute income well in a world inflicted with structural unemployment. But I do mean to suggest that if we can crack that problem as a political problem – especially as a problem of income distribution – then the economic and social problems of structural underemployment could in many ways be turned into sources of real social gain. We really might achieve that identification of unemployment and constructive leisure, which is a bit ticklish to talk about in present circumstances.

14

THE CASE AGAINST VERY FREE TRADE AND VERY SMALL GOVERNMENT (1980)

This broadcast talk was given on 4 May 1980, with Stretton the ABC's Sunday-evening 'Guest of Honour'. Here he sounds a warning against the rise of neoliberalism. Through the late 1970s, the advanced economies struggled with rising inflation and declining productivity. In Canberra, the Fraser Liberal government was riven by conflicts between supporters of big and little government ('Wets' and 'Dries'). As an adviser to shadow treasurer Ralph Willis and shadow science minister Barry Jones, Stretton advocated interventionist policies to curb inflation, promote employment and share the returns of technological change more equally. Three years later, when Labor returned to power under Bob Hawke, treasurer Paul Keating reversed almost a century of Labor orthodoxy by embracing many of the free-market doctrines attacked by Stretton.

SOME VOICES LATELY HAVE BEEN CALLING FOR A return to an older, freer kind of capitalism. Free trade is an old ideal and its modern advocates nowadays seem to have two kinds of reform in mind. Baldly, they want to liberate private business and reduce public business.

If we reduced the regulation and protection of Australian capital and labour, they argue, we could then import more low-priced goods. That would make some Australian firms cut costs and compete harder; others would go out of business, but their capital and labour would find other work, such as mining. Many of these theorists also want less production of goods and services by public corporations, and less welfare and pensions. They think cutting the public sector would allow more growth of private enterprise.

Put those two programs together and you can see that the new free-traders want a rather daring gamble. They want to put some private enterprise out of business, and also some public production and services. Nationally, that would mean less output altogether, and more unemployment. But these theorists think the unemployed capital and labour would somehow find new and better things to do, so we'd be richer in the long run.

But I needn't elaborate that classical case for free trade, because its own advocates are doing that. In fact, I think they're overdoing it, so I'm here to remind you of the classical case *against* free trade – the reasons why our economic activities need some government, and sometimes need defending, just like our other activities do.

That case can be put in two ways. First, historical: we can ask which economic systems have generally done best. If, contrary to Adam Smith, they turn out to be the ones with protective tariffs, and big public sectors, and good welfare systems, then we can ask: why? What do the public and private sectors actually do for each other's productivity?

To start with, some history. Mr Free Trade himself, Professor Milton Friedman, was saying on the BBC the other day that the British industrial revolution of the eighteenth century – the original steam-engine revolution – was a triumph of free trade. He was talking his usual nonsense. Through that revolution Britain had high tariff protection, massive public investment and spending through a quarter of a century of the Napoleonic wars, and the most advanced welfare in the world, with something like a guaranteed minimum income indexed to the cost of living. There was also a government pulley-block factory that invented the twentieth-century assembly line a hundred years before Henry Ford did.

It was *after* all that – *after* the triumph of the new textile and machine-tool industries, *after* the invention of steamships and railways, *after* Britain had forged ahead to become the workshop of the world – that free trade set in. Fifty years after the steam revolution, the humane welfare system was abolished, so was the protective tariff, public investment dwindled, and Britain was indeed a genuine free-trading country for eighty years or so. What happened? Country after country overtook and passed her in economic performance, and the countries that passed her – America, Germany, Australia, Canada, New Zealand – all had tariffs and a good many other public aids to their private industries. So free trade and small government saw the decisive loss of Britain's economic leadership.

I think the small government did most of the damage. The successful countries were learning what government could really do to help the new industrial capitalist growth. For example, railways and waterways and other basic services to industry could often be done better by long-term planning and public investment than by the shaky little private companies that were providing them in England. Even in America, where there was not much state-owned industry, there were a lot of state aids to private industries. Above all, the new technology needed science, and it needed skills. British government didn't do much about either. The German and American governments led the world in providing both, from scores of new state colleges and institutes of technology.

A rather different and unusual success of those years was the Australian one. In this country we've had just one generation, from about 1860 to 1890, when we were among the world's leaders in standards of living, and that was the generation when our public sector was comparatively the biggest and most productive, sometimes importing more capital, and investing more, than the whole private capitalist sector. Two-thirds of all investment was non-profit. So that generation defied all the market theorist principles and forged ahead of the world as never before or since.

Since we came to rely on more conservative methods of private industrial development, through the post-war decades under the Menzies government, most of northern Europe has caught up and some of it has passed us in economic performance. Those European competitors didn't have our natural resource advantages, and they certainly weren't free-traders, so how did they do it? Basically, they pioneered a further range of public aids to economic development: national economic planning; excellent public research and technical and management training; some very efficient public industries, like the German rail and commuter services, or French Renault cars. (When the French reached the Australian income level, about half their heavy industry was publicly owned.) And all those European countries spend more on welfare than we do.

Those aren't the only ways that life contradicts theory. Free-traders theorise that a country will do best if it specialises in its best industries, and trades heavily with other specialists. In fact, countries like Britain and Japan, which are compelled to do that, don't approach the material standards of the more self-reliant European and American and Australian economies, which don't specialise too much, and do manage to produce for a wide range of their own needs. The trouble is that the heavy international traders find that there's not much of Adam Smith's benevolent hidden hand helping them out there in the international markets. Instead there's monopoly, dumping, national manoeuvring and international tax dodging and OPEC oil pricing, in a jungle under no responsible government at all. It's not efficient to expose your national economy to that anarchy any more than you have to. Even when the trading works as it's supposed to in a classical market way, it doesn't only discipline your inefficient industries, as free-traders claim. It's just as likely to ruin efficient ones.

Example: for BHP to invest half a billion dollars to make steel in Whyalla, the state had to invest rather more in town development and houses and schools and hospitals and so on. If we now decide to close down Whyalla because we can buy steel a few dollars cheaper from Korea, we don't just waste the BHP investment, and the public and private investment in the steelworkers' skills. We also waste a billion and a half dollars' worth of perfectly efficient civic and housing investment. That sort of free trade is not efficient; it's inefficient. It doesn't cut overall national costs, or increase overall output; it does the opposite. And the trouble isn't an 'imperfection' in the market. It's a gaping hole in the market theory.

Altogether, I think these theorists are making three basic mistakes.

One: they write off *all* protection as selfish, sectional, short-sighted, uneconomic, purely political and so on. That's fair comment on plenty of misuses of protection, including a good deal of our Australian protection, which has not been efficiently adjusted and economised. But rightly used, and kept under tough review, as it ought to be, protection can be an efficient aid to long-term planning, and it can positively economise a lot of long-term public and private investment.

Mistake number two is to believe that the public sector is always inefficient. In fact, there are many efficient public utilities, there are many public firms competing efficiently in the market, and the public sector is infinitely better than the private at producing the science and educated skill for modern industry. Of course there is inefficiency if you look for it, as there is in private industry. But public economic services have improved spectacularly through this century, and there's no reason why we shouldn't go on improving them.

Mistake number three is to think of the public and private sectors as rivals or alternatives, as if less production by one would allow more production by the other. In fact, the sectors interlock in so many ways that they normally go up or down together. If government spends too freely, that overheats the private sector as well. If government cuts public production, private production falls too.

It's that interlocking that really explains the historical success of the well-mixed economies with strong public sectors. The textbooks used to tell us that the public sector produced social goods like roads and bridges, while the private sector produced private market goods like houses and cars. In fact, private contractors build a lot of public roads and bridges, and public firms produce plenty of market goods like houses and cars – but all those products actually come from complicated mixtures of public and private work. The best method varies from case to case – but it's hardly ever the unaided private enterprise that the British tried in the nineteenth century, or the pure public enterprise that communist countries use, fairly inefficiently, now. In countries like ours, most public works use some private supplies, and most private enterprise uses some public supplies.

Especially supplies of skill. There is no private profit way to educate the twentieth-century workforce, or to do the science on which the whole miracle of modern productivity is built. So firms that can get good science and technical education from their public sectors generally do better than competitors who get less of those aids. If you cut back education and science, as Australia is currently doing, that doesn't help Australian business to grow. It can only make Australian business less efficient at home and less competitive internationally.

There's a final problem, which comes partly from the *success* of the modern mixed economies. We now have the capacity to produce necessities and many comforts of life for all our people, so it's a real question what we want to produce over and above that. But the silicon chip and other problems make it doubtful whether our traditional methods can any longer even deliver full employment or economic growth. We may even be using extra productivity to produce extra unemployment.

If my taxes have to go up, I don't really want them spent on doles for more unemployed. I'd much rather see creative public action to maintain full employment by producing more social goods – anything from better local neighbourhoods through education and social services to better national theatre or national parks. Of course, you can't guarantee those good things just by enlarging the public sector any old how. There are real dangers of waste, and heavy bureaucracy, and misuses of protection, and difficulties with inflation. But it's worth facing those difficulties and working at them, because the alternatives are so unpromising.

I've said that I think the free-traders' program would be technically self-defeating as well as socially bad. But even if they did maintain some economic growth, they want to bias it towards more inequality, and towards private rather than social goods. Remember, that doesn't just mean more private possessions for the richer classes. It means less public education and more commercial education for all of us – our tastes and standards would be shaped even less by the schools and universities and the ABC, and more by the commercial media and the advertising industry. That sort of shift from public to private enterprise doesn't increase individual diversity and freedom; it tends to narrow them.

I think plenty of Australians would rather use a fair share of any economic growth in other ways: to restore full employment, to distribute income and services better, to improve the working and cultural options open to young people. But for those purposes – and to achieve the economic growth in the first place – we are going to need an adaptable, inventive, productive public sector, as seen before. Private enterprise especially is going to need it. So this is a good time to be reforming our public economic services, but a bad time to think of selling them off or closing them down.

15

THE CULT OF SELFISHNESS (1987)

This essay, written for Stretton's 1987 Political Essays, *is the angriest and most revealing in the book. The rise of Reagan, Thatcher and their Australian followers, Stretton believed, symbolised something more sinister: a 'cult of selfishness' that weakened the ethic of mutual care on which democratic societies relied. Since his school days, when he helped found a boys' club in an industrial suburb on the other side of town, Stretton had espoused a vision of society that was, in equal parts, liberal, egalitarian and fraternal. Now, he feared, a new and virulent strain of liberalism, supported by the New Left as well as the New Right, challenged the democratic settlement. How had this happened, what damage was it doing, and what could be done about it? The 'cult of selfishness', Stretton suggested, is based on an impoverished understanding of human nature. Did it therefore contain the seeds of its eventual destruction?*

SELFISHNESS IS PART OF HUMAN NATURE. SO IS unselfishness: love, motherhood, comradeship, charity, blood donation, leper surgery and other generosities.

Most cultures have deprecated the selfishness, however much they always had of it, and have tried to cultivate the generosities. Parents, teachers, clergy and other moral authorities have urged our better natures to overcome our worse natures, or at least they have tried to hold the line between the two by always coupling rights with duties, or persuading us that generosity pays. So although selfishness has always persisted, it has not usually been as a cult. The *cults* – the qualities it was thought necessary or worthwhile to *cultivate* – have been love, duty, obligation, sacrifice.

But now, unusually, a lot of voices are condemning altruism and praising selfishness and encouraging people to be greedier and less compassionate; also – which is not always the same thing – to be more self-interested, self-concerned, self-obsessed. There is a cult of self, or selfishness, or both. It has increased, is increasing and ought to be diminished. So what can be done to discourage it?

It is not a simple cult and it does not seem to stem from any single cause. It is more diffuse: a political and cultural sea change. Some old and some new conditions have combined to make more people than usual more receptive than usual to a variety of selfish persuasions.

The cult has been related to the general lurch to the Right in the affluent Western world. But the relation is not simple. Not all the Right is selfish. Not all of the new selfishness comes from the Right. Thatcher's and Reagan's supply-side economics may be designed by and for the greedy rich. But the mass Right, the populist Right, is not especially selfish. It is moral, religious, authoritarian. The Moral Majority wants law and order; work, duty, abstinence, fidelity; family solidarity. It even has some affinities – which neither side is likely to recognise in the other – with the puritan austerity of the very old Left.

At the same time, some of the new selfishness comes from sources which claim to be radical or New Left. The personal liberation movements may have begun as justice and equality for women and more expressive and generous styles of love for everyone. But plenty of liberators have adapted those ideas to liberate chiefly their own ids. The rhetoric of spontaneity and voluntary truly-felt love can be translated to mean 'Follow your inclinations wherever they lead' – it wouldn't be emotionally honest to bother yourself with the troubles of discarded kin or lovers. What began as a doctrine of unselfish, unpossessive love ends by solemnly justifying the routine desertion of fading wives and tiresome children.

So the rhetoric of liberation can be debased by Left as well as Right. But I think it has its nastiest effects when it serves to bring the New and Old Right together: when the new psychology of self-indulgence joins with the old capitalist greed. The main purpose of this paper is to explore the contribution to that vicious combination which has been made, however innocently, by decent folk like us. For that purpose it is convenient to begin by looking separately at its two strands: first at the Old Right, then at the New.

For the revival of the Old Right, signified by the successes of Fraser and Thatcher and Reagan and the rightward flight of so many professors of economics, half a dozen explanations are commonly offered. They look like rival explanations but they may well all be half-true, because different people lurch to the Right for different reasons. Each explanation may be true of some of the lurchers. Here are six well-known explanations just to remind you of them. The first three allege a historical change or breakdown of capitalism. The next three suggest why capitalist malfunctions these days push so many people to the Right rather than the Left.

Explanation 1. The multinationals are reorganising the world to free themselves from any serious national or democratic control. By shifting production to countries with cheap labour and corrupt government, they make more profits, pay less taxes and evade social responsibilities. In the affluent countries they weaken democratic resistance partly by threatening capital flight and unemployment, and partly by paying lots of experts and profit-seeking think-tanks to preach small government, free trade, low wages and less welfare. The local rich love that, and join in, looking for plunder from union-bashing and tax revolts. Thus international capital leads the local bourgeoisie in a revolt against democratic economics and welfare.

That's partly a class and partly a conspiracy theory. A different version runs like this:

Explanation 2. We're merely returning to normal after a long boom. The Western economies were busy for twenty or thirty years replacing war losses and then equipping all their households, most of them for the first time, with well-plumbed houses, cars, consumer durables and modern urban services. By the 1970s they were all equipped. Demand accordingly fell from an 'equip' volume to a 'maintain' volume, leaving many unemployed. If we want full employment again, we'll have to start again, with new technology serving new directions of demand. But so far the new technology employs fewer and fewer people, and there is uncertainty about any new directions of demand. Do-gooders have not had much success in pushing more environmental care or community service or international aid as new uses for our underemployed capacities. Capitalist advertisers do a bit better, pushing electric toothbrushes and home electronics and fast food and faster fashion changes and quicker obsolescence all round. But they're still not very successful, and perhaps don't want to be. Being rich in a booming economy may have been all right, but being rich among plenty of depressed unemployed can be even better: bossier, more voluptuous, with more obsequious service. Those possibilities attract some rich, while depression frightens some of the poor into defensive moods and conservative voting. In this view, a long economic cycle accounts for the reactionary shift: we've lurched to the Right on Kondratiev's bike.

Explanation 3 comes *from* the Right. It says protectionist, fully employed welfare capitalism was always a technical mistake, and by the 1970s its failure was obvious in slower growth and faster and faster inflation. Sensible majorities, rather than multinational conspirators, saw the need to reverse course and return to free enterprise, small government, individual self-reliance and family, rather than state responsibility for welfare.

This explanation has at least two grains of truth. Whether they are true or false, those *beliefs* do indeed lead many people to move to the Right. And the conservative Keynesian policies did indeed run into inflation, as radical Keynesians predicted they would if they didn't include price and income policies.

But why did inflation push so many people to the Right rather than the Left?

Explanation 4. Welfare capitalism didn't fail, it succeeded. But technical change and economic growth steadily reduced the proportion of dissatisfied blue collars who vote Left and increased the proportion of satisfied white collars who vote Right. In this view, there hasn't really been any lurch to the Right in people's beliefs. The conservative voters are the same sort of people as before, voting conservative for the same old reasons – there are just more of them. They've become a majority so they have more influence over government. The blue collars have become a minority with less influence than before, so they can expect worse class treatment than before. That may affect distributive justice, but not the general quantity of selfishness – all concerned are still voting according to their class interests.

Explanation 5. Besides reducing the numbers of blue collars, capitalism has also conservatised some of them. Some have come to support the system because it kept its promise of wealth and growth. Some Alf Garnetts trust the upper classes to run the country better than Labor bunglers would. Some employed workers see themselves as winners and the unemployed as losers, and vote to kick the ladder down. That sounds selfish, but it can also be dignified as puritan.

Some working-class husbands and wives have strong moral opinions about work and marriage: they see themselves as hardworking, productive people who pay their way and should not be taxed to pay unearned incomes to idle dole-bludgers and sluttish single parents.

Explanation 6. A different version of the capitalist success story is kinder both to capitalism and to the new conservative voters. It says the citizens set out long ago to build something unselfishly good, built it, and now rest content. Starting before World War I and accelerating after World War II, they set out to build the system of universal welfare that people like the Webbs and Beveridge and Nugget Coombs proposed to them. Through the decades it took to build that system step by step as economic growth allowed, from the first old-age pension in 1908 to TEAS [Tertiary Education Assistance Scheme] and the single parents' support in the 1970s, majorities kept on faithfully voting for it. But now the job is done. The social safety net is complete. At last the owners and earners – the productive majority – can sit back and say: 'We're there. For three generations we've voted a rising share of our rising output to the poor. Now they've got enough. From now on, growth can be for us.'

Those six are economic explanations, insofar as they say people move to the Right in response to economic facts. Of course their motives are not all selfish – plenty of people believe that the policies of the Right are objectively best for everyone. But whatever their purposes, the usual effects of those policies are to increase unemployment and inequality, and to encourage fear and greed as preferred economic motives.

Those harsh responses to economic problems can be encouraged or discouraged by the prevailing culture. In recent times I think they have been encouraged by some changes which you may call economic or cultural, according to taste. New industries make money (that's economic) by teaching people to be more interested in themselves (that's culture). Perhaps this trend began when psychoanalysis enlarged its market, going beyond sick and seriously troubled people to offer anyone rich enough and bored enough a weekly hour or two of fascinating self-study and self-reconstruction. Since then, many entrepreneurs have developed and diversified the market, especially downwards. Innumerable therapies and enriching experiences are now available commercially. There are cheap ways, medium-priced ways and expensive ways of learning how to relax – or to tense up and heighten your concentration; how to meditate – or how to reach out and relate to people; how to touch and feel, how to become more popular or persuasive or assertive or masterful. The industry has come a long way since Dale Carnegie and the first half-day courses in How to Discover Your True Self and Sell Encyclopedias. Profoundly unconvincing experts now offer to teach you how to plumb your depths, make yourself over, smarten yourself up, develop your hidden potential, optimise your personal assets, focus your psychic force, and altogether Achieve New Confidence. Furthermore, most of them don't challenge you with difficult trials or ordeals. They promise to make it easy, take you by the hand, do it for you, do it to you. If it calls for strength of character, they may install that too, for a supplementary fee. There have long been experts who would feed you expanding bran biscuits, or staple your stomach, to let you lose weight without actual self-denial. Now there are psychic equivalents of that magic fix: you too can Achieve without actually trying.

Of course this abuse is untrue and unfair of many of the new services. By no means all of the therapies have selfish purposes. Many of them have alternative purposes, or ambivalent purposes. On the one hand, they offer to improve your Self; but on the other hand, their purpose may be to make your Self less selfish. Some people feel incapable of loving and giving and take courses to make them capable of loving and giving. Some people take courses to give meaning to their lives, which isn't necessarily selfish. Some people get on badly with their spouses, children, workmates or others, and buy therapies to make themselves more acceptable, which may sometimes help the suffering spouses and others. But however unselfish some of their aims and effects may be, there is still a sense in which most of these activities are self-regarding or self-centred. If I buy a course in altruism, it may not teach me how to study *you* and serve your interests; instead it may make me introspect to study what it is in *me* that fails to care but might be made to care for you. Earlier generations did less of that. If our parents felt meaningless, they joined a tennis club or looked for charitable work to do. If you were unhappy, they didn't encourage you to introspect. On the contrary, they tried to make you *less* self-conscious, to 'get you out of yourself', to switch your attention to other people and problems, usually by finding sociable or useful or challenging things for you to *do*.

Self-concern is not necessarily selfish – people can study to make themselves better, more generous people. But although self-concern does not have to be selfish in principle, it is often selfish in practice. That is especially so since the rise of the 'introspection industries' has been accompanied by a broad intellectual attack on altruism. Most economists, many psychologists, some political scientists and a few philosophers have done their best to persuade people that altruism is all wrong: it's sick or fraudulent or oppressive or self-defeating, or all four. Most of the persuasion has the negative form of an attack on altruism. The positive implication is less often spelled out but is nonetheless clear: look after yourself, enrich yourself, please yourself, enjoy your *Self*: unselfishness does harm, selfishness does good.

If hell is other people, what should you do about them? Employ them, exploit them, buy cheap and sell dear to them, please and amuse them, but only to earn money or applause from them. By all means trade where there is mutual advantage – exchange sex and drinks and jokes and nights at the theatre with them. In a word, *use* them. And don't feel guilty about it – convince yourself that they'll do the same to you, so there's no occasion to be any kinder to them, collectively or individually, than suits you. Be modern, emancipated, free. Keep relationships open-ended, unpossessive, unentangling. Don't let other people's wants imprison you.

I suggested earlier that the effects are worst when the Old and New Right merge: when the old capitalist greed joins with the new self-indulgence. That has now produced yet another New American Man, an especially nasty mutation of the American New Right. He's commonly a small, affluent male, aged between thirty and forty-nine, with the lines of his face set permanently in a relaxed sneer. His sex life has always been so coolly predatory and emotionally unrewarding that he's beginning to need commercial aids and diversifications to keep it interesting. He sincerely desires to be rich. He has the standard reactionary rhetoric about leaving economics to the market, though he's not usually taking market risks himself, or not with his own money – he's more likely to be in personnel or PR or management education or financial journalism. He's into the tax revolt and supply-side incentives boots and all. He's against welfare. He's against environmental protection. He wants strict air safety because he's nervous flying, but he's against most other health and safety regulations.

So far, except for his short stature, he's Old Right. But he's very far from being an uptight Old Right moralist. He doesn't mind what the masses do to one another, including to their women and children, as long as we don't waste welfare on them. He's not troubled about law and order, he's content to buy good private security. He's no feminist but he's all for women's liberation if that means stripping women of their traditional defences and protections. Above all, he objects to any regulation of his pleasures. No wowser government should stop him enjoying lovers of any age or sex or species he fancies; divorce and abortion on demand; pornography by book, magazine, tape, cable, cassette or peephole; anything he may want to eat, drink, smoke, sniff or inject; and anything else the market offers to keep his experienced senses interested. He doesn't mind if the way people exploit these liberties degrades women or children or the national culture – as long as the market offers the private goods he wants, the general quality of the society around him is not a significant source of his satisfactions. If he's unhappy, that's private too: he'll buy some therapy – psychoanalysis, a facelift, TM or whatever. There's still something less than happy about the half-smile, half-sneer that he wears, because basically people bore him, and no amount of analysis or massage can do much to reduce his anxiety about aging. But he's an original, he has perfected something: he's a perfectly self-centred, self-serving hedonist, born of a strange late marriage of big business and anarchist liberation.

Speaking of self-indulgence, it would be fun to go on character-ising the cult in that self-righteous, disapproving way. But it may be more seemly for academics and intellectuals to notice how much encouragement the cult gets from self-righteous academics and intel-lectuals. I will now do that, but I don't want to be misunderstood. The academics deserve all the abuse they're about to get, but that doesn't mean they invented the cult of selfishness single-handedly. It gets its main force from crude capitalist and class interest.

I think the basic mistake of the didactic classes has been to remove the debate about social purpose from the curriculum. Some students may still debate the principles of social justice and morality, but outside a few departments of politics and sociology, most of their teachers don't and most of their courses don't. Even the few who do debate justice and injustice, equality and inequality, much more than they attend to questions of selfishness, unselfishness and cooperation.

I can think of only two notable books in the last forty years about the basic social functions of generosity: Richard Titmuss's *The Gift Relationship* and parts of Fred Hirsch's *Social Limits to Growth*. In Australia there are dozens of valuable books about our unequal and unjust distribution of wealth and income and other good things – but only one that I know of (David Scott's *Don't Mourn for Me – Organise*) about voluntary organisations and the work they do.

Why did we remove from the non-scientific curriculum the social purposes and values that were traditionally the core of the curriculum? I think the mistake arose from a habit that could be described, dully, as over-generalising. What that means can be illustrated by a well-known historical example. When the American middle classes wanted to get rid of colonial rule, or the English middle classes wanted to get rid of aristocratic rule, they didn't say: 'All power to us – let the middle classes rule.' For various reasons they said more general things, such as: 'All men are equal' and 'Government should be answerable to the governed'. That proved to be a rod for their own backs – they had invented a universal philosophy of political equality which the working classes, in their turn, were soon using in their efforts to get rid of middle-class rule, or at least to get a share of it.

That's the model: to get something specific, you make very general claims, which may well have more and sometimes better or worse effects than you had in mind.

I think that model illuminates what we have done to our curriculum in the following way. A hundred years ago, drink really was the curse of the working classes: if a worker took to it, his family was done for. If girls fornicated, voluntarily or not, and got pregnant or diseased, their life chances really were ruined. So it was neither funny nor foolish for middle-class Methodist reformers to preach purity and sobriety to the working classes. A century later, wages were better, pubs were licensed, venereal diseases were more curable, some of the contraceptives worked some of the time, and fewer people believed in the Methodist God anymore. So there was understandably a dwindling audience for any Methodist wowsers who still preached purity and sobriety to the working classes. But did the twentieth-century liberators say: 'We think the workers could have some booze and sex now' or 'Times have changed, so some of our moral rules need changing'? No, they over-generalised. They said things like 'Do-gooding is insulting. All moralising is ridiculous. No one has any business telling other people how they ought to behave.' They developed an abusive vocabulary of words and phrases such as 'do-gooder', 'wowser', 'paternalist' and 'middle-class moraliser' to discredit any moralising at all, and any serious debate about social morality and justice. That's the language in which the anarchist Right now asserts its hedonistic privileges, and the likes of us now sneer at the Moral Majority. All parties are fully hypocritical, because they're all moralising like mad – but no longer admitting it. Instead of saying: 'We need to change some of our social purposes and our educational approach to them' or 'We think some of the Moral Majority's morals are bad, we'd like to propose some better morals as follows', we say: 'Down with *all* moralising and *any* educational approach to it'. Of course, some say more cautiously: 'Yes, people need morals. But I'll decide my own, and so should everyone else – nobody needs telling. Telling is totalitarian.' The point is that both parties – the anti-moralists and the individual moralists – agree that there's no place for social values or moralities in the educational system, or not beyond primary school. Thus they teach the young – actively and authoritatively, however inadvertently – that moral thought is childish. If morality is for children, what's for adults? Why, self-service, of course.

That message does come from many practitioners of the arts and social sciences. Ayn Rand's best-known novel announces on page one that 'altruism is the enemy'. The psychologist Norman Brown and other spontaneous thinkers urge you to do what you feel like doing, and take what you feel like taking, carelessly on impulse. Those and some other schools of psychology identify altruism (especially to strangers you don't know) chiefly with guilt, and often as irrational and unhealthy. Ideas of justice or equality merely rationalise guilt or envy (guilt if the believer is rich, envy if poor). Prudence is worse. Prudent care for others is worst of all.

Some political scientists take all expressions of altruism or care for others as threats: threats to know other people's interests better than they do themselves, threats to decide things for them bureaucratically, threats to govern them without their consent. Nobody should pretend to care for other people's interests except by way of trade, or as paid agents of those other people. The economists Gordon Tullock and James Buchanan [authors of *The Calculus of Consent*] and others think votes *are* spent like dollars in the market to buy private advantages, and rationally *should* be.

Orthodox economists are as fond as ever of the hidden hand. That is still the most ambitious of all the arguments for selfishness, because it makes greed look benevolent: getting the most I can for me is also the best I can do for you. Those economists have thus abolished effective selfishness, so perhaps they've abolished sin.

Many of them now go further. They don't just commend greed, they say it defines and limits their discipline. They say economics is about 'rational optimising behaviour', which means greed, and it's not about anything else. Not long ago I heard an eminent academician go further still, and declare that producing more is economic, and fit to be studied at universities; but distributing it better is ethical, and not fit to be studied at all, or certainly not by economists. Other disciplines have said much the same – it's part of the positivist delusion. But I think economics is the worst case. The delusion persists there, and does three kinds of harm, all of which connect with the cult of selfishness:

(1) One reason why economists cling to 'axiomatic selfishness' is that it seems to offer a basis on which they can build a precise deductive science. The assumption is false, the scientists' values merely get distorted and concealed; so the science is less competent than it could be if it accepted the realities of mixed human motivation and the realities of a conflict-ridden political economics.

(2) But the preference for 'rational optimising behaviour' is persuasive, and helps to induce more of that particular kind of greedy behaviour. Through many of the media much of the time, many of the academically qualified voices are telling the politicians and the public that the market will work better the less we govern it: that the main enemies of prosperity are government, taxation, welfare, and the commitment to ideas of equality and social justice and to a contrived and protected full employment. As the politicians compete for the public's votes, the experts recommend the meanest motivation to all concerned, and assure them that generosities or ideas of justice or cooperation would be illusory and self-defeating. Why does the successful Labor political leader these days offer no real vision of good? Why does he compete for votes in such a me-too way, offering most voters lower taxes and fewer sacrifices than his competitors do? Why does he thus add his voice to all the other voices that are telling people that selfishness is right and sensible? Presumably it's not his own mean spirit: it's his sad judgement of what he thinks the public wants. But he and they are both persuaded – a lot or a little, to a degree we can't measure – by the degrading ideology they hear incessantly from so many of the experts of the relevant profession.

(3) In the end, the worst effect of that ideology may prove to have been its reconstruction of the curriculum of higher education. The graduates' heads are full of algebra and dubious psychology but

empty of the questions that bothered Hobbes and Marx, and the answers that Burke and Mill and Richard Tawney proposed. I don't know whether their higher education actually degrades their morals, though if not it's not for want of trying. I think it must impoverish the inner life of their memory and imagination. It certainly makes many of them less competent than they might be – those classical thinkers understood some aspects of human motivation and behaviour which are simply not accessible to Chicago 'realists'.

✳

So what can be done? What will discredit and outmode this nasty cult? What will make justice and generosity fashionable again?

There are three obvious sources of hope.

The first is perennial. Parents can't bring up children at all without moralising them to some degree, if only for practical safety and self-defence. I have longed for a public opportunity to commend motherhood, and here it is. Mothers and fathers, lovers and spouses, aunts and grannies, friends and workmates, for all their sinful, unregenerate human nature, are still the most reliable source of generosity and ideas of right and wrong. So common sense and the natural affections are a first cause for hope, as they operate through families and friendships and some of the caring professions whose work brings them face to face with the innocent kinds of suffering every day.

Second, the cult of selfishness does a heartening amount of damage to a lot of its own begetters. Adam Smith, Schumpeter and Fred Hirsch are not the only economists to have noticed that the most rapacious capitalism works only if it can rely on a great deal of inbuilt honesty and cooperation in most of the citizens most of the time. Modern retailing breaks down if most of the staff steal most of the time. Modern industries run badly if they accept the orthodox economists' mean-spirited assumptions about the motivation of labour by fear and greed. Frightened but greedy managers are not the best custodians of shareholders' interests. And so on – even the nastiest of our owners and managers are, for their own purposes, quick to recommend self-sacrificing wage restraint to the rest of us.

Finally we the intellectuals should work at it. Novelists and poets and journalists can apply the acid to the cult of selfishness, to make it ugly and unlovable and – what may be even more effective – make it out-of-date unfashionable. The academics should restore the great questions of social purpose and justice to their proper share – which I think is about half – of the curriculum. That's not hard to do. In Oxford you have never been allowed to study economics by itself, without immunising doses of philosophy or politics or both. Adelaide has courses in the history of political and social ideas. Students are expected to enter the arguments. Besides knowing what Burke and Mary Wollstonecraft and Mill and Marx thought, they are supposed to know what they think themselves about the questions in hand. Nobody tells them what to think. In the end some incline to Burke's views, some to Marx's, some to Wollstonecraft's, some think they can reconcile the three; some think all three were on about the wrong questions. But whatever conclusions they come to, the cult of selfishness doesn't usually survive the experience.

16

—

URBAN CONSOLIDATION (1988)

Who consolidates who?

From the late 1980s, state governments across Australia begin to embrace policies of 'urban consolidation'. Instead of allowing cities to 'sprawl', as they had since the beginnings of settlement, they would have to be 'consolidated' or 'densified' within tighter metropolitan boundaries. Denser cities, its supporters argued, would be tidier, more sociable, more efficient and more sustainable than sparser ones. Stretton disagreed. Here, in one of his occasional contributions to Christopher Pearson's vigorous independent paper, Adelaide Review, *he offered an incisive critique of how urban consolidation might apply to his own city.*

URBAN CONSOLIDATION IS FINE IF PEOPLE really do want to have less space and more spending money, and if government is clever enough to prevent the saved money disappearing into higher rents and higher prices. But no modern population anywhere in the world has yet desired to reduce its living space. If government tries to force such a historic reversal, trouble is likely. The policy-makers who want to consolidate Adelaide have not accepted various professional warnings, so this is a plea for some public anxiety about the project.

Some opposite forces converge to determine how densely people live in modern cities.

The strongest force is economic growth. Real incomes grow, people have more to spend. They always spend more of it on more space: bigger houses and gardens, bigger apartments, more parks and playgrounds, more golf courses and bowling greens and riding schools, acres of grass instead of a half-acre of asphalt around primary schools.

As with income, so with technology. For more than a century, improvements in commuter transport have not been used to cut travel time. Instead they've been used to lengthen the average distance between home and work, partly to allow cities to grow bigger, partly to let people spread out to get more living space per head. The worker's slum cottage gives way to the 10 square house with room for a car; the next generation adds an en suite and a rumpus room and room for two cars and boat.

Social and demographic changes reinforce the economic trend. People have fewer children, so smaller numbers occupy each family house. More couples split, often replacing one household with two. Children leave home earlier to form households of their own. Single workers have self-contained flats instead of boarding-house rooms. Old people live longer and more often in independent households. So for a given population there are more households. Some of them want smaller premises than big family households used to have, but in total they still want more space per head than their forebears had.

For all those reasons, urban densities continue to decline all over the Western world – from London to Los Angeles, from Stockholm to Sydney. (Only Hong Kong can reverse the trend.) There's nothing wrong or regrettable about it. Choosing to spend more income on more independence, privacy, outdoor entertaining and active recreational space is at least as wholesome as choosing to spend it on more fast food and passive electronic entertainment.

As cities grow, there's competition for central space and their central parts get more densely built. New flats replace old houses and gardens. But that usually slows rather than reversing the outward spread, for two reasons.

First, as noted, growth finances people to buy more living and car-parking space in any of the housing forms. A 1960s study found that the housing along Manly esplanade went from two storeys to eight, with no change in population numbers.

Second, in the inner parts of growing cities, other uses replace housing. Partly, business for the growing metropolitan population concentrates near the centre, pushing housing out. As each resident gets richer and spends more, the spending has to be accommodated. Houses have to make way for more shops, supermarkets with car-parks, public and commercial recreations. In a half-circle north of Sydney Bridge, a decade that saw 24,000 new flats built also saw the population decline by 15 per cent.

Both these processes – the growth of urban space per head, and the 'densing' of cities' inner areas – can be done in better or worse ways, to produce better or worse urban fabric and social life. Unfashionably, I think Australia has done the first better than most, and South Australia is doing the second better than most. Reasoning follows.

An Australian achievement

THE ACHIEVEMENT IS SIMPLE: A COMPARATIVELY classless housing stock with an unusually equal distribution of urban living space.

Through the middle half of the twentieth century, as one product of economic growth, the Western world rehoused much of its urban working class. Europe put most of them into flats, without choice. Australia offered them flats or houses with gardens, and most opted for the suburban house and garden which middle-class Australians already had.

The choice was real, and free. From the 1950s at least, flats were available, usually cheaper than houses, and offering landlord-investors good returns and tax treatment. (The theorists' myth that taxes or building regulations *forced* Australians out of flats into houses and gardens is rubbish.)

The same choice almost certainly helped rather than hindered economic growth. Around the world through those decades, there were only one or two exceptions to this rule that the more gross national product a country put into housing, the faster gross national product grew. (Rubbish on that subject still flows freely from our Commonwealth Treasury.)

Thus, a large majority of Australians, encouraged by both political parties, welcomed a housing system which gave most households a genuine choice from the full range of housing forms: gave four out of five of them the option of ownership at some stage of their lives, and distributed private land, housing and home ownership more equally than other countries do, and more equally than Australia distributes wealth and income. The achievement was so remarkable that an army of urban theorists, economists, Canberra hierarchs and

New Right tax-cutters (affluent home owners all) have been reviling it and hoping to dismantle it ever since.

So much for creating a freely chosen and fairly shared fabric. Different problems come with growing pressures to make over the older inner suburbs to greater density of buildings or people or both.

The South Australian achievement

ADELAIDE'S DENSING HASN'T BEEN PERFECT, BUT seen as whole, and compared with others, it has so far been done rather well.

It was right to segregate industry and housing at least into different streets.

Since controls began, about half metropolitan Adelaide's residential territory has been open by right or consent to attached or terraced housing and flats, including (in R2 zones) high flats. [The reference here is to local residential controls which ascend from R1, low density, to R3, medium-high density]. The supply of land for those dense housing forms has thus been well ahead of demand – the R2 and R3 zones still don't have as much as a tenth of the dense development they have room for.

(Why do dense theorists say otherwise, and want to call off the zoning? An R1 owner would love to cover his block with flats. A developer would like to buy land at R1 prices and then convert it to R3. When they're blocked, they both complain of selfish restriction of development, and mutter darkly about capital flight to the Gold Coast. In fact, if each got his way it would merely shift some flat building from one place to another – there is no reason whatever to think that the whole demand for flats would increase.)

Under this regime, metropolitan Adelaide has acquired as many cheap flats and as many bigger, better-landscaped, dearer flats as investors have wanted to build, which have often run some hundreds ahead of the number people wanted to rent. Their vacancy rates are much the same or easier than the vacancy rates of rental houses. There is no evidence whatever of frustrated demand for denser housing forms.

There are also many thousands of small new pensioner units or 'cottage flats', packed in at a dozen or so per standard suburban block. For those, there is frustrated demand, but only because most of them need some subsidy, and subsidy money is limited. They're well located in small groups through nearly every neighbourhood to allow people to move into them without necessarily leaving their old neighbourhoods.

(Compare the Sydney authorities, who began by building one monster block for 600 widows from all over, destroying acres of good, dense terrace housing to make room for it.)

There have also been some inventive land gains and conversions: new land at West Lakes and North Haven, reclaimed pugholes [claypits] and industrial sites, and MATS [Metropolitan Adelaide Transportation Study] highway routes in Bowden and Hindmarsh, quarry-floor housing in some eastern suburbs, and housing conversions of old factories, a warehouse, a tram barn. More than sixty local governments have provided land for pensioner flats in joint ventures with the Housing Trust.

Quite a lot of inner-urban renovation and replacement has been positively charming. The charm is important if you want the 'densing' to continue. Urban folk who hanker for the street and cafe life of the King's Road or the Left Bank can't hope to get it simply by crowding people. (Tokyo is lamenting the loss of that sort of life from districts with ten times the density of ours.) TV, videos, CDs, private cars, big suburban hotel bars, beach and barbecue life have changed our lifestyles and meeting places. Where busy urbanity is achieved nowadays, it is by positive attraction: by building charming precincts.

We do that well so long as we don't trust it entirely to developers or bureaucrats. Sixteen years ago popular revolts stopped bureaucrats from bulldozing Hackney and North Adelaide for apartment towers, and stopped developers replacing old villas with ugly blocks of walk-up flats which offended their neighbours and asphalted their sites to their boundaries.

Having learned those lessons, Adelaide's city planners decided that the City and North Adelaide should be rebuilt with the best of the old fabric conserved, with more terrace houses than flats, with better flats with new design sympathetic to the old, with a good deal of compulsory vegetation and with beautiful streetscapes. Those principles have since achieved *both* attractive neighbourhoods *and* (unlike Paddington or North Sydney) a rare increase of inner urban population.

Similar achievements are underway in Port Adelaide, Hindmarsh, Unley, Norwood. Are they all yuppie gentrifications, merely? No more than unregulated market takeovers would have been. In fact, rather less: those neighbourhoods have acquired more than the metropolitan average of new and restored housing.

Notice, finally, that much of the good physical and social quality of the redevelopment comes from resident political action, ever since the rebellion of the City and St Peters voters sixteen years ago. Neither the developers nor the government were building anything half as good until direct local democracy reformed them – and made them a lot more popular than their own efforts were doing.

So why not steady as we go?

The lurch to the right

THE COMMONWEALTH GOVERNMENT IS SOME YEARS into a bipartisan attack on Australia's public sector. The worst effects tend to be on capital investments in infrastructure, because those are the biggest items and the easiest to defer.

The Commonwealth economists believe, wrongly, that less public infrastructure and services will somehow generate more private investment.

The politicians compete for votes chiefly by cutting taxes, never mentioning what the cuts will cost in poorer services and public and private investment. But there must somehow be less dams, sewage treatment works, power stations, roads, bus routes and schools than are actually required by people's effective market demand for residential growth.

How can the South Australian government cope with that? Its urban consolidators hope (1) to limit the outward growth of Adelaide to less than the market is demanding; and (2) to contrive redevelopment of existing suburbs both faster and denser than the market is demanding.

That's been attempted at various times in a number of the world's cities. In dictatorships and democracies, in capitalist and communist economies, the attempt has *invariably* failed. To the extent that it tried to frustrate or reverse the actual democratic and market demands, it will fail here. The only question is what damage the attempt will do – to the poor by forcibly crowding them, and to other households and their public services by jacking up land prices against them – before the impractical parts of the policy are abandoned.

The first damage is a dramatic decline in the quality and competence of the policy papers.

Fifteen years ago Cedric Pugh, an able economist at the Institute of Technology, researched the comparative costs of suburban development and inner suburban development. Even on public account, the new is not always dearer than reconstructing the old. If you count private costs as well, there's not much in it either way. On the whole, it's sensible to let people's market and lifestyle preferences determine the proportions of outer and inner development.

In 1981 the Australian Institute of Urban Studies got Raymond Bunker, then head of the Institute of Technology Planning School, and Lionel Orchard of the Department of Environment and Planning, to investigate the scope for urban consolidation in Adelaide. They found some real possibilities, most of which (as reported above) are now in train. But the possibilities which they identified – although already a bit optimistic to a realist eye – did not reduce the public investment required to the level which, under Genghis Keating, the Commonwealth now dictates.

So another report was sought, from private consultants. They were bullied and bullied to amend and amend drafts of their report until (1) it said what the relevant bureaucrat wanted it to say; and (2) nobody in the firm would sign it. Further reports of that predetermined and anonymous kind have followed. This is not the place to review their calculations, which I believe are sprinkled with optimistic misjudgements and evasions, but some samples can indicate the general quality of their professional and social thought.

A consultant report (which I don't identify to spare the blushes of an otherwise excellent firm) arrives at its conclusion by the following super-scientific method. It finds that letting people build the houses they wish to have and are willing and able to pay for will be best for the residents – they are not mistaken about their interests, and urban consolidation is squarely against their interests. But consolidation is better (i.e. cheaper) for the providers of (1) water and sewerage; (2) power; (3) roads; and (4) public transport. That's *four to one against the residents*, so the democratic course is clearly to consolidate!

That report did at least concede that residents know their own interests and will be hurt by consolidation. Departmental reports no longer concede that. Instead, they assume that a household without at least two residents children which still has a three-bedroom house and garden is antisocially under-occupying its patch, and is blind to its own interests. Some paragraphs hope to *persuade* people to want less space; others argue that they merely need to be *informed* about the attractions of having less.

Thus people who live in a city which has scores of thousands of flats, terraced houses, townhouses, semi-detached houses, old slum cottages and new pensioners' units are believed not to know what those housing forms are like. They merely need to be told – 'demystified', one report says – and their interests will become clear to them. The day the kids leave home, their parents will gladly get rid of all those sheds, pools, boats, hobby and rumpus rooms, studies and workrooms, spare beds for kin and visitors, playspace for grandchildren, and their silly liking for views, vines, gardening, fruit-growing and outdoor entertaining. That is to say, they will realise how unnecessary the last forty years of economic growth have been, how mistaken was the long trudge from the old Bowden cottage to the spread at Golden Grove. They'll flog the house and return to some minimum functional shelter with sighs of relief and enlightenment.

One of the things the department thinks the people need to be told is the difference in costs between the big old place and the small new one. What actually *is* the difference? Having never researched it, the department does not know. (Their statement, not mine. Mine would be: the department does not know whether there's a difference, or how the difference depends on which public and private, direct and indirect costs you choose to count.)

But I underrate their surefooted approach to research. Academics who are currently worried about the Commonwealth and state proposals to have public servants take over the direction of university research may be interested in a preview. Paragraph 3.5 on p. 13 of the *Urban Consolidation Working Party Report*, published in September 1987 by the Department of Environment and Planning, reads in its entirety:

> Constraint: lack of data on the cost savings achievable. The working party considers that lack of hard evidence of the potential public savings of an urban consolidation strategy will hinder the promotion of the concept. Although savings will occur, a cost-benefit analysis should be undertaken *on a limited basis* using fringe and potential urban consolidation sites to *provide statistics to justify the policy.*

Only the italics are mine. All the papers are in a similar spirit. Where consolidation may have wholesome effects, specify them. Where it may have expensive, unfair or divisive effects, don't mention them, or don't specify what they'll be. Ingeniously, the obligatory note on 'social equity considerations' doesn't actually consider any social equities. It merely lists headings under which they need to be considered. It's factors which raise social equity issues include:

- changing household structures;
- the decline in inner and middle suburb populations;
- the extension of development into fringe areas;
- the high cost of home ownership;
- restrictive residential development standards and zoning policies; protection of the rights of existing residents at the

expense of the rights of potential residents through the operation of the third party appeal system.

I think you are meant to reflect that 'the extension of development into fringe areas' removes some women and children from easy access to transport and services. True, it does, especially if the Commonwealth is preventing the state from keeping the services up to the spread of settlement; and it is indeed an equity issue.

But I fear that you are not meant to reflect that the same extension, backed by the 'restrictive residential development standards', also does other things. It gives many low-income households a housing option they otherwise would not have: a house-and-garden alternative to slum-dwelling or flat-dwelling. And for those who want it, it equalises Australian families' share of private space and school and neighbourhood space to an extent that unregulated market development never did, and consolidation may not do either.

Those also are equity issues, unmentioned in the new reports. So would any policy be which permitted private housing development to meet market demand without rationing, which imposed lower standards on public housing as the element of development which government can control.

But unlike the competent Bunker/Orchard report, these newspeak papers are quite vague about whose housing, where and in what quantities it is expected to shrink. They mention all 'improvements in equity which consolidation may bring'. They mention none of the inequities and social costs it may bring.

What might those costs be? What harm might flow either from determined consolidation, or from half-hearted, under-financed consolidation? What winners and losers may there be? What fail-safe precautions might reduce the damage?

There are five causes for anxiety. To sum them up:

By deferring headworks, and therefore servicing too little new suburban land to meet demand, it may raise land prices. That may well cost households more than it would cost them to finance the necessary headworks; i.e. the compelling financial purpose of the consolidation policy may well be self-defeating for the people, if not for the politicians.

Meanwhile, the intention to consolidate discourages strong decentralist planning and may hurt the people, especially the poorer people who must still live in present and future outer suburbs.

It may shrink some poorer homebuyers' shares of land, while allowing the rich to use land as extravagantly as ever.

It will increase inequalities further if it ever takes backyards from more public tenants than actually want to lose them.

And it may reduce Adelaide's actual and potential provisions for public parks and outdoor recreations.

All that is threatened not because the nation is too poor to afford the necessary public investment, but because the dominant faction of the Commonwealth government (and the opposition parties) puts tax-cutting and financial deregulation ahead of other needs, especially the well-researched and widely acknowledged need to renovate and extend the nation's material infrastructure.

In the private sector, the consolidators hope to permit closer settlement, but not force it. They hope that fewer home-seekers will want the standard house and garden; that those who do will accept smaller blocks; and that developers won't compete (as many do now) by offering blocks above the minimum regulation size.

I don't believe that this part of the project will have much success. Developers' and local governments' experience suggests that the customers know what they want for themselves and for the neighbourhood around them, and that most of them will continue to demand what they've always demanded. If that happens, consolidation won't work. If the supply of land for subdivision is nevertheless restricted for want of headworks, prices are likely to rise – prices all over the metropolis, for old as well as new houses. But experience does not suggest that the higher prices will have textbook market effects: they won't force smaller blocks. New Sydney blocks are costing twice what new Adelaide blocks do, but their average sizes are much the same, and many of them in both cities are bigger than the regulations require.

The state authorities are well aware of these dangers, and in all but one respect they are well equipped to avoid them. The Land Trust and Housing Trust own more than half the next ten years' development land. By selling to individuals and developers and joint venturing with private developers, they can keep the supply of developed land well ahead of demand. The government's 1987 *Long Term Development Strategy for Metropolitan Adelaide* proposes to maintain a supply of 20,000 developed allotments for sale, plus 12,000 in the development 'pipeline' and 12,500 awaiting development. Those are good allowances; if the authorities maintain them, there should be no land price revolution. But if the current patterns of demand continue, that land supply will soon need precisely the new headworks – a Murray pipeline, a sewage treatment works – which the government can't afford and which consolidation is designed to avoid.

A shortage of capital funds, not of land, caused by policies of the Commonwealth, not the state, is what threatens to restrict the supply and raise the price of developed blocks if current patterns of demand continue, as they are likely to do.

Sprawl

CONSOLIDATION IS MEANT TO REDUCE SUBURBAN sprawl but may actually encourage it. 'Sprawl' means – or ought to mean – haphazard suburban growth without good planning, design, centres or services. 'Sprawl' is Mansfield Park as opposed to Elizabeth, Surrey Downs as opposed to Golden Grove.

If the policy is consolidation, outward growth is likely to happen grudgingly, bit by bit. The purpose of consolidation is to reduce public investment at the outskirts, where previous policies encouraged it. It was more orthodox to insist that Elizabeth and Noarlunga get their full share of public and private investment and services. Now, Adelaide Council can work to attract every dollar of investment and every square metre of office and shopping and entertainment space that it can, regardless of the district centres' needs and without a word of dissent from state planning or service authorities.

If it's suggested that some government offices, or private-sector banking and insurance paperwork, be decentralised to Salisbury or Noarlunga, anyone who would rather go on working in Grenfell Street or Victoria Square can protest that decentralisation is out – that consolidation is government policy now. In a metropolis whose outer suburbs are short of jobs and services but continue to expand in response to private housing demand, centralist policies of consolidation *are* policies of sprawl.

The policy also discourages imagination and innovation in outer-suburban planning. The last imaginative planning of a new district as a whole was done for Golden Grove five years ago, before consolidation set in. The last to include strong town-centre and job-creating elements were longer ago, at Elizabeth and Noarlunga.

Since then, all we have tended to get are small extensions as they're needed. If another quarter or half-million people do one day live south of Noarlunga, they are likely to have sprawled there, a few subdivisions at a time, each bit much the same as the last. Their pipes and wires and main roads must have been coordinated economically – the engineering utilities are the effective planners now – but there will have been no William Light, no grand designs like old Adelaide's, no coherent long-term strategy to give them a city and a life of their own.

17

A USE FOR HISTORY (1990)

In February 1992 Stretton was invited to give a seven-minute talk to the 'Ideas Summit' convened in Canberra by his friend Donald Horne. He used the opportunity to make a plea for the importance of history in public policy. While often diffident about his own claims as a historian – 'I've never written any,' he replied to one interviewer – he remained, from first to last, an energetic defender of the discipline and its educative value.

THERE WAS SCARCELY A TIME WHEN ORIGINAL thought about the most basic moral and social questions, and the basic social capacities and incapacities of humankind, seemed so urgent, and perhaps potent for good or evil. I think such thought needs, among other things, three qualities which have been scarce in modern social science: it needs to be holist, uncertain and eclectic.

'Holist' scarcely needs explaining. As far as possible we should think about whole people and whole societies and stop supposing that any mental abstract from their whole behaviour – such as their economic behaviour alone, their political behaviour alone, their affectionate or acquisitive or altruistic behaviour alone – is likely to be so regular and independent of the rest of their experience that determinate theories can hope to predict it.

'Uncertain' means knowing that what we study may be changing as we study it – sometimes because we study it. That's another reason to stop looking for rigorous, formal theories which could only work with stable subject matter, i.e. if people never changed their minds or directions. I say it briskly, but if you believe it you must discard a great deal of this century's social science.

'Eclectic' has two meanings. First, the people we study are eclectic: they learn and think and choose, and what they will choose next is not always predictable. Second, whoever studies them must also choose. Social behaviour responds to its whole context. Innumerable conditions have to be present for people to behave exactly as they do. Alter any one, and they may behave differently. That is another way of saying that the causes of human behaviour are innumerable. To explain the behaviour, you have to choose which of its conditions to take for granted and which to explore, just as if you want to influence it, you have to choose which of its conditions to act upon.

To design new social arrangements or decide between rival reform proposals, you of course need to know our society well. But if that is all you know, there is one thing you cannot know about that society. You cannot know how much of its behaviour is conditioned by local, changeable conditions, and how much by capacities built into human nature. The wider the variety of actual societies – past and present and far and near – that you know about, the better equipped you are to judge what is fixed and what may be changeable in any one of them.

Consider, for example, the motivation of work. If all you know is the here and now, money may look like the main motive for productive enterprise. But medieval Europe saw innovation in many fields, from optics and glass technology through rational farm accounting to cathedral engineering, done mostly by men sworn to poverty. When Meiji Japan needed a new breed of capitalist entrepreneurs, the aristocratic samurai rather than the profit-seeking merchant class supplied most of them. If you see housework and childcare as work, other motives including love appear. And so on: subject to all the usual requirements that the thinkers have brains and good intent, the wider the vicarious experience, the better the social engineer.

Who study societies of every kind, study them whole, know most about how they conserve or change their ideas and institutions, write in plain language, and generally know how uncertain and selective their knowledge is at best? Historians do. Their vocation is – roughly speaking – to give as good foundation as scholarship can to the kind of selective-but-holistic discourse about society that politicians, public servants, journalists and citizens use every day to arrive at their political judgements and policies. We should stop tagging historians as the people who study the dead past, and see them as the people who do their best – at whatever cost in certainty and precision – to study how whole societies conserve and change their social life.

So when, as now, we face great social choices, three disciplines should chiefly educate us. The first is the natural science of our physical environment, and our means of manipulating it. The second is the high art and literature of individual human nature and experience. I leave those to other advocates. I am here to barrack for more historical education. The historians have done a good deal as relatively rapid innovators, to match their work to changing need. They have become quite competent measurers and quantifiers where appropriate, while still avoiding the trips of jargon, pseudo-science and sterile theory. There was never much ground for the hostile stereotype of them as anecdotal chroniclers of battles and royal marriages: those were not the main concerns of Thucydides, Machiavelli, Clarendon, Catherine or Thomas Macaulay, de Tocqueville or Henry Adams. Their successors have supplied much of the best understanding of modern industrial and social transformations. They are our main source of wisdom about religious violence, now threatening much of Asia. They are now exploring mankind's diverse experience of childhood, marriage, ordinary life, the unrecorded experience and forgotten achievements of women

So I am for more Australians learning more history, of other countries and times as well as their own. It would be nice if the modern economic miracles had all been achieved by societies with a broad and deep education in natural science and the humanities. Unhappily, that's not true: some narrow-minded utilitarians have also got rich. But it *is* true that a broad education, a rich culture and an interesting intelligentsia never held a country back, and those who get rich with that sort of culture are happier and more interesting societies than those who got rich without it. One promising local enterprise just now is a joint Japanese/Australian comparison of Japanese and Australian history, to see what thoughts the Australian experience may prompt in Japanese minds growing uneasy and uncertain about the uses of their wealth and the quality and direction of their national life. Just as the Japanese example is used to scourge lazier societies, might some alien achievements stimulate them to reflect on the range of good human potentialities which *their* culture does not yet engage as happily as it might?

18

TRANSPORT AND THE STRUCTURE OF AUSTRALIAN CITIES (1994)

In the 1970s Stretton was Australia's leading defender of the suburban way of life. Twenty years later, as the world awoke to the threats of climate change and peak oil, planners and environmentalists began to ask whether the car-dependent suburb was sustainable anymore. Australian cities, they argued, must become more like European ones, with higher densities to discourage car use and to support better public transport. The most prominent advocate of this view, the West Australian Peter Newman, suggested that if you want to make Australian cities less car-dependent, you must first make them denser. Stretton disagreed; here he explains why.

THE SAFETY, EQUITY AND ENVIRONMENTAL EFFECTS of our urban transport need to be improved. Should we do that directly, by reforming the transport, or indirectly, by rebuilding the cities more compactly?

People who want to reduce the demand for powered transport indirectly, by rebuilding the cities in more compact form, argue from comparisons which have been researched most extensively by

Peter Newman and his colleagues at Murdoch University. Australian cities average about a quarter of the population density of European cities, and per head of population they have:

- about twice the kilometres of private motoring;
- about four times the length of roads;
- three quarters of the public transport route length, but only half the passenger kilometres and much less than half the number of passenger journeys; and
- about a quarter as many journeys by foot or bike.

Altogether, we make 12 per cent of our urban journeys by foot, bike and public transport, where the European figure is 46 per cent.

Those figures are generally taken to indicate that our system is comparatively expensive and inefficient. But one implication of the figures suggests that the Australian arrangement may be more efficient than the European: we enjoy four times the urban space per head, with only 18 per cent more travel time and 64 per cent more travel mileage than the Europeans. A relatively small increase of travel time and distance thus buys a fourfold increase of space. Some of that is road and parking space, but most of it is private house and garden space, school playgrounds, public parks and playing fields, golf courses, tennis courts and other recreational spaces; and the public and private space is probably shared more equally than urban space is shared anywhere else in the world. So if the space is worth having, we get it at much lower travel time and infrastructure cost per hectare than Europeans pay for their urban space. I will return later to the question of whether the space is worth having.

To return to the case for consolidation, it is that our sprawling suburban cities are environmentally unsustainable, economically inefficient, inequitable and unsociable. We can unpack those charges in turn.

Environment

T RANSPORT IN MORE COMPACT CITIES USES LESS fuel and emits less pollutants. Transport uses about 30 per cent of the energy used in Australia. About a third of that – 10 per cent of the total – fuels urban car travel. If we could halve that, and consequently have to fuel some more public transport, we might save 3 per cent of national energy use. We could alternatively save a little more than that by contriving for all our private motoring in town and country the average 30 per cent improvement of fuel efficiency that is technically feasible.

Further gains are possible by limiting the size and power of vehicles. If we reformed the cars and converted the cities to European density, we might save 6 or 7 per cent of total energy use. But less than half of that would come from the higher density, and some of that gain would be reduced by the energy cost of rebuilding cities and servicing high buildings, and the environmental cost of losing some home production of fruit and vegetables and flowers. There is also some evidence that people with gardens care more for the natural environment than flat-dwellers do, and bring up children with more concern for it.

There is still a net gain in sustainability to be won by reducing the private motoring use of fuel. But increasing residential density may not be the best way, or even a possible way to do it.

Economy

THE CLAIM THAT AUSTRALIAN CITIES ARE LESS economically efficient than denser cities relies on childish accounting tricks. The Australian government and most economists make housing and urban infrastructure look unproductive by refusing to notice their products. First, public infrastructure is part of the capital which every private producer and every household uses – but neither public nor private accounts ever say so. One reason is that all accounts of the productivity and rates of return to private capital overstate the private and understate the public capital contribution to private output. Second, household capital – house, equipment, garden, car – is the capital for more than a third of the national output of material goods and services. Properly estimated, that capital averages about the same productivity as our public- and private-sector capital does. But our authorities do not measure its output, do not know how the output varies with the amount or distribution of the capital employed, do not include it in their accounts of national product, and do not compare it with the household output of other countries. They do not compare what a densely housed English family can produce for themselves in a tower flat over a vandalised car park with what they can produce for themselves as emigrants to a house and garden in an Australian suburb. Australia is blessed with one government economist who is a spectacular exception to this, and whose work I will presently cite. But the orthodox accounts define 'household production' as consumption, and call its equipment 'consumer durables' to avoid identifying it as productive capital. The taxicab produces, the private car consumes. The McDonald's cook produces, the home cook consumes. The league game you pay to see is a product, the school playing field which is the league's nursery is unproductive infrastructure.

Australian households are unusually well and equally equipped and are probably among the world's most productive, but there has been very little research to compare their productivity with that of households elsewhere. There have, however, been studies of the amount and distribution of household space and capital, and of the public capital which people also use, unpaid, when producing goods and services for themselves and one another. The best Australian work is by Dr Ian Castles, former Commonwealth Statistician, in some scholarly non-government publications which deserve to be better known than they are.

Because he doubted the OECD story that Japanese are now richer than Australians, Castles used available household expenditure and time use surveys to arrive at comparisons of productivity and material standards of living in Australian and Japanese cities. The opening items of the comparison offer great comfort to believers in compact cities.

Among affluent societies, the Japanese have the most compact cities. Australian cities have the second-lowest density, after the United States, and their density has declined continuously since the 1940s. By the 1980s Tokyo had about five times the population density of Sydney. Through those decades, Japan, building the densest cities, rose from far behind to the top of the international table of income per head, while Australia, building ever more expansive urban sprawl, declined from fourth or fifth to fifteenth on the income table. What more do you need to know about economically efficient urban structure?

Answer: you need to know the rest of Castles' findings. His first concern was with items which do figure in orthodox accounts. How productive are Japanese and Australian workers, and what will their

wages buy? Australians have always been and are still more productive per hour. (The higher Japanese money income per head of
population comes from working longer days, weeks, years and lifetimes supporting fewer dependents.) What will the money incomes
buy? Castles compares the wage price of a Sydney basket and a Tokyo
basket of household necessaries, mostly food. To earn the price of
a year's supply of what Australians consider basic, Tokyo residents
would have to work two and a half times the hours Sydney residents
do: 600 hours in Tokyo, 245 in Sydney, at 1987 wages and prices. To
earn the price of what Japanese households consider basic, the difference is predictably less – but not much less: Tokyo people must still
work twice the hours that Sydneysiders would have to work to buy
that Japanese basket of goods at their local prices. For other goods,
the differences are less, but still significant and all in Sydney's favour.
Very roughly speaking, an hour's work in Sydney buys about one and
a half times the market goods that an hour's work in Tokyo buys.
Castles concludes:

> [T]he available evidence indicates that the purchasing power of
> earnings, as measured by the command over goods and services
> obtained on average by a given amount of working time, is
> much greater in Sydney than in the Japanese cities … [Through
> the 1980s, despite Australia's slower economic growth] even on
> the conventional measures, Australians apparently continued
> to enjoy higher real consumption levels per capita, in respect of
> virtually every significant category of expenditure. This was
> true notwithstanding the facts that they worked fewer hours
> per week, took longer holidays and had shorter working lives.

So much for the belief that more compact cities necessarily promise
more efficient production of market goods.

Castles next compares the private and public space and facilities with which people can produce non-market goods and services for themselves and each other with their unpaid labour, and occupy their time interestingly and enjoyably.

A majority of Japanese share the Australian preference for a separate house and garden. But in cities, fewer achieve it, and those who do have smaller houses on smaller allotments, and pay much more for them. Seventy-four per cent of Sydney households have some sort of house and garden; 35 per cent of Tokyo households do. Thirty per cent of Tokyo households live in buildings more than three storeys high; 3 per cent of Sydney households do. New Sydney dwellings of all types average more than twice the floor area of new Tokyo dwellings, and those with their own allotments average more than four times the lot size. Though a quarter the size, the Tokyo allotments were costing ten times as much – i.e. forty times the land price of comparable Sydney allotments, at the time of Castles' study.

Thus, housing and other necessaries together take a higher proportion of spending in Japanese cities, leaving less for discretionary spending. The longer working days, weeks and years leave less time for discretionary use. And what urban households can produce for themselves at home has to be produced in less space, and consequently with a narrower range of equipment and creative possibilities, than are open to Australian households.

What can people do for themselves away from home, in a non-market way, in their cities, public spaces and facilities? Per million of population, Sydney has 2040 public recreational sites; Tokyo has 250. The Sydney sites average more than two hectares; the Tokyo sites average less than one. Sydney has ten times the playing fields, nineteen times the tennis courts.

Most of these different land uses are long-lasting: it takes a long time to replace or reconstruct a city's residential fabric, and the denser it is, the longer it is likely to take and the more it will cost. But the Sydney pattern is potentially more flexible: Sydney could fill its parks and playing fields and school grounds with housing more quickly and cheaply, with less demolition and replacement, than it would take to insert Sydney's public spaces into Tokyo's built-up fabric. Sydney could add a flat or two to most of its detached houses more readily than Tokyo could provide its residents with private gardens.

A final economic argument alleges that Australia can no longer afford to build new suburbs. Compare the $40,000 to $70,000 it is said to cost to service each new suburban allotment with the negligible cost of connecting a new house to the underused services of the existing city; multiply the difference by the number of additional households to be housed in the coming decades, and it is plain that we cannot afford it.

I do not know how this argument has escaped the derision it deserves. If you want to compare the likely alternative costs of suburban extension and compact rebuilding, you must compare the cost of new suburban services with the cost of connecting not one but some hundreds of thousands of new customers to the old urban services. That will require reconstructing and expanding some of them through built-up areas, which is dearer than installing them on greenfield sites. Any substantial increase of density will require some demolition and replacement as well as infilling, and the replacement costs should be brought to account. So should the loss of quality or quantity of some existing services, if a serious increase of numbers are going to compete for space in the existing recreational spaces and the asphalt yards of the old inner-city schools. Then, having arrived at an honest estimate of costs, our capacity to pay should be investigated. Our grandparents, with less than half our present productivity, enabled the Australian working class to afford and acquire their first suburban houses and gardens. It would be interesting to do some Castles-style work to compare the hours of work which built their dams, pipelines, treatment works, power stations, roads and bridges with the hours of work that produce those items now. Competent investigators will find that we can perfectly well afford to continue meeting the market demand for standard housing, and supplying it with standard services, if we want to, and if we can find political leaders who will set the necessary levels of taxation and public investment.

What I believe we cannot afford for much longer are some prevailing economic theories and political practices. First, prevailing theories tell us, I think mistakenly, that reducing investment in housing and infrastructure will increase other investment and employment. (Opposite effects are likelier. A sensible public investment program, sensibly financed, could contribute usefully to private employment and growth. In almost all developed economies through the last half-century, the rate of economic growth has varied with the proportion of national income invested in housing, not inversely to it.) Second, the leaders of both parties have been telling us for a decade now that taxation is not the necessary price we pay for the public goods and services we need, much of it is money that governments simply take and waste. Tax-cutting – or promising or pretending to cut taxes – has become the main mode of competition for votes. Talk of urban consolidation has become a thin excuse for deferring the investment and services which existing outer suburbs need, and our further suburban growth will need.

That is a pity, because market productivity, household productivity and urban adaptability to changing industrial and household needs seem to do well at Australian urban densities. But can the same be said of social equity, or the culture and lifestyles that the cities allow?

Equity

J UDGEMENTS ABOUT EQUITY ARE OF COURSE DISAGREED by people with differing values; and the urban issues to be judged are complex. In the argument about density, I do not think either side has a knockdown case on equitable grounds. I can merely remind you of some advantages and disadvantages of each.

In European cities that are governed and serviced in a European social-democratic way. most residents have good physical access to whatever the city has room for. Compared with Australian conditions, many more working, shopping, educational, service and recreational journeys can be made on foot, bike or public transport by the quarter or so of all households and the half or so of individuals who have no cars of their own. Their access is also cheaper than car-borne access is. So for many poorer people, access to the city's attractions is both physically and financially easier than it is for many poor Australians. Ease of exit from the city is more variable. Australia has a lot of suburbs with bush or beach boundaries, but also a lot without, and a lot of those without have no ready access to bush or beach by public transport. Exit is often easier in Europe, with shorter distances, better public transport and many smaller cities. But it may need to be more frequent: Europeans have to leave town to reach some recreations that Australian cities have room for in town. Quite a high proportion of Australian households, including some of the poorest, have cars, and access to a wider variety of in-town, open-air recreations than urban Europeans or Japanese have. Perhaps a heroic simplification would allow that dense cities can offer their poor better access but to a narrower range of facilities, while Australian cities offer a wider variety of facilities, but worse access to some of them for people without cars.

Shares of space matter at least as much as shares of access. In principle, a city's density need not determine the distribution of whatever space there is: there can be equal or unequal shares in crowded or in extended cities. The central parts of old European cities may seem to distribute space fairly equally: everyone lives in apartments without private outdoor space, and the public spaces are accessible to all, and sometimes very civilised and sociable. But many of the European rich and rising numbers of the middle-income apartment-dwellers also have country retreats of one kind or another, and most of the rest do not. There are fair shares of space within the city, but not overall. Europe is also now building a lot of row houses and villa suburbs. That may produce the kind of spatial inequality that Australian cities used to have when the working classes lived densely in inner-suburban struggle-towns and the middle classes retreated to house-and-garden suburbs.

The best of the European cities offer some of their citizens marvellously interesting, attractive and sociable urban life. Australia has some fashionable patches of that in Paddington, Carlton and the like, and some less fashionable patches in (for example) Italian Norwood or Aboriginal Redfern. But there is overwhelming evidence that Australian major cities through most stages of life want public and private space more than they want that dense urbanity. And Australia and New Zealand distribute that space more equally than any other country does. That is doubly equitable. It is good that most households, if they want to, can have the space to share the country's most preferred lifestyle. And in equipping people to do a good deal for themselves, house-and-garden forms can have special importance for households with low incomes. If you're poor and carless in an upstairs flat in a neighbourhood without much open space – and especially if you're a child or bringing up children – you can do a good deal less for yourselves than you can do with a house and garden and shed in a suburb with the parks and playgrounds and school grounds that Australian densities allow. Finally – still speaking of equity – if governments do succeed in imposing some higher density on Australian cities, there is not much doubt that the rich and the middle classes will hang onto their houses and gardens, and it will mostly be the poorest households who lose their private space.

Community

AS A FOURTH OBJECTION TO SUBURBAN LIFE: do the private garden, the private car and the travel distances isolate people in an unsociable lifestyle – watching TV, motoring to visit a few friends and relations – while more civilised Europeans and Japanese commune with more acquaintances and strangers in more crowded neighbourhoods and public spaces?

Not altogether. People watch more TV the less private indoor and outdoor space they have. Australians eat and drink away from home more than ever before. They mingle with strangers in the big shopping centres and meet neighbours they know in neighbourhood supermarkets. They join with others in more sporting and recreational activities than Japanese, and perhaps Europeans, do.

Ian Halkett's studies twenty years ago, of the extent to which public space and facilities could replace private house-and-garden space, found that in many respects the two were not alternatives but complements: people with most resources at home went out and made most use of public and convivial resources away from home.

Now, in the 1990s, research of unprecedented scale, skill and sophistication is being done on the material living conditions of urban Australians and their reasons for their residential preferences and choices. Cooperation between Professor Riaz Hassan, the South Australian government's review of its metropolitan planning, the Australian government's House Strategy Review, the Australian Bureau of Statistics and McCann Eriksen have surveyed in great detail the residential preferences and satisfactions of large samples of Adelaide, Melbourne and Sydney households. The Australian Institute of Family Studies, in the course of its study of Australian living standards, has published an exceptionally thorough survey of a new outer suburb in its Berwick Report. Sue Richardson and Peter Travers – an economist and a welfare administrator turned sociologist – have used some of the Institute of Family Studies data to survey the material conditions of life of poor Australians, and to explore relations between the material elements and the other elements of all Australians' welfare. (It's a change to find a work of number-crunching social science whose first reference is to Thomas Aquinas' *Summa Theologiae*).

These investigators find what Halkett found. As expected, people's experience and preferences vary with their tastes and circumstances. But a large majority of households are happy with where they live and how they live there, and specifically prefer their suburban houses and locations to denser housing forms or inner-city locations. Most of them have quite a strong sense of neighbourhood and neighbourliness, and value it. The troubles of which some of them complain mostly concern health, marriage, education, income and employment: very few of them arise from the type of house or its location.

Scarcely any would be helped, and a great many would lose conditions which they value highly and use fruitfully, if they had to leave their suburban houses for inner-city apartment life. Most of them could have chosen that alternative if they had wanted to.

Most of the few who are disadvantaged by their suburban loca-tions could be better served if they could afford to move nearer to particular friends or relations, or if their suburbs had better public transport to local centres, and had the welfare and childcare services, the kindergartens, women's shelters, community centres, libraries, craft centres and other public services that most suburbs now have, and that three levels of government and sufficient levels of taxation should routinely be providing to all suburbs, including the newest. Extending and improving those standard services would cost very much less than the public and private costs of rebuilding old inner suburbs at two or three times the density, and compelling unwilling people to give up their gardens.

There remain two terminal arguments – in both senses of the word – about the compact city project.

First, its proponents rarely get their sums right. Some who do get them right are the officers of the current South Australian planning review. At first sight, Adelaide's prospects of consolidation looked good. The market is demanding and supplying quite a big flow of small new housing units in existing suburbs, and Adelaide has an unusual amount of vacant public land available for infilling. But most of the market infilling is replacing a big house which housed five people with three small ones each housing one or two: scarcely any of the new small units are actually increasing population density. The planners find that, with the maximum practicable public and private infilling and replacement of existing suburbs, their sleepy state, with the nation's slowest population growth, will still have to meet two-thirds of its predictable demand for new housing on green-field sites at the metropolitan outskirts.

Second, none of the relevant politicians intends to apply any of the coercion that would be necessary to achieve enough consoli-dation to have significant effects on transport costs and emissions.

They won't ration new urban land (though they've long done that in Canberra). They won't compulsorily acquire occupied houses or their backyards for denser development. They won't ration internal space, as has sometimes been done in wartime, by requiring small households with big houses to take boarders or get out. They will sell some surplus schools for housing, but not the playgrounds of continuing schools, and not many public parks or playing fields. The 'Better Cities' demonstration schemes of denser housing will do very little to increase the already considerable output of smaller housing units by private and public suppliers meeting the market demand of many smaller and older households.

Alternatives

THE POLITICIANS MUST KNOW BY NOW THAT THEY cannot consolidate the cities by permissive or persuasive means, and they dare not coerce them. So the cities are plainly going to continue their general character and mode of growth. I do not think that is extravagant, stupid, culturally bad or economically unproductive. But its present costs in fuel consumption, pollution, and road accident and injury are high and ought to be reduced. What might prudent, long-sighted government lead us to do about that? I will presently list some well-known technical possibilities and discuss their political difficulties. I am not as pessimistic as some about those difficulties: I have personal as well as intellectual reasons for disagreeing with younger, more determinist experts who assume that urban transport systems are inevitably determined not by choice but by the cities' physical structure and the available transport technology.

I live now with about a million people in a city eighty kilometres long. Its transport does all the harm its critics, including me, say it does. But as an old Melbourne native, I have also lived happily and fairly efficiently in a city eighty kilometres long with a million people, of whom only one in ten belonged to a household which owned a car. Things have changed since then, but not all for the worse. The post-war suburbs are not as well related to the radial rails as those Melbourne suburbs were. But the radials are less important now that their hub houses a much smaller proportion of metropolitan jobs, shopping and services than it used to do. Market and government have together equipped suburbs with much better centres and commercial and public services. Transport technology is better. If we had the will to tame and cleanse our urban transport, what might we do?

- We could shape planning and transport policies to further improve the district recentring of employment, shopping, services and recreations that are in progress.

- We could improve footpath and cycle routes through many old suburbs and plan better ones through new developments.

- We could increase taxation to finance large losses, for a time, to provide good public transport throughout the metropolis, capable of accepting a coerced shift from private transport.

- To force that shift, we would have to ration car fuel or mileage, or both. The means of rationing are unpleasant, unpopular and imperfect, but they are well-tried and reasonably effective. With some further cost and irritation, the rations can be roughly adjusted to household and business need.

- Finally, we could reform the vehicles. If a 30 per cent improvement in fuel efficiency is available, we could insist on as much of it as saves fuel without increasing pollutant emissions. With the usual long notice we could limit the permitted performance capacity or fuel consumption, or both, of new cars and motorbikes.

We could similarly regulate a range of commercial vehicles which are currently overpowered for their functions. We might even stop affluent, greener-than-green young male ecologists ravaging their private hillsides in two-tonne, four-litre, four-wheel-drive wagons with tyre treads like tank tracks, as they commune with nature.

For most of these purposes, rationing and regulation are both fairer and more effective than taxing and pricing policies. It may always be reasonable to tax fuel quite heavily, but that is not an effective way to get well-off people to use less of it. Also, a lot of the industrial demand for it is necessary and inelastic, and raising those industries' costs and prices may not be the best way to distribute the costs of environmental reform. Rationing by price is inequitable, grossly so if the price has to be high enough to have much effect on upper- and middle-income demand.

Fantasy

A BOLDER STRATEGY OFFERING ECONOMIC AS WELL as environmental gains might combine good, temporarily subsidised public transport with a new kind of Button plan for the automotive industry, as follows.

Over a ten-year period, ask the carmakers, or as many as wish to stay under the forthcoming conditions, to produce, with public financial and research support, a range of super-virtuous vehicles: from motor-assisted pedal cycles and lightweight low-powered motorbikes through electric runabouts to minimum-function cars like underpowered Mini Minors and Morris 1100s, with state-of-the-art fuel economy and emission cleansing, and with van and utility and station-wagon variants. Catch up with the European leaders in electric automation; design cars around a standard range of slide-in, slide-out batteries; equip service stations with one-minute battery exchange gear and recharging units. The new vehicles can be as cheaply or expensively furnished as the market demands, but they must be low-powered and long-lasting. Support the participating firms with any public aids they need. Take a 49 per cent share in the Australian operation of any of them who would welcome that.

In a staged program over the same period, close the frontier to imports which do not meet the same virtuous requirements. Even virtuous imports can be made subject to a quota if necessary, to protect the scale and market base of the Australian producers. What might we have at the end of the transition, when the last old V8 gas-guzzler is in the museum, and the good public transport is carrying the numbers to pay its way? At worst, we would have a safer, greener, fairly unpopular passenger and light-goods transport system, with some better transport than before for people without cars, and some improvement in our employment and exchange figures. At best, our carmakers might be inventive pioneers of virtuous vehicles at a time when the world is driven to follow our example; and because their vehicles would by then be cheap and durable, they might find big export markets in Asia and elsewhere. That would not only bring further improvements in employment and foreign exchange. It would signify that we had recovered confidence in government's capacity to fulfil its proper role in a modern mixed economy.

I know all too well how absurdly improbable that fantasy is, and how little chance anything like it has of being adopted by our prevailing economic rationalists, tax-cutting politicians or business leaders in their tax-evasive six-litre Mercedes and Jaguar twelves.

But I also know two other things. First, that fantasy would actually leave us with perfectly livable, lovable and efficient cities, more helpful to many of their poorer people than the present cities are. I know that from family life in pre-war Melbourne, when most of its passenger transport was public, and from family life in post-war Britain, when most people's cars, though far from fuel-efficient, were about as small and slow and tame as virtuous, state-of-the-art, minimum functional cars could be now. We need designers like Issigonis again, who start from the dimensions of a man's body rather than his ego.

Second, Australians would rather lose their cars than lose their cars and their houses. However hard it may be to get them to trade their big cars for little ones and rationed mileage, or to give them up altogether, it would be harder still to get them to do it by first giving up their houses and gardens and neighbourhood parks and playing fields. I think they are right, for social and economic reasons, and also – though arguing this has not been my task here – for environmental reasons. Suburban life without private cars can be quite tolerable, and without cars it promises better environmental performance than dense cities do.

This is not an excuse for doing nothing. A radical transformation of our wasteful, pollutant and accident-prone urban transport is something I believe we owe to our Australian successors, and to the world at large in its task of global environmental reform.

Summary

I F WE AND OUR POLITICAL LEADERS EVER GENUINELY wish to reform Australia's urban transport for local or global reasons—

(1) we should reform the transport system directly, not indirectly by offering tax and price inducements, or indirectly by trying to build the cities compactly;

(2) it needs more radical, inventive and unpopular action than we have yet considered; but

(3) it nevertheless offers the least-cost, less inequitable and even the least unpopular way, in our Australian conditions, of significantly reducing transport harm.

19

THE FUTURE OF SOCIAL DEMOCRACY (1994)

By the mid-1990s, Stretton had turned his attention to the future of the social-democratic tradition he had upheld since the 1940s. From the high noon of the Whitlam government, it had suffered a long and perhaps terminal decline. Under Hawke and Keating, the Australian Labor Party embraced many of the guiding policies of its traditional adversaries, such as floating exchange rates, free trade and the privatisation of state enterprises. Now Stretton recognised that social democracy was in need of renewal. How should that generous egalitarian vision adapt to an era of galloping technological change, rising gender, generational and global inequality, and looming environmental disaster? Into his seventies, he pursued these questions with undimmed energy, imagination and moral insight.

B Y 'SOCIAL DEMOCRACY', I MEAN THE ATTEMPT, through the long mid-century boom, at managed full employment, cradle-to-grave welfare, declining inequalities of wealth and income, and confident government for an expanding range of collective purposes.

Different parties offer different explanations of the troubles – the slower growth, inflation, unemployment and loss of political support – that have since beset the enterprise.

Hard liberals suggest that too much government reduced economic efficiency and that its costs prompted tax revolts. Too much employment enabled labour to demand and get more pay than there were goods to spend it on. Too much welfare sapped work incentives and tempted people to defraud employers and government in various squalid ways.

Some soft conservatives and Christian socialists think that the moral decline actually came with the liberation movements of the 1960s, whose progressive pretences masked the assertion of strictly selfish and individualist purposes and rights. It was only when the neoclassical economist's assumption of an exclusively self-seeking *homo economicus* thus came true that perceptive people realised – as Adam Smith had – how much the success of capitalism depends on a pervasive personal morality not derived from capitalism itself.

A simpler explanation reminds us that there were always opponents of the purposes of John Maynard Keynes and William Henry Beveridge. All that has happened is that the opponents have at last got the numbers and are winning, which happened as economic progress reduced the proportion of blue-collar voters and increased the proportion of satisfied conservatives. Thinkers on the Right see the people experiencing the capitalist success and learning to support it. Hard Left thinkers see the capitalists recovering their nerve as the long boom struck trouble and pouring resources into a successful counterattack.

A variant of that explanation focuses on the elite. The patrician leaders who implemented the ideas of Keynes and Beveridge through the long boom had been schooled by Depression and wartime comradeship to be generous; often, they were Christian social democrats. Their successors are the spoiled brats of the welfare state and of 1960s self-indulgence, kicking down the ladder as they welcome Friedrich von Hayek's and Milton Friedman's encouragements to cut taxation, minimise welfare dependence and restore some bracing unemployment. Or, to take a more charitable view of their motives, they have simply been persuaded by the dry reasoning that less government and more unhindered self-seeking will help Smith's 'invisible hand' to enrich everyone willing to work. That belief has shifted a critical number of people, including generous and socially concerned people, out of the old winning alliance of middle and poor against rich into the new winning alliance of middle and rich against poor.

There are also more technical explanations of some of the troubles that have beset social democracy. Some economists – from Left, Right and Centre – suspect that new causes of permanent unemployment may be at work. For example, affluence increases the proportion of spending that is discretionary, and people may not continue to demand the proportions of capital-intensive and labour-intensive goods that would keep everyone employed. We are accustomed to jobless growth in agriculture and industry freeing labour to meet rising demand for labour-intensive services. But that happy coincidence may not continue. Some services that are labour-intensive to produce are also labour-intensive to consume: if only from time constraints, the demand for them may not be expandable. Some services are shedding labour as they computerise. Demand for some services is declining as the continuing elaboration of household capital equips people to do more for themselves. Many of the labour-intensive services are partly or wholly public, and effective demand for them is reduced by tax-cutting governments. So overall, demand may be sated; or its further growth may be met by jobless growth in technically advancing industries; or its further growth may depend on some downward redistribution of spending capacity or some expansion of public services, both of which are contrary to prevailing policies. There may also be a fluctuating amount of transitional unemployment from misfitting lead times as reskilling lags behind changes in demand or in techniques of production.

At an opposite pole from those grave diagnoses are three diagnoses that see the recent changes of direction as simply mistaken.

Some on the Left do not think the troubles of the 1970s were serious: social-democratic intentions were being steadily fulfilled, and where they were not the need was for more determined action in the same direction. The conservative reversals of policy were technically mistaken, and were a main cause of the ills they aimed to cure.

Joseph Schumpeter also expected capitalism to self-destruct by following the wrong path: unlike Marx, who thought capitalism's contradictions would kill it, Schumpeter thought one of its virtues would. Its success derived above all from the role of its innovators and entrepreneurs. Schumpeter thought that the drive to innovate had become so powerful that it would overrun its usefulness. When capitalism was mature and needed only conservative maintenance, its restless innovators would not leave well enough alone. If there could be no more improvements to capitalism, they would be driven to think of something else. Capitalism would innovate itself out of existence.

And third, some political theorists suggest that the self-interest of the most ambitious new members of the elite will drive the destructive process of restless change. In intellectual, bureaucratic or political life, how do ambitious young contenders dislodge and replace the old guard? In an innovative, competitive culture, they do it by discrediting prevailing beliefs and presenting themselves as the bearers of new and better policies. But in a mature, well-managed political economy, changes of direction are likely to be for the worse. For example, a modern mixed economy in a globalising world needs pervasive government and a great many public goods and services. These have been developed, bit by bit in the course of economic growth, to meet evident needs. Without them the machine is likely to run down or run wild. But a privatising, deregulating, tax-cutting determination to 'roll back the state' is driven not only by a few groups who expect to profit by it but also by a restless impulse to try something new.

There are strands of truth in all these positions. A great many forces converge and interact to shape our present situation and policies. There are also disagreements between them, about what causes what and what might cause what else in future. But most of the debaters have agreed for some time now that *something* needs to be done about the Western economies' troubles. As to *what* to do, it is of course absurd to simplify the possibilities to three that can be characterised as moving onwards, sideways or backwards. But that is the best this short paper can do.

Think back twenty or thirty years to the emergence of a number of the troubles – for example, to 1968 or 1973: *social-democratic* expectations are upset as the rates of inflation and unemployment defy theory by rising together. Capitalist expectations ought to be upset by now by the performance of capitalism wherever it operates without effective government, as in much of South America. *Socialists* should be upset by now by communist economic performance. In these confusing circumstances, what might it mean in practice for social democrats to press on, turn aside or turn back?

Onwards

U NREPENTANT SOCIAL DEMOCRATS COULD PLAN to repair the Keynesian system, refine the welfare services and begin some serious redistribution of wealth. Keynesian economic management at the time had four faults, of which Keynes had foreseen only one. Keynes was wrong to dismiss what the economists Joan Robinson, Thomas Balogh and Michal Kalecki told him about the need to accompany full employment with effective wage restraint. By the 1970s there was enough cost-driven inflation to prove them right, and enough executive plunder to justify some public restraint of high as well as low incomes from employment.

Second, it was becoming apparent that Keynes was wrong about 'the euthanasia of the rentier'. Inequalities of wealth were still declining, but by dispersal, not from declining rates of return. It was time to repair the collection of death duties, to consider other capital taxes and to introduce, perhaps along the lines proposed by Rudolf Meidner in Sweden, a slow but sure transfer of share ownership to collective institutions designed to reduce inequalities of private wealth and power without increasing bureaucratic command of the economy or reducing the market freedom with which firms need to be directed. That might also have contributed to the 'socialisation of investment' by which Keynes himself – unlike a lot of his post-mortem followers – wanted to stabilise growth and employment.

Third, at Bretton Woods the US negotiators had fatally weakened the international financial regime that Keynes had proposed. By 1971 it was clear who had been right, and a social-democratic US government might have moved to complete the Bretton Woods structure instead of beginning to dismantle it.

Finally, Keynes did not foresee the amount of structural unemployment that might develop for technological or other reasons. By the 1970s, the level of employment needed different management, perhaps including some work rationing and government as the employer of last resort, besides the various kinds of national and regional protection that some governments already applied.

It was also reasonable, as it still is, to reflect that in the course of the century the advanced economies had crossed an important threshold. For the first time in human history they could produce enough to keep all their people in material comfort and security, with access to the basic elements of a common lifestyle. Evidence was accumulating, much of it since brought together by Robert Lane in *The Market Experience*, that above that threshold more income does not increase happiness. The poorest fifth in rich countries are unhappier than the rest, but there seems to be no difference between the average happiness of the other four quintiles. Pay increases bring some temporary pleasure, but it passes; for four-fifths or so of the population, satisfaction with life seems to be determined by other things than income.

That was not true when low productivity still condemned the mass of the people, even in the most advanced economies, to cold, hunger, disease and discomfort. It is not true in the Third World now. So it becomes reasonable for social democrats to argue that, in the West, distribution now matters more than growth: the well-off *can* now afford, without pain, to abolish poverty, at least within their own societies. And there are new questions about the best use of any further growth. The questions are not just for the rich who might give a bit and the intellectuals who might persuade them to it. While the West's workers were still cold and hungry, they had a merciful coincidence of material self-interest and moral principle: they could battle for more for themselves quite consistently with an egalitarian ethic. But how should they think and act now, as they become a comfortable middle class between the Western rich and the Third-World poor? And if we are their policymakers or persuaders, should publicly directed education and television urge them to think and sympathise and give – or should commercial press and television urge them to earn and spend, earn and spend, earn and spend?

That is a practical as well as a moral problem. International aid has not been as generous or as effective as was hoped, and the two shortcomings are linked. Globally, I think aid has done net good, despite the levels of failure and corruption. It has helped to develop the recipient countries' productivity more often than it has hindered it, as is evidenced by countries from Japan and the other tigers to Malaysia, Indonesia and India – wherever there was competent government to receive and use it. And aid has done massive good of kinds that economists cannot see and do not count – what sort of mind values and accounts clean village water over much of India or the massive reduction of smallpox, typhoid, cholera and other diseases at the factor cost of the aid that engineered those blessings? Aid is not always and everywhere a 'mechanism for transferring money from poor people in rich countries to rich people in poor countries' – that is merely the standard excuse that rich people in rich countries give for reducing or refusing aid.

The most beneficent and effective way 'forward' for traditional social democrats who are still centrally concerned with poverty and inequality would be to join with their counterparts in poor countries in thinking hard about how to make aid more effective, and how to persuade Westerners of all classes to provide more of it.

Sideways

NE TROUBLE WITH A FURTHER STRIDE FORward – especially if it includes capital redistribution – is that it will provoke powerful opposition and may not attract much mass support, once the masses are comfortable. But by the 1970s new *discomforts* for rich and poor were threatened by concerns about women's issues, about the natural environment, and about science as sorcerer's apprentice. Social democrats stand for fairer shares. Perhaps their best course now is to extend that principle sideways, broadening its application to comprehend relations between the sexes, between users of common resources and between generations, and to govern the uses of such scary items as genetic engineering and uncensorable communications. That might attract less resistance and broader support and appeal to some new coincidences of self-interest and high principle.

Thus, extending sideways rather than onwards – broadening the scope of social democracy rather than advancing its vanguard against the capitalist citadel – should have been a promising direction for the democratic Left, for a number of reasons.

First, it promised to give new life and urgency to the movement's traditional commitments to equality and to a positive economic role for government. Neither feminist nor green concerns could safely be left to the market; nor could genetic engineering or worldwide broadcasting. Old reasons for wanting to regulate employers' treatment of workers would be strengthened by the women's demands. So should the old debate about the desirable limits of equality. For feminists on the Right, gender equality meant giving women a fair share of the established capitalist inequalities – half the rich surgeons and barristers and half the chief executives taking a million a year from their companies should be women. Among other effects, that would greatly increase inequalities among women. That troubled feminists on the Left, who wanted both more equality with men and more equality among women. Anyone might be anxious about the potentialities of unregulated genetic engineering or the criminal potentialities of unregulated pay TV: social democracy must surely benefit from a revival and rethinking of the classical debates about necessary and unnecessary freedoms, constraints and inequalities.

Resource and environmental imperatives should have similar effects. People cannot change the way they use resources without changing their relations with each other. Energy can be conserved in ways that provide frugal shares for everyone or in ways that freeze the poor to death. Environmental policies can be designed to deal anywhere from fairly to very unfairly between rich and poor and between generations. To leave these choices to market forces is to choose with a vengeance, often with radical increases of inequality. And so on – on all these fronts, the modern predicament calls for active, fair-minded, forward-planning government of the economy, and should attract more support for that sort of government than social democrats can now attract from their dwindling blue-collar constituency alone.

The new issues also have interesting effects on patterns of interest and altruism. Capitalists' and workers' self-interest motivated plenty of the development of modern productivity, but the social-democratic use and distribution of modern output also owes a good deal to support and leadership from well-off people acting against their own individual and class interests. Now men are being asked to give up material advantages over women, and workers are asked to forgo some margins of pay and employment in the interest of ameliorating polluted neighbourhoods and sharing with generations unborn. In both cases there are recalcitrant minorities. Some men continue to discriminate against women. Some workers in threatened monocultures or company towns face losing too much altogether to green reforms, and so resist them. But most male workers and, as far as I know, all their unions have dropped their one-time opposition to industrial equality for women. In Australia and Western Europe, there was never much truth in the US picture of conservation as an upper-class hobby; the green movement has more often been led from the Left, including by some unions. All things considered, I think that men's response to the women's movement and workers' response to the environmental movement have been of a kind that no public-choice theorists could possibly explain: a complex mixture of self-interest with quite surprising amounts of sympathy, cooperation and generosity. Compared with the old working-class movement, which felt no strain between its self-interest and its egalitarian principles, social democracy can claim to have become – so to speak – a Better Person.

Backwards

BUT IT IS ALSO, DISCONCERTINGLY, A WEAKER force, beaten time and again these days by its old and new opponents on the Right, and compromised or betrayed by some of its own leaders, as a century of progress towards greater equality is halted and reversed, and the institutions that achieved it are one by one sold off or dismantled. It is time to look at the third response to recent troubles, the one that says: 'Wrong way, go back.'

I need not spell out this program in much detail because increasingly it is the one we live with. Its vision is of a world economy in which free exchange will locate production wherever in the world it can be done most efficiently, expose it to unhindered competition, and subject it to worldwide consumer sovereignty. According to David Ricardo's thinking, that should maximise world output; according to Paul Samuelson's thinking, it should reduce international inequalities by generating equal pay for equal work.

If this program worked as predicted, it would deserve to count as a great leap forward rather than backward. There have been periods of widespread free trade in the past that have not worked in that way, but production and distribution have since been transformed by modern technology and the instantaneous transmission of money and information, and an open world economy might have different risks and benefits now. Nevertheless, most of the deregulation of the last twenty years repeals regulations introduced in the previous forty years, and dismantles or privatises institutions created or nationalised during those years, so it can be seen as a return to past policies, if not necessarily past outcomes.

Critics of this reverse direction have diverse objections to it. Its vision is said to be bogus: governments are actually cutting taxes and changing rules selectively, for sectional or national advantage rather than genuine global liberation. Welfare cuts and user charges are an attack on the poor by the rich. So are the downward shifts of taxation. Deregulation both increases and maldistributes inequalities as it liberates unproductive and antisocial business behaviour by which wrong people get rich. Not all the privatisations improve efficiency, and even those that do are often improvident in that governments use the capital proceeds of asset sales to fund tax cuts, thus dissaving nationally by diverting private investment funds to consumption. And so on. But I would rather talk more generally about the theory and practice of the retreat from government that these policies represent. What follow are some reasons for believing, of the enterprise as a whole, that its theory is incoherent and its practice often self-defeating.

The theoretical objections are mostly familiar objections to neo-classical economic theory. I will refer to two of them: the inconsistent application of the assumption that individual self-interest is what drives most economic activity and policymaking, and the incoherent theory of what neoclassicists choose, I think misleadingly, to call the labour market.

The limits of self-interest

Adam Smith thought self-interest operated within the constraints of a morality intrinsic to human nature. If this morality is actually a product of culture as well as nature, then to the extent that modern life erodes it, it needs to be replaced and enforced by regulation. The nearer economic actors actually get to the *homo economicus* of modern neo-classical and public-choice theory, the more government they need, not the less. Fred Hirsch complained twenty years ago (in *Social Limits to Growth*) that capitalist theory and practice were eroding the exogenous morality on which capitalist efficiency depended. Similar conclusions can be drawn from the British economist Ronald Coase's theories. Modern production is very complicated and needs elaborate coordination. Coase simplified the modes of coordination to two: exchange and organisation. Firms use both, buying items or organising their production within the firm. Each has transaction costs. Fear of immoral behaviour raises the costs of both. Preventive regulation, reflecting and reinforcing a moral culture, lowers those costs. Deregulation, which makes cheating easier and rewards it, and therefore compels all parties to take expensive private precautions against being cheated, raises the costs and lowers the efficiency of both methods of coordinating production – that is, the efficiency of both market and firm.

There is also a self-interested inconsistency in the privatisers' assumptions about the role of self-interest. Especially in the public-choice literature, public employees are assumed to be so individually self-seeking that public policies and public enterprises rarely serve – or are even intended to serve – their ostensible public purposes. But private owners are assumed to harness their directors' and employees' interests to their own without difficulty, even with Delaware charters and directors commanding the proxies at annual meeting. Directors have actually been taking anything from two or three to twenty or thirty times as much money from their owners as the highest-paid public directors do, and taking it as freely from failing and over-indebted companies as from successful ones. And the purpose and effect of many of their debt-financed takeovers have had little to do with their owners' interests or their firms' efficiency. Why expect individual self-interest to work *for* the owners' interests within private firms but *against* the owners' interests in public firms? But faith in the ungoverned invisible hand persists, and shapes policies that are designed to increase efficiency but that in practice quite often reduce it.

Privatisation

There are similar strains in dry attitudes to privatisation. Everyone agrees that natural monopolies of essential services need some public control. Government can own public monopolies, or it can regulate private monopolies. Which works best depends on local conditions and capacities. For technical reasons, it is easier in some services than in others for regulators to prevent private monopolists from misusing their advantages. Governments vary in their capacity for skilful and incorruptible regulation. Public services – as alternatives to regulated private services – vary widely in their efficiency. But doctrinaire privatisers persist, apparently assuming that private employees serve their owners' interests more faithfully than public employees do, and that all governments are less efficient as owners than they are as regulators. But I know of few attempts – and no very successful ones – to justify those beliefs on practical or theoretical grounds. In any case, as already mentioned, many public enterprises have been privatised for a cruder reason: to spend capital in relief of taxation.

There are also inconsistencies in many deregulators' understanding of relations between corporate and individual competition. Economists do now recognise industries in which monopolist or oligopolist advantages allow more inventive and provident performance than incessant competition would allow. But public enterprises – from the Cavendish Laboratory to the French and Japanese fast trains and the universities' lead in developing solar-powered vehicles – are rarely credited with the same long-sighted or creative use of their advantages. At an individual level, some economists understand why the firms that compete most successfully tend to be those whose employees compete least with each other, cooperating readily because (among other encouragements) their jobs and expectations are secure. But what is thus admired at Toyota gets less credit from labour-market theorists when it elicits good performance at Renault or in public hospitals, research services or telecommunications. The productive effects of fair and secure conditions of employment (when well managed) are noticed or not by these theorists depending on the conditions of ownership in which they occur.

Contradictions

Those are not the worst of the inconsistencies in theories about workers' motives. On some pages of their standard textbooks, students learn about the alternative income effect and the substitution effect of price and wage changes and the indeterminate relation between them: if earners' pay is increased or their taxes are cut, they may respond by working less, or the same amount, or more. Theory cannot predict which. But on other pages, students learn that Alfred Marshall's supply/demand cross, which depicts the relations between supply and demand and the price of carrots, also depicts the relations between supply and demand and the price of labour: if wages rise, workers will offer more work but employers will hire less; as wages fall, workers will offer less work but employers will hire more; so to end unemployment, it is only necessary for workers to lower their asking prices until demand and supply come into equilibrium.

That is not the end of the contradictions. On another page students learn that rising wages have historically *reduced* working hours; nevertheless, the supply curve for US labour has been vertical for half a century despite a doubling of real wage rates. But from tables on other pages, students can work out for themselves that the reasons for that stable supply of labour changed radically during that half-century. These contradictions are not from warring schools of thought; they are all from the same eminent authors and cohabit within the same textbooks. They are there not by mistake but of necessity: worse contradictions appear in the neoclassical model if it tries to do without them.

These confusions do double harm. They prompt some bad policies. More generally, they encourage an unjustified belief in the regularity of economic behaviour and discourage open-eyed and open-minded observation and understanding of the actual springs of economic behaviour: how widely they can vary with time, place, occupation and other circumstances; what a range of relations can hold between self-interest, culture and government; how people's conceptions of their individual and class and communal interests are shaped and change; how the quality and intent of government can vary; and so on. It is not promising to try to govern such a changeable system with an unobservant, doctrinaire preference for market over government. (Nor were the reverse preferences any more sensible in the command economies.) Kyoko Sheridan's book *Governing the Japanese Economy* shows how often, through the century and a half of Japan's modernisation, her economic bureaucrats saw the economy develop from needing one sort of government to needing a different sort, and how successfully they have adapted their policies to the changing needs. Axiomatic theorists, whose conception of science must include a core of universally applicable theory, can rarely bring themselves to behave so flexibly, and sure enough, Japan's economic ministries appoint scarcely any economists to influential policymaking positions. Meanwhile, in English-speaking countries the axiomatic approach to policymaking is having some of the perverse effects in practice that its theoretical confusions would lead one to expect.

There may well be disagreement about the successes and the imperfections of the US economy after Ronald Reagan, the UK economy after Margaret Thatcher, and the New Zealand economy after Douglas. But notice that even their successes did not all accord with their theoretical expectations. The revolutions that took British Steel from being the least to the most profitable steelmaker in Europe and took British coalmining some way in the same direction were engineered by public rather than private owners. British carmakers, bankrupted under private ownership, were restored to saleable health by public owners. And of course there have been cases of the opposite contrast, between worse public and better private management. The worst effect of a doctrinaire belief that public ownership is always best or that private ownership is always best is that it directs reformist energy to shifting activity from one sector to the other by privatising or nationalising – energy that could be more fruitfully applied to improving the performance of both sectors.

Allocating resources

NEXT, THERE MAY BE FUNCTIONAL RELATIONS between the degrees of freedom enjoyed by different industries. Sweden offers an example, if one forgets the recent Swedish troubles and focuses on the past successes of Swedish capitalism. For forty post-war years, Sweden was the freest free trader in Europe – but it managed to be so, without severe exchange difficulties, by maintaining the tightest public financial controls in Europe. Australia through the 1980s could have freed *either* her trade *or* her financial system without much harm to her balance of payments – but freeing them both at once, to allow unlimited foreign borrowing to finance a rising import bill, has brought serious trouble. I think – controversially – that it has always been a mistake to suppose that free trade in money would have the benign effects that market theorists expect of free trade in goods. It takes a very, very true believer to believe that the world's financial resources have been allocated and used more productively since the financial deregulation of the 1970s and 1980s than they were before those changes. To stick to the case I know best, Australia's financial deregulation has had effects opposite to each of the five main purposes for which it was done. Among the effects are about 20 per cent more central-city office space than can be used, $30 billion or more of bank losses, $120 billion of new private foreign debt – debt whose servicing now costs much of what Australia's exports earn and that continues to escalate – and a sevenfold increase in real interest rates over those prevailing for the previous half-century.

A different abdication of national financial control is in progress in the attempt to give Europe a single currency unaccompanied by a central government with the standard instruments – or what used to be the standard instruments – of macroeconomic policy. I agree with Wynne Godley's observation in the *London Review of Books* that 'there is only one theoretical position which would make sense of such a program: one which ... holds that any attempt to conduct positive macroeconomic policy would, except in the very short term, only add to inflation and, in the end, make unemployment even worse than it otherwise would have been'.

I believe that similar arguments apply to prevailing theories and policies about national economic structure, the distribution of income, the motivation of private corporate performance and other issues.

Modern technology and organisational complexity increase rather than reduce the need for pervasive macroeconomic and microeconomic government and for public input to private and household production. The worst thing about trying to expand output by shrinking the public sector is not its cruel effect on distribution or welfare or national independence, but its incompetence in its own terms, as incoherent theories shape policies whose effects differ, often radically, from their intentions. Whether one wants Right, Left, green or feminist outcomes, or some national and international regulation of genetic engineering or of what is transmitted into the world's households, nurseries and thieves' kitchens by the new broadcasting modes, one needs government whose capacities and morals can be trusted. If present government falls short of that, the need is to reform it rather than weaken and reduce it. A modern mixed economy cannot be productive, equitable or environmentally prudent without it.

20

TWO LEADERS (2000)

Stretton was a keen observer of Australia's leaders. 'Australian business and political leadership has been generally mediocre and uninventive,' he lamented in 1985. This was not an elitist putdown, he insisted. 'Caring about the qualities of a society's most influential people does not necessarily signal a distrust of democracy.' On the contrary, democrats should be interested in the qualities of the nation's leaders precisely because their decisions affected everyone. In this essay, he compares two of the most influential: Herbert 'Nugget' Coombs and Paul Keating, both the sons of working-class families, with a shared interest in the future of Australia's Indigenous people, but opposing visions of its economy and society. Coombs exemplified the traditions of disinterested public service that had created Australian social democracy; but how to understand Keating, a product of that tradition who had overturned some of its most cherished beliefs?

HERBERT WAS A SHORT, SKINNY BOY WHO GREW up in Western Australian country towns, attending the schools where his father taught. He went to Perth for his secondary schooling but came back to the country in 1922 as an apprentice teacher. That year he played football in a town team with an able Aboriginal captain. Aboriginal children were not doing as well as whites at their schoolwork, but Herbert found that some brief one-to-one tuition could resolve their difficulties and level them up with the rest.

In Western Australia at the time, Indigenous people had no state or Commonwealth votes. Whatever the law said, its institutions did not give them much protection from white violence, exploitation or sexual misuse. They were officially regarded as racially inferior and likely to die out, but half-caste children had enough white blood to be worth rescuing, and an act of parliament allowed them to be removed by force to white-run orphanages whose whereabouts their parents were not allowed to know. Young Herbert nevertheless respected Aborigines and held more hope for them. But he was also clever, got a degree by part-time study and switched from teaching to other work before long.

Late in the century, another ex-teacher was researching how Commonwealth public servants had deprived Aboriginal Australians of their right to vote. She came across a file of letters from Shadrach James to the Department of the Interior. He and his father had also been teachers. His father, an Indian, had moved to Australia as a young man. When he soon afterwards caught typhoid, Aboriginal people befriended him and treated him with traditional herbal medicine. He recovered, and worked in Aboriginal schools, where he taught some of the first leaders of Aboriginal political movements. He married the daughter of an Aboriginal woman and a white man. Their son Shadrach progressed much as white Herbert did a few years later (attended his father's school, qualified as a teacher and then taught for a time). Out of work in 1928, Shadrach moved with his young wife and children to a Victorian country town, where he could earn his living in a fruit-processing cooperative. He was soon an elected official of his union, of the local government and of the Aboriginal Progressive Association of Victoria. At intervals through the next seventeen years he wrote to the Commonwealth government to suggest practical things which it could do to improve the lives of Indigenous people.

Public servants treated Shadrach James's letters and their author with contempt. Cursory notes dismissed him, first because he was unknown and then because he was known – 'he's been writing to us for years'. They doubted his word, hinted that he had a police record, denied that he was a real Aborigine, and insisted that the Commonwealth leave Aboriginal issues to the states. Half a century later, reading through this miserable record of black intelligence insulted by white stupidity, the researcher grew increasingly angry and depressed until – with shock, disbelief, then tears of joy – she came to a memo dated 27 October 1945, which seemed to come from some different civilisation altogether. It was addressed to the head of the prime minister's department. For the first time in sixteen years it referred to James as Mr James. It recommended that the government adopt his intelligent proposals. A bureau of Aboriginal affairs might be established to do the work, but ministers should first consult Mr James about its design.

The memo was signed H.C. Coombs. Skinny little Herbert, nicknamed Nugget, now a Doctor of Philosophy in banking from the London School of Economics, wartime Director of Rationing and Director-General of Postwar Reconstruction, had not forgotten his football captain or his black pupils. He was one of a number of able, educated men, imported to the public service during the war, who transformed it after the war. He did not think his nickname meant that he was worth his weight in gold; his country childhood taught him that a bullock team's nugget was the quiet, stocky beast that never stopped working and gave the team its strength. Seven prime ministers kept him in office for thirty-five years, valued his advice and usually followed it. But it took twenty-two of those years after he read Shadrach James's letter, and a new generation of Aboriginal leaders, to create the white goodwill and the Commonwealth powers to begin doing what Mr James had recommended.

Through those years, Nugget was more occupied with money than with race. He was one of Keynes's earliest disciples. Prime Minister Chifley was another. Together they managed to make most of Australia's wartime banking controls permanent. Introducing the necessary legislation in 1945, the prime minister said:

> If, after the war, the trading banks' holding of liquid reserves with the Commonwealth Bank were placed freely at their disposal they would be able by increasing their advances and purchases of securities to build up a secondary credit expansion of formidable dimensions … The Commonwealth Bank must be given authority to immobilise the liquid reserves of the trading banks to whatever extent may be desirable. No responsible government could afford to move forward into the postwar period without adequate means at its disposal to cope with inflationary and deflationary movements in the monetary and banking system.

The public bank could thus expand or contract the amount of private lending without destabilising the rate of interest or (therefore) the likely productivity of the credit. There were also national controls on the entry and exit of capital funds, on borrowing from foreign banks and on foreign ownership of Australian banks and some other industries. Life insurers were given tax incentives to lend at low interest to government and for housing.

A conservative coalition soon replaced that Labor government. It retained a number of the wartime public service chiefs, with Coombs as head of the Commonwealth Bank, then the Reserve Bank. Prime Minister Menzies had promised the electors 'a bonfire' of the remaining wartime controls. Coombs persuaded him not to burn the bank controls, but he kept his promise about prices, rents, rationing and some other items. The bonfire coincided with the Korean War and a record world price for wool. The Australian economy responded with 21 per cent inflation in a single year. Appropriate action stopped the inflation as promptly as it had started, and lessons were learned both from its sudden outbreak and from its quick end. The Liberal prime minister and the Country Party treasurer had grown up in country towns, then lived through the Great Depression. They distrusted bankers and had Coombs regulate them throughout the long life of their government. Helped by other wartime recruits to the public service, a mostly bipartisan strategy gave the country thirty years of steady growth, full employment, rising home ownership, declining inequality, restrained inflation, low real interest, balanced trade and payments, and negligible foreign debt. Thus, the productive economy delivered better income and housing to more of its poorer households than most advanced economies did through those years. There was less for public welfare to do, and it was accordingly cheaper.

In the 1970s that strategy came to need repair or replacement. The economy was hit by stagflation – an unexpected combination of inflation and unemployment. That had a number of causes. The United States withdrew some critical support from the international financial system. Some international prices changed to Australia's disadvantage. Technical progress had farms and factories employing fewer people to make more and cheaper products, while rising incomes made labour-intensive human services relatively dearer. Demand shifted accordingly, making full employment harder to maintain.

A new generation of political and public service leaders had to respond to the new conditions. They were advised by a generation of Australian economists whose education had come under increasing

American influence. Many of them thought that the continuing Keynes/Coombs policies were main causes of the stagflation. They set about dismantling them. Through the last quarter of the century, they freed the financial system from effective government and cut the protection of Australian agriculture and industry. The banks responded with exactly the inflationary expansion of unproductive credit that Coombs had predicted. Without the lost controls, inflation had to be tamed instead by methods which halved the rates of investment and growth, and quadrupled the numbers unemployed. Together, the financial and trading freedoms ran the country into serious payments deficit and self-expanding foreign debt.

*

In 1968, before that rakes' progress began, Nugget had retired from the Reserve Bank. He spent the rest of his long life doing his best to help Australia's arts and its Indigenous people. Those two good causes also got good service from a boy who was born a year before Nugget read Shadrach James's letter, and was elected to parliament a year after Nugget retired from the bank. Paul was the first child of Matt and Min Keating, working-class Irish Catholic Australians. Matt was a boilermaker, working for wages when Paul was born, later a partner in a firm he helped to found. He was a tough, hard-working man with no respect for the intellectual classes. Min was a lively, sometimes fiery woman, and adored Paul. Friends see Paul as a combination of the two. Until he was twenty-two, they lived in a twelve-square fibro house in a working-class bit of Bankstown. They were a solid family, faithful to what Paul's biographer calls 'the three traditional adages of Catholic childhood (go to mass, join the union, support Labor)'.

Paul's sister Anne remembers him as 'a normal larrikin kid'. At his Catholic school he was in a clever class which sometimes gave its teachers trouble. He got by without distinguishing himself, and chose to leave school before he turned fifteen. He worked for local government, then for a Hong Kong trading company, then for the Electricity Commission, and managed a rock band in some of his spare time. He got some part-time secondary and technical education but didn't persist with it. He was a quick learner, but more from listening to people talk than from formal study.

Neither study nor his father's business really grabbed him. Politics did. He letterboxed for the Labor Party at twelve and joined it at fifteen. He was president of what is now Young Labor at seventeen, a federal MP at twenty-six and a minister (the youngest in Labor's history) at thirty-one, in the last three weeks of Whitlam's government. He had become a friend and disciple of Jack Lang, the radical Labor premier sacked by the governor of New South Wales back in 1932. He admired and learned much from Rex Connor, the Whitlam minister who fought but failed to keep Australian oil and minerals in Australian ownership.

Early in 1983 a general election returned Labor to power. Its electoral platform promised 'the restoration and maintenance of full employment'. For that purpose:

> Labor believes that a dramatic change is required in the direction of economic policy, with new methods and programs ... The achievement of our objectives therefore requires a national economic and social strategy. Such a strategy must involve an expanded interventionist role by government through the processes of economic planning and specific industry, manpower and regional policies.

Under Hayden as leader, that manifesto was the work of two able economists, shadow treasurer Ralph Willis and backbencher John

Langmore. But in the weeks before the election, Keating and Hawke replaced Willis and Hayden. Starting dramatically in their first months in office, the new pair led the government and the Labor Party to adopt most of the New Right program of deregulation, privatisation and small government (more of it than the Liberal–National government they replaced had yet adopted). Then for thirteen years (eight as treasurer and five as prime minister) Paul put into practice as much of that program as he could.

To many old Labor hands and young intellectuals, that seemed the worst betrayal of the century. There had been others. In 1917 Labor prime minister Billy Hughes changed sides to lead a conservative government. Labor treasurer Joe Lyons did the same in 1932. In the 1950s 'split', some members left (or were driven out) to form the rival Democratic Labor Party.

Those departures at least left the Labor Party intact in opposition to battle for the causes it had always stood for. Scullin and Theodore led Labor back to power twelve years after Hughes' desertion. Curtin and Chifley did it nine years after Lyons' desertion. Whitlam did it seventeen years after the split. But since Hawke and Keating led the whole parliamentary party to change sides in 1983, the electors have had no chance to vote for any alternative to the Right strategy, which both major parties now offer them.

How could Matt Keating's boy lead that betrayal of the party's history and aspirations? He was not its only leader, nor the sole cause of it. But such changes may be easiest to understand in the minds which made or believed in them, and we can try to understand this one in Paul Keating's experience of it.

He had been seven years in opposition as a shadow minister for mines and energy. He learned about that industry as he learned most things, by going and seeing and asking and listening. He talked with other ranks as well as bosses, and boasted of having been down every mine in the country. He made friends with the industry's leaders by believing most of what they said and promising most of what they asked for, while expressing continuing respect for Connor and the other Labor leaders whose policies he was quietly promising to reverse. A Shell executive admired how 'Paul Keating turned it all around without appearing disloyal'. A BHP executive thought that 'by the time [he] got into government in 1983 he understood mining and energy better than any politician. And the more he learned about the industry, the more he knew that Connor had been wrong.' While he continued to revere the past leaders and traditions of the party, his biographer reports that he was 'spreading the message that there was now a new generation of Labor politicians who had not grown up in the trade union movement and who were not bound by dogma. He was openly scathing about the party's Left wing, whose members he referred to as troglodytes with outdated attitudes.'

But for one 'not bound by dogma', the daddy of all dogmas was lying in wait. How much of the prevailing neoclassical economic theory Paul Keating knew before he became treasurer is not on record. What is on record is his opinion of its chief Australian exponent in 1979:

No department in the Western world has had such a rein on economic policy, with a more compliant cabinet, than the treasury in this country has had for four years ... it has doubled the unemployment level in Australia, has failed to contain inflation and has dragged Australia deeper into recession.

After a few months as treasurer in 1983, he was a true believer in the department's dogma and most of its policies. Once again, he had learned quickly by listening to the relevant experts. At the heart of what was learned was (in a crude summary) this.

Everyone is born with a mouth and a pair of hands (a need to consume, and a capacity to produce). As means of production some own land, physical capital, money to lend or invest; and all can learn skills and work.

Firms bid for those factors of production. Equitably, the people who contribute them are paid their market prices. In rent, dividends, interest or wages, they each get what they contribute to the value of the final products. The firms compete to use those means of production most efficiently, inventively, productively, and compete to sell their products to consumers. Those which produce most efficiently and give the consumers the greatest value for their money are the ones which survive.

It follows that in dealing with business, government must often be cruel to be kind. Open the national economy to all comers. Enforce competitive principles within it. Let inefficient firms and industries fail, freeing their resources for more competitive uses.

How could another Paul on the road to his Damascus (a quick learner passionate to get it right and do it right) resist such a brilliant resolution of the human dilemmas not just of economic scarcity, but also of conflict and cooperation, good and evil, self and other?

He did not have to abandon all his traditional commitments. In the market miracle there is still a role for government. It must provide defence, law and order, some public infrastructure and services. It may even intervene in the economy, in accord with old Labor values, to prevent monopoly or other market failures. And a productive economy is not all a society needs. A lot of its output needs to reach people who are outside the productive system, and perhaps also some losers from the competition within it. Families, charities and government all do some of that welfare work. It follows that you don't have to be hard-hearted to believe in the neoclassical imagination of untrammelled competitive efficiency. That high productivity can be accompanied by social policies anywhere from mean to generous. Now that communism is dead, Right and Left may well agree how to produce most wealth and income. But they can still fight elections about its distribution. And with transitional hardships in mind, they may also disagree about how quickly to drive the economy in the agreed new direction.

Paul certainly came to believe the essentials of the vision. Its logic and elegance helped. But at its heart is an act of pure imagination: how perfectly might an economic system work if government left it alone? There has never been such a system. But history and observation can support the dream if you want them to. All actual economies have lots of government. They all have lots of imperfections. Connect the two and what more proof do you need? It's at least worth a try.

Thus, the rationalist or 'neoliberal' version of neoclassical economic theory seemed to promise optimum investment, employment, growth and wealth – and abundant means of compensating losers, if that were desired. It also promised least inflation.

Except for inflation, all the promises have been broken. A dozen good books have lately explained why, and done their best to measure the ill effects of doubled and trebled rates of real interest, diminished investment, continuing unemployment, rising insecurity, steeper inequality, unbalanced trade and payments, a dangerous increase of foreign debt, and a great switch of capital from new productive investment to incessant unproductive gambling on asset values and unstable rates of interest and exchange. It turns out that deregulation can reduce the efficient allocation and use of resources. In some circumstances, including twentieth-century Australia's, free trade can kill more employment than it creates. It can increase the import bill faster than it increases export earnings. That can depress exchange rates and raise import prices as far as tariffs used to raise them. Privatisation can degrade some services, and taxpayers can lose more than they gain by it. Small government can leave too few public servants, with too little skill or institutional memory, to do what a quick-changing, high-tech economy needs its public sector to do. This essay need not repeat that familiar history, or detail the flaws in the theory that guided it. Instead, it tries to understand how it came to happen by imagining Paul Keating's experience of it.

He hated the ill effects but refused to surrender to them. As far as resources and tax restraint allowed, he did his best to keep the government's social promises. He financed Health Minister Blewett's creation of the country's first satisfactory system of universal medical insurance. He financed better family and other allowances for a wider range of needs than before. He was a generous supporter of the arts. With his colleagues he did a lot of things, some kinder than others, to train and occupy people while they were unemployed, and to give special options and incentives to the young and the long-term unemployed.

Above all, especially as prime minister, he worked hard for Indigenous people's land rights and other opportunities. He did that for the best of reasons, knowing it brought no net gain of votes. His radical Redfern speech in 1992 was a milestone on the road to reconciliation. He still speaks of that work as his best work, for which he most hopes to be remembered. The young Paul, passionate for good causes and doubly effective for them as statesman and streetfighter, was there to the end.

One strong critic of the Right economic strategy went out of his way to praise Paul's personal commitment to his Indigenous policies. Nugget Coombs, in his nineties, still spent time out of town with the Indigenous people for whom he continued to work. In an article written not long before his death, he praised the prime minister's response to the High Court's *Mabo* decision, and went on to wonder about the enigma of the man: how could he have such vision and human sympathy but use such gutter language?

*

As the mistaken economic strategy blundered on, the other Paul became as deceptive and quarrelsome and unconvincing as the worst of his colleagues in defending the indefensible. But his friends' accounts of him suggest that even in that role he was more mistaken – or 'resolute in error' – than dishonest. His 1983 conversion to free trade and global integration endured. If the miracle was working imperfectly, that could not be theory's fault or the market's fault: home and foreign governments, bemused by troglodytes, must still be hindering it.

Besides the pure attractions of the vision, it offered more practical temptations. I can't know what part each of them played in moving Paul to act as he did. Readers can do their own guessing. But it is not hard to list the available temptations. Imagine that you believe in the new strategy and expect it to succeed. What additional attractions might it have for Labor contenders for power? How might you persuade people to tolerate its early hardships? When it fails to perform, how might you pretend that it still will? When it plainly won't, what might you do instead of pretending?

A first thought might be that if the Right strategy is likely to succeed, the Labor Party had better grab it and run with it before the enemy do.

For the Right faction of the party, the strategy has double political value. It got more support from business, the media and academic economists than Willis's and Langmore's official election platform could attract. And those respectable media, business and academic voices could help the Right faction to rubbish the Left faction as (according to the occasion) unworldly socialists, union racketeers or nostalgic troglodytes.

Some of the respectable voices were beginning to blame the unemployed or their welfare incomes for their unemployment and other unsatisfactory behaviour. Labor ministers could call the criticism cruel and unfair, while dodging some of it themselves by doing moderately punitive things to train the unemployed and keep them hunting for the jobs the strategy was failing to create.

Paul's years as treasurer saw unemployment and its welfare costs increase by half or more. How might you defend policies which let that happen? You could explain that, in the worldwide transition to a global market economy, there are bound to be transitional stresses and costs. Cowards and sentimentalists may falter, and long to retreat to the cosseted, protected, unprogressive past. But a changing world allows no way back. Only market forces, finally freed of short-term, sectional, restrictive state intervention, can deliver the growth which can keep us up with the world leaders, and keep employment up with the rate of technological advance. But to prevail, that new vision requires some old-fashioned virtue: tough government, steady purpose, hard decisions, the long view. There must be no flinching even from the Recession We Had to Have (Neal Blewett remembers himself, Don Watson and Annita Keating imploring Paul not to outdo that PR disaster with the Unemployment We Had to Have).

All parties play silly rhetorical tricks. The cycle bottoms and begins to recover. Official unemployment descends from 11 per cent to 9 per cent. Some reclassifications, disqualifications and drop-outs get it down to 7 or 8 per cent. Growth recovers to 3 or 4 per cent for nine continuous quarters! (Sounds a lot longer than two years.) The upward progress looks wonderfully steep on tall, narrow graphs whose vertical axes run only from 0 to 4 per cent (growth) or from 12 to 6 per cent (unemployment). If you're in office, the great transformation is at last rewarding your stoic endurance of the transitional pain. If you're in opposition, the government's incompetence is endangering a normal cyclical upturn with needless increases of insecurity, current account deficit and foreign debt.

Five and ten and fifteen years pass. The promised benefits of high investment, full employment and balanced payments continue to recede. The promises are harder to defend by serious argument. Two retreats from reason beckon. You can switch from repeating the arguments to characterising the arguers. Your lot are the bold, the innovators, the future-makers. The other lot are yesterday's men, troglodytes, stuck in the past. When even that wears thin, you can retreat to realism. Face it, social democracy is dead. Corporate America rules. Best comply, and glean what crumbs you can from the new masters.

Besides the PR conflicts, there are three serious ones. Each springs from a contradiction at the heart of the Right strategy.

First, the continuing unemployment forces expensive dole and welfare spending, but you have promised not to increase taxes.

Second, technical progress keeps increasing the need for higher education and training. Many of the students and their parents can't pay for the extra education the economy needs them to have. If they don't get it, our industries can't stay competitive. But you have promised not to increase taxes.

Third, research keeps adding to the expensive things doctors can do to improve people's health and prolong their lives. In half a century it has raised the amount that can usefully be spent on health services from about 3 per cent to 10 or 12 per cent of national income. But you have promised not to increase taxes.

Each process increases some costs which are best paid, or can only be paid, by government. And the three together dramatically increase the proportion of non-earning years in most people's lifetimes, and therefore the proportion of income they need to transfer from their earning years to their children's and their own non-earning years. Families make some of those transfers in cash and kind. But for many of them, public income transfers and superannuation schemes can be cheaper, safer and fairer than their private equivalents.

Hence the compound contradiction. On the one hand, most people want the education and training that their career choices call for. They want as many years of life and health as medical advances can offer. They want a secure income in retirement, which they're likely to enjoy for much longer than their grandparents averaged. On the other hand, their political, professional and business leaders keep urging them to vote for less taxation and smaller government, and the ruling theory defines those negatives as necessary conditions of economic growth and sustained employment.

Why don't you, as a politician, defy the theory and tax citizens for the public services they plainly want to have? Here comes what seems at first sign to be the dumbest paradox of all. There are quite promising signs that solid majorities would welcome that strategy. They may vote 'No' if party pollsters simply ask them if they want high taxes. But whenever they have been asked if they would pay a few more percentage points of tax to improve services to children, improve schools, keep technical and university education up to standard and open to competent students however poor their families, cut hospital waiting lists, improve the incomes and care available to old people, keep research and development up to US or European standards, keep banks and post offices open in country towns, and save Australia's soil and forests and river systems, 60 per cent or more have always said 'Yes'. For twenty years majorities have been telling pollsters that they would pay higher taxes for good purposes. Why do their politicians fear they wouldn't, urge them not to, and accuse each other of plotting to tax them nevertheless? In five of the six elections which Hawke and Keating won, they were offering slightly higher tax than their opponents were. Their successor's GST has been accepted much more calmly than either side expected.

It's a fair guess that the politicians privately fear what the influential rich might do to politicians who dared to tax them effectively.

But their public excuse, endorsed by rich Right think-tanks, is that progressive personal taxation would drive foreign firms out of the country, deny Australian firms any serious executive talent by driving that out too, and ruin us all.

So if higher tax is unthinkable, how else can you, as politician, sustain the public infrastructure and finance the desirable increase of educational, medical and welfare services and superannuation, and the public contributions to private research and development?

You can make more users of the services pay for them directly or by private insurance. Where there's no profit for insurers, you can cap or cut the funding so that the people who manage the public services must degrade their quality as fast as they're compelled to expand the things they do or the numbers they serve. Where that might offend conscience or lose seats, you can finance unavoidable improvements by cutting less noticeable public investment and services. Where that also might lose seats, the best advice is to wake up, at last, to what you're missing. Think laterally. Shed your public-service blinkers and open your eyes to the wealth you have ready in your hands. Counting only the profitable services, state and Commonwealth governments began the 1990s with better than a hundred billion dollars' worth of saleable public enterprises. Leading economists want you to privatise them for reasons of economy, efficiency and freedom. Whether or not you believe that stuff, the project pays big bikkies. So do it.

Using the capital proceeds for current spending would be improvident. But you can make it look holy if you use the cash to repay public debt, then spend the revenue which would otherwise have had to service the debt. (Other professions call it laundering the loot.) In the long run, it's likely to lose money: you give up more revenue than you save in debt service, or there'd be no buyers for the services. And with or without laundering, all those options use capital instead of current revenue to finance current spending.

After the capital is spent comes the permanent loss of revenue. But that's five or ten years ahead: someone else's problem. (In 1994, when Mrs Thatcher's successors finished spending the capital proceeds of her privatisations, they had to legislate the biggest peacetime tax increase in Britain's history.) Meanwhile, the sales may cut new private investment by diverting funds to buy the public enterprises. The new owners typically cut the numbers they employ and the pay and security of some of those who remain, especially the least skilled and lowest-paid. Government has to pay the public welfare costs of that.

Among the casualties are also some of the most rewarding occupations. Keating's last and financially his worst privatisation was of the Commonwealth Serum Laboratories. That story of blood and money tells how far Matt Keating's boy had been driven by the ramifying effects of his private conversion and his great public mistake eleven years before. Two years after he did it, he lost power to a government even further to the Right, and retired from parliament.

All competent polls report that a majority of electors distrust the strategy of deregulating and privatising the Australian economy, but since 1983 neither side of parliament has offered any alternative to it. The strategy is 'inevitable and irreversible' only because our leaders make it so. National policies do not need to respond to the global changes, and the best responses may well need to be inventive. But the bipartisan abdication of economic responsibility has prevailed for so long that for any inventive change of direction, we probably need – which means that the major political parties need – new leaders.

What should our next leaders try for?

Except in its treatment of its Aboriginal people, Australia has been a comparatively independent, inventive, egalitarian democracy.

We were early with religious equality, manhood suffrage, secret ballot, votes for women, the eight-hour day.

We developed an effective Labor Party and the world's first Labor governments.

We invented public institutions, sufficiently independent of government, to regulate wages and working conditions.

It has been to protect our wage levels and balance of payments and develop our productivity, rather more than to enrich our manufacturers, that we have protected some of our industries.

And for all but one group of our people, we have achieved a peaceful and interesting multiculture.

But in the face of the new global conflicts of the last twenty or thirty years, we have so far been copycats rather than inventors. I believe that the Anglo-American economic theory which recommends a general weakening of economic government is wrong. All business needs government, some of it heavy and some light-handed, much of it detailed to the needs of particular industries and markets. Without it, the secret of capitalist efficiency – the harnessing of private interest to produce more efficiently the goods and services that the people most want – breaks down. Many of the new freedoms are actually damaging the efficiency they were meant to improve, as well as degrading valuable social bonds and qualities of life.

We should instead be using our resources and inventive capacities to develop for ourselves – and perhaps to show the world – some better uses of the new technology, better uses of affluence and better responses to global conflicts of interest. But such adventures have to be well led, technically competent and democratically desired. It's the first two of those that most need repair.

21

HOW NOT TO ARGUE (2001)

Over fifty years, though a neoliberal revolution that turned some former allies into opponents, Stretton remained true to his social-democratic beliefs. Accusations of being backward-looking, unrealistic or resistant to change did not trouble him: 'New ways of doing things are neither necessarily better, nor necessarily worse, than old ways.' More worrying than the drift of debate, he argues here, was the way in which it was now conducted. There were fair and unfair ways of arguing, he insisted. In this essay, one of his last, he returned to the theme of his first book: the need to be honest and self-critical about 'the necessary mix of facts, judgements, values and social purposes that shape our imperfect knowledge of cause and effect, our judgements of alternative possibilities, and our policy choices.'

W E AUSTRALIANS ARE COMPARATIVELY peaceful, skilful, workable people. We should be able to contrive full or fairly shared employment, tolerable conditions of work, prudent environmental care, creative arts and science and social thought, interesting recreations, and the material conditions for happy childhood, single or family life, and old age. Any strategy designed to achieve all that – economically, with least restraint of desirable freedoms, and with no more than a necessary minimum of inequality – is bound to occasion plenty of argument. But it may be worthwhile to identify four kinds of argument that I believe we could do without.

This may be easiest to do by example. Some critics will condemn a return to a traditional social-democratic program of full employment and greater equality as (1) backward-looking; (2) scared of change; (3) elitist; and (4) unlikely to be competently managed. Opposite charges are just as likely. Far from looking backward, the program may be accused of ignoring plain lessons of history. Far from avoiding change, its reckless proposals would threaten our social and economic stability. Far from being elitist, it would cut down many tall poppies. And far from depending on competent management, its lunatic strategy would be unmanageable by anyone, however competent.

However far apart, those radical and conservative critics share a common fault. They generalise much too simply about their four subjects: about the value of past experience, about change and conservation, about elites, and about methods of national economic management. As follows: new ways of doing things are neither necessarily better, nor necessarily worse, than old ways. We can pick up ideas and historical experience from any place or time, if they promise well for us. What matters is to understand, as perceptively as we can, the circumstances in which past ideas and institutions have served their purposes well or ill, the reasons why they did so, the conditions in which we think of using them here and now, and the reasons why they might or might not serve our present purposes in present conditions.

Suppose that I recommend stricter public regulation of private banks. Market theorists may accuse me of wanting an impractical return to rules in force in the 1950s, when our income per head was scarcely a third of what it is now. To respond in kind, I could accuse them of wanting to restore the financial freedoms of 1930 with a quarter of the workers unemployed, or of 1890 with many of the country's financial institutions insolvent. We both should know better, and spell out the causal analyses that are at the heart of our disagreements.

A second example: stung by a scandal in the 1720s, the British government abolished the private powers of corporate identity, joint stock and limited liability. (Corporate identity gives the firm its independent legal existence. Joint stock allows it to manage for all its shareholders, and reward them in proportion to the number of shares they own. Limited liability exempts the shareholders from liability for the firm's debts: they can only lose the capital they have contributed by buying their shares.) A century later, Britain's industrial revolution was seriously hampered by the lack of those private powers. Did their past misuse make it wrong to reinvent them, as parliament did in the nineteenth century, when there was urgent need for them?

Democracy is the simplest example of all. Should the Germans have shunned it after 1945 because it failed them in the 1930s? Should Eastern Europe have refused to restore it in the 1990s after half a century without it? Should everyone abandon it now because it's 2500 years old? Or because its Athenian inventors, and for nearly a century its American champions, enforced slavery?

Most of the best social thought and institutional design draws on complex mixtures of past and present experience, home and foreign experience, and creative invention. It is not sensible to write off all experienced wisdom as stupidly nostalgic and backward-looking. It is not sensible to write off all inventive ideas as wild, impractical, dangerous. Any fixed attitude to change – for it or against it – tends to be unhelpful. It is good to conserve good things, it is good to reform or get rid of bad things. Sensible people oppose change for the worse and support change for the better. Sensible arguments are about which is which, or likely to be.

Likewise for the people who propose or support the ideas: it's unhelpful to replace reasoning by hostile characterisation, dismissing all cautious thinkers as sentimental troglodytes or all inventive ones as raving Trotskyites. What we need in every case is cool thought about the actual prospects, for particular purposes in our particular circumstances, of particular ways of doing things – old or new, radical or conservative, simple or complicated, inspired by our own or by others' experience or imagination.

Next, 'elitism'. It is sensible to think coolly about the quality of a society's most powerful or influential members. Australians tend to have primitive attitudes to that subject. Some who want greater equality talk as if we should somehow do without leaders altogether. Some who want steeper inequality don't want any hindrance at all to escalating executive plunder or other 'tall poppy' self-service. Both parties should be more discriminate.

Caring about the qualities of a society's most influential people does not necessarily signal a distrust of democracy, or a preference for greater equality or inequality. We employ professional thinkers, teachers, publicists. The force and direction of their influence surely matter. So do the uses which our captains of industry make of their powers. We can't do without government. The quality and competence of the politicians offering to command it, and the public servants who deliver most of it, should concern the rest of us, whatever side we're on.

Especially the politicians. Should they see themselves as leaders, deciding what's best and showing the people the way to go? Or as obedient administrators, finding out what collective action the people want and organising it for them?

In Britain, those questions got some intelligent attention back in the 1830s. A *Reform Act* had extended the right to vote to more than half a million men. For their first experience of mass democracy, leaders began to develop party organisations to campaign for votes. What should be the relation between party members and the leaders they elect, and between citizens and the governments they elect?

Three schemes had their advocates. Some radicals wanted more direct democracy, as some do now: frequent plebiscites could let the whole electorate determine national policies one by one. But that could be incoherent – what if a 51 per cent decision for low tax was followed by a similar majority for high public spending?

For more coherent policymaking, moderate democrats wanted each party to campaign (as they often do now) with a detailed program to be fulfilled through its term of office.

Sir Robert Peel, a manufacturer's son on his way from the middle to the upper class and from conservative to liberal leadership, disagreed. Should a government really be bound throughout its term (which could be up to seven years at that time) by facts known and promises made before its election? Have no new thoughts, however the problems it faced changed from year to year? Five years into its term, should it act only on five-year-old knowledge and five-year-old forecasts and electoral promises, however wrong they turned out to be?

Rather than that idiocy, Peel argued that leaders should certainly be committed to broad values and purposes. Electors could observe how faithfully (or not), how coherently (or not) and how competently (or not) the rival parties and their leaders stuck to their declared principles as they coped with the changing problems that any government faces through its term of office. There need be nothing unduly respectful or subordinate about that scrutiny. Elections should thus determine the broad directions of policy and the choice of the leaders for whom majorities have learned least distrust.

That could be seen as elitist, surrendering power to the best people. It is just as sensible to see it as strictly practical: the most democratic government must still be able to respond, inventively if necessary, to changing dangers and opportunities. In war you don't tell your generals what to do hour by hour in battle; in football you don't tell your fullback what to do second by second in the goal-mouth. You appoint the people likely to know their business best, and do it best, in the service of general purposes which you share.

Finally, questions about better and worse systems and institutions should not be confused with questions about the best management of those we have now. For example, the Australian government and Reserve Bank used to regulate the entry and exit of foreign capital funds, and the foreign purchase of a wide range of Australian assets. With those controls, we were freer than we are now to manage our national economy for our own purposes. For example, we could fix low interest rates, control the amounts that banks could lend and regulate some other business conditions, without fearing 'capital flight'. That may well have been a better system than we have now. But given the open system we have now, we have to run comparatively high interest rates and vary them up and down from time to time. That is not only to avoid capital flight. It is now government's main means of influencing the amounts that banks lend, which can affect rates of investment, employment and inflation. That may well be a bad system which we ought to change. But while we have it, competent managers have to manipulate the high and variable interest rates that the system requires. It's wrong to insist either that low fixed interest is always best, *or* that it is always dangerous. Like a lot of other economic policies, the role of the interest rate depends on the prevailing national strategy of which it is a part. And strategies are likely to vary widely, and *ought* to vary, with national conditions, capacities and purposes.

*

For most of our agreed and disagreed purposes, we need to know what causes what in our economic activity. But like other human activity, economic activity is so complicated that most causal analysis of it – most accounts of what causes what – has to be selective.

Some of the necessary information is strictly factual. Some of it can be hard to know exactly, or for certain. Some is intrinsically uncertain or changeable from day to day because the relevant 'causal forces' are changeable human feelings and choices and inventions. And many require some imagination: you can't know what a particular force is actually causing without imagining what would be happening without it.

For an example, imagine a small business as follows.

Working from her suburban home, a dressmaker picks up fashion ideas from women's magazines, designs garments and has them made by a dozen immigrant women whose language she speaks. She sells the garments to local retailers.

Three experts are asked to explain the cause(s) of her success.

A male economist explains that she needs next to no fixed or working capital. She buys her cloth on credit. She can pay for it and pay her workers after the retailers pay her. Her workers live within walking distance, work at home and rent or hire-purchase their own sewing machines. They're independent contractors, paid for each garment they make. The whole operation succeeds because its low capital, labour, transport, organisational, communication and transaction costs allow low prices and quick market responses. The dressmaker and her workers get income. The retailers get good designs, and orders filled at short notice. The consumers get good clothes at low prices. They're all making the best of their opportunities. Efficient market relations are the main cause of all their rewards, not just of the dressmaker's profit.

Next, the local secretary of the Textile, Garment and Footwear Union is asked why the dressmaker is so successful. Because he knows that she's breaking the law, he explains how she gets away with it. Australia's Clothing Trades Award for outworkers and contractors extends the award to all garment workers, wherever they work and whatever their legal relations with the people they work for. Whether these immigrant women are employed for wages, or paid fees for their services, or sell the garments they make to the woman who orders them, and wherever they do the work, the law entitles them to award rates and conditions. (Textile and garment workers are the last workers in Australia who still have that protection. The Howard government tried to strip them of it in 1998, but failed because of the strength, even in its own party ranks, of sympathy for the women concerned.) The law can be broken by 'cash work' done without the required paperwork. Most of the cash workers are from one of two groups. They are from whichever are the most recently arrived foreign-language immigrants – once Greeks and Turks, then successively Lebanese, Arabs, Vietnamese, Chinese and other East Asians. Or if Australian-born and English-speaking, they are single mothers with young children.

The work tends to entrap them. The pay is low, but it's work they can get when they can't get any other. As law-breakers, they dare not report any ill-treatment they suffer. Some of the immigrants' husbands keep them at it whatever they suffer, for the money or for fear of reprisals. The employers risk tougher official penalties than the workers do, so some of them threaten any informers with unofficial penalties. 'Like most vices,' says the union officer, 'the cash work comes with a lot of bullying and harassment.' Doesn't working at home at least free young mothers' time to adapt to their children's needs? For some, perhaps. But many of them are bullied to do more and faster work than they want, or they'll get none at all. If sacked, they can't expect any pay they're owed. Even when they do as they're told, the cheats they work for may underpay them 'because the quality was bad', 'because the order was late', 'because your bad work lost me other orders – you really owe me!' Fearing official and unofficial punishments themselves, there's not much the workers can do about it.

But there are things that others can do. Recent tax changes, though not designed to benefit the working women, are making it harder for employers to conceal illegal work. The union is cooperating with the biggest capitalists in the business – the retailers rather than the garment-makers – in the FairWear campaign to label goods whose production complies with relevant awards in Australia, or with other codes abroad. Suppliers to Target or Coles Myer have to agree to enforce the FairWear rules, and to allow union investigation on request.

The union rep thinks government could do more to equip the victims to defend themselves. He wants foreign-language immigrants, especially women from poor or oppressed countries, to be greeted on arrival with free compulsory courses of study in their new Australian rights as workers, as women, as spouses, as mothers. Also where to find and why to trust the institutions that can protect them on all those fronts.

Thus, in the union rep's explanation, the main causes of the dressmaker's success are her law-breaking, and the defective law enforcement that lets her get away with it.

The third of our causal analysts is a politician, an Australian Democrat. Ask her why those women are getting about half the pay they would earn for doing the same work lawfully, and she insists that the basic cause is the destruction, since the 1970s, of the historic 'Australian settlement'. We had a discriminate boundary around our country, and through the mid-century we used it well. Among other things, we restricted imports to what our exports could pay for. We enforced a fair minimum wage, protected where necessary from foreign competition. With control over the import and export of capital and credit, we could manage the national economy to maintain full employment without too much of either inflation or foreign debt. And after seventy years or so of gender-biased industrial arbitration – but better late than never – we came closer than most countries to equal pay for women. So nobody had to put up with the sort of exploitation these women suffer now. They're suffering it now because we opened the boundary to uncontrolled flows of goods and money and credit. Imports soon exceeded exports. We paid for the excess by borrowing instead of buying the necessary exchange from foreign banks and other lenders. That pushed our dollar's exchange rate way below its real purchasing power, so a lot of the imports now cost us as much as they used to cost under the tariff – but we've lost the jobs, the tariff revenue, and the necessary protection of our fair-waged industries.

To stop the rot, we need to limit our imports again. But the only way our ruling parties are willing to do that now is to use tax and other budget and monetary controls to cut our people's total spendable incomes by enough to cut our import spending down to the amount our export earnings can pay for. Less than a third of our spending is on imports. That means that action to cut (say) a billion dollars off our import bill will also cut *more than two billion* off spending on our own output. That keeps unemployment needlessly high. That's why there are no basic-wage jobs for these poor women. And since the Howard government's welfare cuts in 1998, there are no welfare incomes either for most of them, for the first two years they're here. A few find work as cleaners or household servants. For the rest, the options are to work for cash at prostitution or illegal needlework, or beg or starve. Government policies are the main cause of this dirty business. Don't blame the Australian people for the policies – neither major party is offering our generation anything better to vote for. Blame the responsible economists and politicians and public servants and the rich interests they choose to serve, or fear to offend.

Thus one expert sees efficient market forces as the main cause of the dressmaker's small-business success. Another sees defective law enforcement as its main cause. A third sees economic deregulation and welfare cuts as main causes of it. All three rely on true facts, but focus on different causes because they would like to do different things about the business: let the market rule; or improve law enforcement to protect a particular group of disadvantaged women; or replace the national economic strategy with a different one.

*

Selection – deciding where to look, what for, which strands of causation to follow and so on – is not the only problem for people exploring the complex patterns of cause and effect in economic life. Three other traps lie in wait for overconfident reporters of that life. Some of the important facts are hard to know for certain. So are some of the actual relations between cause and effect. And most understanding of what causes what in particular cases calls for some imagination as well as hard knowledge.

There are measurable facts. A drought cuts farm income. A new machine cuts production costs. A fall in market prices cuts somebody's profit. But some causation presents technical problems. If a drought and a new crop disease together cut farm output, it may take some serious science to judge what each cause contributed to the effect, and what each might have caused in the absence of the other.

At another extreme are human tastes, beliefs, choices, inventions. What causes people to vote as they do? Choose the occupations they do? Prefer more income to more leisure or more leisure to more income? Like or dislike the paid work and the unpaid work they do?

Guessing or pretending what actually motivates particular people occasions some of the worst tricks of political persuasion. (Argue as if you and your allies act with just and generous intentions, and your opponents are driven by nothing but greed or lust for power.) Similarly simple assumptions occasion some bad economics. In theory, most economists assume that people act to achieve whatever they most desire. In practice, they tend to assume that the desires are few, constant and selfish: commonly for some balance of money and leisure, without moral concerns or care for other people's fortunes or feelings.

That's guessing at facts you can rarely know for certain. But at the heart of any causal analysis of complex social life is a more fundamental role for imagination. You don't really know what something has actually caused unless you know what would have happened without it. But in complicated political, social and economic life you can rarely know that for certain. The same difficulty arises as with prediction.

For example, suppose an orthodox economist predicts that if the government collects more money than it spends, and thus has a budget surplus, that will restrain inflation without necessarily increasing unemployment. Events confirm his prediction. But they don't necessarily prove that his reasons for it were right. Other forces may also have been at work restraining inflation; others again may have sustained employment. The economist's prediction may have been rightly reasoned, or it may just have been lucky. And the same is true years later, when a historian explains those past events. Her causal explanation can't necessarily be proven true or false by reference to facts alone.

Return to the example of the unlawfully employed immigrant women. The first expert, the economist, assumes that the reason they are employed at all is their willingness to work for a wage that allows their output to compete successfully with imports from low-paid workers in poorer countries. If they refused to work on those terms, or if government succeeded in preventing them, he imagines that they would be unemployed or facing even worse options of lower-paid work.

Surprisingly, the Democrat politician agrees with that. Award rates of pay might not put the dressmaker out of business. But if she had to pay award wages, she might well hire different people from the pool of unemployed – English speakers, more experienced, with good work records and references. Imagining this likely alternative to illegal work prompts the Democrat to ask: what has caused a situation in which slack law causes the women to be overworked and underpaid, but effective law would put them out of work altogether? What has caused this intolerable dilemma? Unemployment has caused it. Whatever ended full employment back in the 1970s, and has since prevented its return, is the main cause of the immigrant women's suffering. So it is on that cause that she would like to operate, by replacing the national economic strategy.

No doubt the trade union rep would also like to see that happen. But with or without it, he'd like to see the award enforced for another reason. He can well imagine how illegal maltreatment of workers is likely to spread to other workers and other trades if employers find they can get away with it.

Thus, the Democrat imagines that if low pay were not hurting the immigrant women, they might well be hurt by employers' preference for other workers. Their troubles are treble-caused: by illegal exploitation, by potential discrimination by law-abiding employers, and by the prevailing level of unemployment. She imagines the likely effects of each combination of those three causes, and concludes that full employment is a necessary condition of getting recent, foreign-speaking immigrants lawfully employed.

Are the economists who see market forces as the sufficient cause of the women's experience necessarily heartless, uncaring, class-prejudiced male supremacists? Some, perhaps, but by no means all. Theory tells them that those women are getting the market price for their labour. With one exception, the alternatives which they can imagine look worse, for the women or for the national economy or for both. The exception is the law that the dressmaker is breaking. If that were repealed, the freer operation of market forces might well serve the immigrant women a little better. On balance, illegality probably strengthens the dressmaker's power over her workers, and enables her to misuse her power in some bullying, non-market ways.

Conservative economists are not alone in accepting the market explanation of the immigrant women's situation. For example, a fine and compassionate Australian historian read and commented on a draft of this essay. He prefers the market explanation because it identifies the conditions that allow those unfortunate women some work and income, which he can't imagine them getting any other way. He doesn't welcome the Democrat's explanation and the program of action which it would justify, because he can't imagine that program succeeding. His soft heart is with the social democrats who hope for it, but his hard head expects that their attempts at reform will continue to fail, as they have been doing for a generation now.

Thus, the different imagination of possible alternatives, past and future, can prompt people with different values – but also people with similar values but different imagination of the alternatives and different judgement of the possibilities – to focus on different elements of the many conditions and processes that have converged to shape those women's options.

The possibilities multiply in larger, more complicated disagreements. Between social democrats, who want better government of our economic activity, and neoliberals, who want less government of it, the divisions are not simple or all of a kind. In my experience, those who would like to see less government include some of each of the following. Greedy capitalists, who know exactly what they're doing and finance Right think-tanks to persuade press and politicians to tolerate it. True believers in versions of neoclassical economic theory, who expect that such policies will benefit everyone and finance Right think-tanks for generous reasons. Troubled believers in the theory, who know that it's an imperfect guide and that all progress has losers, but think it the best direction, all things considered. People who want economic efficiency but also progressive taxation and compassionate welfare policies. Social democrats who want to throw out the Labor leaders who have sold out to the Right, and who think the Right are at least doing what comes naturally to them, and may do it more competently than turncoat Labor leaders will do. And above all, the many people who, whatever their natural moral and political inclinations, don't claim to understand economics but trust the advice of our mainstream economists just as respectfully as they trust our doctors, lawyers, chemists, engineers and other professionals. Plenty of those respectful people may be open to civilised persuasion. But they're least likely to be persuaded by voices that call them capitalist lackeys and monsters of greed simply because they respect economists and vote Liberal.

∗

To understand the economy, you have to know many hard facts and figures. You have to approximate or guess more uncertain facts by whatever means you can – perceive qualities, estimate imprecise quantities, judge balances of strength between boss and worker, buyer and seller, commercial persuader and resistant consumer. Many of the causal forces at work can only be known by knowing – as well as you can – the minds of the people concerned. That's complicated by their many differences: their common and conflicting material interests, their shared and conflicting values and judgements of right and wrong, their diverse imagination of what their individual and collective options actually are. And to know what causes what, you must often imagine alternatives to what is actually happening. To avoid doing that is merely to assume the alternatives without thinking about them. (Neoclassical economists tend to decide what harm government is causing by imagining how, with less government, the private sector would produce more of what people most want and distribute it more fairly. Social democrats tend to decide what good government is causing by imagining how, with less government, quite a lot of production would be less efficient, more of it would be dangerous, and its output would be distributed less fairly. Rather than noticing only the quantity of government, both parties should sometimes pay more attention to the particular purposes and quality of government in the particular countries that they have in mind.)

To cope with such complexities, it's necessary to select and simplify. The selections and simplifications should be rationally guided by the purposes of the investigation. Those vary with investigators' values and social purposes. They are intrinsically controversial, and so must be some elements of the causal analyses that they shape. That's unavoidable, however true their facts, admirable their guiding values, and shrewd their judgements and imagination of alternatives.

In an ideal world, we should argue accordingly. We should understand the necessary mix of facts, judgements, values and social purposes that shape our imperfect knowledge of cause and effect, our judgements of alternative possibilities, and our policy choices. Unless there are good reasons for doing otherwise, we should credit opponents with as much good intent as we believe we have ourselves. We should acknowledge any costs and risks of our own policy proposals as candidly as we attack our opponents' proposals. That's to show competence as well as goodwill. And so on: fair's fair.

Good behaviour need not inhibit strong argument – for some values and social purposes rather than others, for some strategies as more practical than others. True facts and logical reasoning don't guarantee agreement. Different values and tastes, and attitudes to risk, are part of the human condition.

SOURCES

Introduction

For biographical details, I have drawn on interviews with Stretton by
Neville Meaney (NLA, 1986) and Susan Marsden (NLA, 2002), and on
material in my previous chapter in City Dreamers, listed below in the Select
Bibliography.

'a theory of everything', Marsden, p. 117 ; 'pragmatic social democrat':
Gibilisco, p. 134; 'moderate socialist', *Ideas for Australian Cities*, p. 5; 'Left',
Capitalism, Socialism and the Environment, p. 2; Christian atheist', HS
to Robert Dare, 11 Aug 1989 (copy supplied by Robert Dare); essays on
Wainwright and Ramsay in *Meanjin*, no. 4, 1991, pp. 565–581 and *Australian
Quarterly*, vol. 50, no. 3, 1978, pp. 90–100; Coombs: see below 'Two Leaders';
Leonard Stretton: *Australian Dictionary of Biography*, vol. 16, pp. 336–337,
also *City Dreamers*, pp. 199–203; 'almost perfectly non-political': Meaney,
p. 3; 'life consisted of doing things': Marsden, p. 4; Yarnold: Recollections of
Stephen Yarnold [1982], Stretton Papers; 'trotting about the class structure':
Marsden, p. 25; 'genius': Kathleen Fitzpatrick to Rhodes Scholarship
Selection Committee, 9 Nov 1945, 'exceptional promise': Crawford to same,
5 Nov 1945, both in Rhodes Scholarship Selection Committee 1911–46,
Melbourne University Archives; 'card-carrying membership': Marsden p. 16;
'Bliss to be alive': 'From London with Hindsight', *Overland*, no. 101, 1985,
p. 15; 'I shall never understand': Nora Stretton to Max Crawford, 4 May
[1951], Crawford Papers, Melbourne University Archives; 'no historical
imagination': Meaney, p. 3; 'I'm a historian': Marsden, p. 16; 'aghast at Oxford
historians': Meaney, p. 13; Streeten's influence: compare his 'Programs and
Prognoses' *Quarterly Journal of Economics*, vol. 68, 1954 with Stretton,
Political Sciences, pp. 259–260 and *Capitalism*, chs 1–5; 'a fashionable thing':
Meaney, p. 18; 'intellectual fraud', Meaney, p. 19 ; 'sloth and incapacity':
Interview with Huw Evans, 23 Jan 1984, Stretton Papers; 'few memorable
books': Submission to ALP Working Paper on Higher Education, Jan 2001,
Stretton Papers; Oxford and Melbourne intellectuals: Meaney, p. 16;
'working effective' citizen and 'came home happily', Marsden, p. 27; 'lively
democratic department', Ken Inglis, 'Hugh Stretton's University of Adelaide';
'suspended seminar program': Personal Communication Patrick Troy,
2016; 'brilliant' but 'wrong': Stinchcombe in *American Journal of Sociology*,

vol. 76, 1971, pp. 1137–1140; C. Wright Mills, *The Sociological Imagination*, Oxford UP, New York, 1959; Jean Martin's reminder: Jean Martin to HS 16 February 1966, Stretton Papers; 'as clearly as they can': *Political Sciences*, p. 425; 'social scientists should write "good': *Capitalism*, p. 2; 'I want what I've got': 'The Good City' below; 'Dress respectably', Marsden, p. 43; Greg Melleuish: *Australian Journal of Social Issues*, vol. 35, no. 4, November 2000, pp. 363–369; on leaders, 'Two Leaders' below and his 'The Quality of Leading Australians' in Stephen Graubard (ed.) *Australia: The Daedalus Symposium*, Angus and Robertson, Sydney, 1985, pp. 197–230; 'amateur book': *Ideas*, p. 1; 'see beyond the clichés', Foreword to *Ideas*, 3rd edn, Sydney, 1989, p. vi; not a mindless conformist, Australia as a Suburb, below; 'housing policy for the middle class': Michael Jones in *Community*, no. 9, 1975, p. 17; neo-liberals: John Paterson, *The Economic Consequences of Mr Stretton*, Melbourne 1975; a technical fix: Stretton, 'A Capital Mistake and Sloped Credit' in his *Political Essays*, pp. 54–69; Stretton's arguments against densification: Ideas, pp. and chapters on consolidation and transport in this volume; 'inflation and unemployment destroyed', *Economics*, p. 118; 'Tasks for Social Democratic Intellectuals' in his *Political Essays*, pp. 195–224; On his aims in *Economics*, Stretton, 'After Samuelson?' *World Development*, vol. 24, no. 10, 1996, pp. 1561–1578; 'the book is right': John Legge in *Dissent*, vol. 2, 1989, p. 20; 'always respect', 'How to Argue', below; Judith Brett, *Australian Liberals and the Moral Middle Class*, Cambridge University Press, Melbourne 2003, p. 11; 'What do you think of Stretton?', Patrick Troy Personal Communication; Paul Keating says so, *The Sydney Morning Herald*, 30 March 2017.

Chapters

Chapter 1 Stretton on Himself: 'Is a fair society a happy one?', unpublished talk in Papers of Hugh Stretton, National Library of Australia; 'Biography and Opinions of HS', undated paper in Papers of Hugh Stretton; Hugh Stretton, Rhodes Scholarship Application November 1945, Papers of the Victorian Selection Committee, University of Melbourne Archives; 'From London, with love and hindsight', *Overland* no. 101, 1985, p. 15; 'Capital Mistakes' in Colin Bell and S. Encel (eds.), *Inside the Whale: Ten Personal Accounts of Social Research*, Pergamon Press, Sydney 1978, pp. 68–72, Hugh Stretton, *Economics: A New Introduction*, Pluto Press, London 1999, pp. 61–63.

Chapter 2 A Political Science of Society: *The Political Science: General Principles of Selection in Social Science and History*, Routledge and Kegan Paul, London, 1969, pp. v–vi, 426–431.

Chapter 3 'A Tale of Three Cities': *Ideas for Australian Cities*, The Author, Adelaide 1970, pp. 142–146, 210–213, 256–257, 261–266.

Chapter 4 Australia as a Suburb: *Ideas for Australian Cities*, pp. 7–11, 13–18, 20–23.

Chapter 5 Who is My Neighbour?: *Ideas for Australian Cities*, pp. 103–118.

Chapter 6 Ideologies: *Ideas for Australian Cities*, pp. 271–284.

Chapter 7 A Good Australian City: ABC Radio Transcript. 'The Science of Cities', 1972 in Papers of Hugh Stretton.

Chapter 8 Advice for Activists: Amalgam of Extracts from Hugh Stretton's Talk to First General Meetings of the Adelaide Residents' Society [sic] and the Residents' Association of Dulwich Rose Park & Toorak Gardens, n.d. State Library of South Australia.

Chapter 9 'Planning to Break the Rules': Sidney Luker Memorial Lecture, Royal Australian Planning Institute, *RAPI Journal*, October 1972, pp. 135–139; also in Stretton, *Political Essays*, Georgian House, Melbourne 1987, pp. 130–138.

Chapter 10 Letter from Australia, 1976: Typescript in Papers of Hugh Stretton.

Chapter 11 Democracy and Homeownership: *Capitalism, Socialism and the Environment*, Cambridge University Press, Cambridge and Melbourne, 1976, pp. 183–206.

Chapter 12 Cities as Distributors: *Capitalism, Socialism and the Environment*, pp. 221–231.

Chapter 13 Social Implications of Technological Change: Paper to Department of Community Development Torrens CAE 11 November 1978, Papers of Hugh Stretton.

Chapter 14 The Case against very free trade and very small government: ABC Guest of Honour Talk, 4 May 1980, Papers of Hugh Stretton.

Chapter 15 The Cult of Selfishness: *Political Essays*, pp. 184–194.

Chapter 16 Urban Consolidation: Who Consolidates who?: *Adelaide Review* September 1988.

Chapter 17 A Use for History: Seven Minute Paper for Donald Horne's Ideas Summit, 1990, Papers of Hugh Stretton.

Chapter 18 Transport and the Structure of Australian Cities: *Australian Planner*, vol. 31, no. 3, 1994, pp. 131–136.

Chapter 19 The Future of Social Democracy: 'Onwards, Sideways and Backwards: Alternative Responses to the Shortcomings of Social Democracy', *Society*, 1995; also in *Development*, vol. 45, 1994, pp. 33–38.

Chapter 20 Two Leaders: 'Leaders' in Peter Craven (ed.), *The Best Australian Essays 2000*, Black Inc., Melbourne, 2000, pp. 43–66.

Chapter 21 How not to argue: *The Best Australian Essays 2001*, Black Inc., Melbourne, 2001, pp. 205–224.

HUGH STRETTON: A SELECT BIBLIOGRAPHY

Principal Books

The Political Sciences: The General Principles of Selection in Social Science and History, Routledge and Kegan Paul, London, 1969.

Ideas for Australian Cities, 1st edn, The Author, Adelaide, 1970; 2nd edn, Georgian House, 1975; 3rd edn, Transit Publishing, 2001.

Housing and Government: The Boyer Lectures, Australia Broadcasting Commission, Sydney, 1974.

Capitalism, Socialism and the Environment, Cambridge University Press, Cambridge 1976.

Urban Planning in Rich and Poor Countries, Oxford University Press, New York, 1978.

Political Essays, Georgian House, Melbourne, 1987.

Public Goods, Public Enterprise, Public Choice: Theoretical Foundations of the Contemporary Attack on Government, St Martin's Press, New York, 1994 (with Lionel Orchard).

Economics: A New Introduction, Pluto Press, London, 1999.

Australia Fair, University of New South Wales Press, Sydney, 2005.

Writing about Hugh Stretton

Obituaries by Patrick Troy, Economic and Labour Relations Review, 26, 4, 2015; Tony Stephens, *The Sydney Morning Herald*, 2 September 2015; Wilfrid Prest, *Australian Academy of Humanities Annual Report, 2015–2016*.

Interviews by Neville Meaney 1986 and Susan Marsden 2002, National Library of Australia and Peter Gibilisco, *Journal of Australian Political Economy*, no. 51, June 2003, pp. 132–142.

Sol Encel, 'An Establishment Radical', *Island Magazine*, no. 36, Spring 1988, pp. 72–74.

Lionel Orchard and Robert Dare (eds), *Markets, Morals and Public Policy*, Federation Press, Sydney, 1989.

John Tregenza, 'Committed Historians: Charles Pearson and Hugh Stretton', *Journal of the Historical Society of South Australia*, no. 18, 1990, pp. 13–17.

Ken Inglis, 'Hugh Stretton's University of Adelaide 1954–56', *Journal of the Historical Society of South Australia*, no. 18, 1990, pp. 7–12.

Bruce Wearne, *Hugh Stretton: An Australian Social Theorist*, Monash University Department of Anthropology and Sociology, Working Paper no. 5/92, May 1992.

Peter Gibilisco, 'Hugh Stretton and His Social Theory', *Journal of Economic and Social Policy*, vol. 5, no. 1, 2000.

Lionel Orchard, 'Public Philosophy and Australia's Cities: Hugh Stretton's Ideas for Australia's Cities Twenty Years On', *Australian Planner*, vol. 28, no. 4, December 1990, pp. 44–46.

Greg Melleuish, 'Hugh Stretton and the Wise Administrator', *Australian Journal of Social Issues*, vol. 35, no. 4, November 2000, pp. 363–369.

Wilfrid Prest (ed.), *Pasts Present: History at Australia's Third University*, Wakefield Press, Adelaide, 2014.

Peter Beilharz, 'Hugh Stretton – Social Democracy in Australia' in his *Thinking the Antipodes: Australian Essays*, Monash University Publishing, Clayton, 2015, pp. 275–285.

Stephen Hamnett, 'Hugh Stretton: Ideas for Australian Cities', *Built Environment*, vol. 41, no. 3, 2015, pp. 419–434.

Graeme Davison, 'Planners: Hugh Stretton's Ideas for Australian Cities' in his *City Dreamers: The Urban Imagination in Australia*, New South, Sydney, 2016, pp. 195–216.

Doug Munro, 'The House That Hugh Built: The Adelaide History Department During the Stretton Era, 1954–1966', *History of Education*, vol. 46, no. 5, 2017, pp. 631–652.

INDEX